In Common

The architects of our lives are divided. There are those who insist that there is still no alternative to neoliberalism. Despite the many crises it has provoked, they continue to push for competition in every sphere of life, to widen the wealth gap, to ignore climate change and to pursue the steady dispossession of our rights and commonwealth.

Then there are those advocating change, those who seek to persuade us that capitalism can be saved from itself. They conceal capitalism behind a human face. They tell us that environmental disaster can be averted through technological solutions. They say that deeply rooted social injustices can be cured with a little more economic growth. That we'll be safer with more police on our streets.

And yet, we know that capitalism is dying, that its lies have been unmasked, that its grip on our world and our lives is maintained only through expropriations, dependency and commodified desires. In Common is a collection of works that see an end to capitalism without apocalypse. It provides us with techniques for building another world, and it narrates practices of alternatives and theories of hope. It is a glimpse into our shared present, for a future in common.

In Common is published by Zed Books under the creative commons license. You are free to share this material, transform and build upon it for non-commercial purposes.

Series editor: Massimo De Angelis

Already published: Stavros Stavrides, *Common Space: The City as Commons*

Omnia Sunt Communia

On the Commons and the Transformation to Postcapitalism

Massimo De Angelis

ZED

Zed Books

LONDON

Omnia Sunt Communia: Principles for the Transition to Postcapitalism
was first published in 2017 by Zed Books Ltd, The Foundry, 17 Oval Way,
London SE11 5RR, UK.

www.zedbooks.net

Typeset in Minion by seagulls.net
Index by John Barker
Cover design by Dougal Burgess

A catalogue record for this book is available from the British Library.

ISBN 978-1-78360-063-2 hb
ISBN 978-1-78360-062-5 pb
ISBN 978-1-78360-065-6 pdf
ISBN 978-1-78360-064-9 epub
ISBN 978-1-78360-066-3 mobi

Printed and bound by CPI Group (UK) Ltd, Croydon, CR0 4YY

Contents

Tables, figures and boxes

Tables

Figures

Boxes

Acknowledgements

This book is the creation of many discontinuous encounters, with people, books, situations and life processes. Each of these encounters brought home to me a confirmation or a dissonance, a question or an exclamation mark. To search for the commons meant to leave the normalised part of me sitting silently in its cynical sulk about the world's condition, and to open out for the warmth of human commoning. This was the only way for me to do research on the commons. As this work is not a literary piece, this warmth will not be greatly expressed through the book. But I would never have been able to carry out this research without having experienced the love, the friendship and the experience of community with many of the people who taught me about the commons. In the first place, unlike with many other subjects in science, the student of the commons cannot avoid examining also the position in which he or she, the author and researcher, is located in much of daily life and their immediate circle of affects and love. The micro-commons of my family, and the commoners therein, became the most immediately approachable mirror for my ongoing internal dialogue on the system, on aspects such as the properties of the commons and the aporias of the process of commoning. I must therefore thank Dagmar and our two sons Leonardo and Nicola for their support in critical times and for their patience in having to deal with my never-ending work on 'the book' in the midst of multiple other work and life pressures, and my often inappropriate attempts to consider the kitchen floor as a seminar room, although we still had lots of fun to common.

In 2008, my family went to live in a small village in the Apennines near Modena. Since then, I have absorbed the schizophrenic and creative shock of working and living in two so incredibly different places: Monchio, a tiny dot on some – not all – maps, where life runs slow and an open valley crowned by mountains makes you smile in the morning; and London, the global city that never stops, in which community-less crowds run to get the tube in order not to be one minute late to work. This shock has been extremely formative for me and my understanding of the commons, as I realised through my body the poverty of the metropolitan 'well-off', and the richness of the villagers 'worst-off'.

The key moment of realisation occurred one day when I felt hungry on the tube when travelling to evening class, while surrounded by people going home from work who were all eating crisps. I pulled my sandwich from my bag, and at the first bite I realised how rich I was: for every ingredient in my succulent sandwich, bread included, I knew the faces of its producers, I had joked with them and shared smiles; with some I had planned together, I could trust their method of production without the need for any organic certification, I could even celebrate some commoning for the tomatoes and salad leaves. From that moment, London appeared to me to be a mystery, even though I had lived there for almost thirty years and had enjoyed quite a good time: the traffic, the shopping malls, the full buses, the expensive transport, the replicant shops and brands, the alien food producers, the poverty in the midst of plenty, the high cost of living, the venal buzz of commerce, the young charity workers on busy streets appealing for money for some desperate cause to the spaced-out crowd, attempting to distract it from its collective delirium with a fun costume. While the fast and precarious life in the global city made it difficult to sustain commoning with others, the boring life in the village appeared to me as an amazing opportunity for commoning. Our kids went to school in the village, thus introducing us to other parents, and Dagmar and I began, with others in the village, to common. Almost ten years later, we have an association with a (not certified) biological community garden, a theatre group producing drama and comedies on critical aspects of our lives, and we are involved in the organisation of events on edible and medical plants growing spontaneously in our locality, defence against school closures, critical rethinking of contemporary models of education, ecological days, antique wheat production, and welcoming refugees to counteract widespread fear and anxiety. To explore with others such a tiny territory in search of problems and solutions opened to me – a urbanite academic with years of research and experience of urban struggles and capitalist strategies – a completely new creative dimension rooted in the fabric of daily life in a given context, rather than in the big claims of academic work in the decontextualised world of abstractions. To my friends of Montagna Viva, our association for commoning (and especially to those with whom I worked with more closely along with Dagmar), that is, Carlo, Claudia, Daniela, Giorgio, Giuliana, Loretta, Melissa, Patrizia, Stefano and Roberto, I give a warm thanks for sharing with me the effort to develop and sustain an 'association of free individuals' (Marx 1976) and a big hug for having given me first-hand experience of the complexity of maintaining cohesion and motivation even in such small groups, as well as the excitement of commoning and of the new projects spinning out of it. I hope to continue our journey in always new territories.

This book is also the result of years of research in the field beyond my immediate circles. I had the privilege to visit commons spaces and talk to commoners in Italy, the UK, Greece, France, Germany, Spain, Switzerland, Austria, Croatia, the USA, South Africa, Mexico, Brazil, Ecuador, Bolivia, and Peru. At meetings I have attended, I was able to talk to commoners beyond these countries: Columbia, Argentina, Paraguay, Uruguay, Chile, Canada, Nigeria, Uganda, Tanzania, India, are only the ones I can remember. Some of my informants gave me key insights into aspects of the commons, while others broadly confirmed them. In this book I have illustrated some of the cases that were very formative material for me, that forced me to travel further along my theoretical journey and explore and select new ways of thinking, so as to understand the new insights as aspects of the commons. I must therefore thank Patrick Bond and the Rosa Luxemburg Foundation for making possible my visit to Durban and Johannesburg in 2004, and Prishani Naidoo for introducing me to the South African anti-privatisation struggles around water and electricity, and for guiding me to the township of Orange Farm, where I was able to gather key early insights into the internal dynamics of a commons movement.

During the summers of 2007 and 2010 I participated with friends and colleagues around *The Commoner* journal in the commoner convivium, generally a week-long experience of very intense encounters, in which we shared cooking and child care, we played with words and balls, we napped on hammocks and forest turf, and we talked endlessly about the different crises of the time, the different movements, and the commons. In these contexts I matured, either by symbiosis or dissonance, the stimuli to develop further my theoretical framework, in order to make it possible to include all our voices in the commons. At the convivia I realised in my body – although I already knew it in my mind – that among the different opinions and positions expressed on a given topic, it was impossible to select just one to define the commons. A difficult process of consensus seeking, even at this theoretical level, was necessary to move on, although when that consensus was reached, the different positions often kept alive at least in the individual internal debates. This taught me that complexity is to be found also in small groups in communication, and that it is impossible to define the 'politically correct' commons with the 'correct' line, or understanding of the world. Hence the need emerged in my mind to define frameworks that allow for a continuous flux of argument and a diversity of beliefs and values, but with a mechanism that is able to reach consensual decisions. Commoning is thus, therefore, an ongoing dance of values, kept together by the rhythm of our daily reproduction and the decisions that need to be communally taken in given contexts. With this preoccupation in mind, I later encountered the work of Humberto Maturana and Francisco Varela, providing a systems view of cellular life which I began to translate – with some difficulty – in terms of the commons system within the context of our capitalist political economy. The step from studying Maturana and Varela to utilising one of the insights of Luhmann, and later complexity theory, was relatively short. Many people participated in our convivia, but I must especially thank those I worked closely with during that period and who pushed my thinking in the years that followed: Camille Barbagallo, Nick Beuret, George Caffentsis, Mariarosa Dalla Costa, Olivier De Marcellus, Emma Dowling, Silvia Federici, Viviane Gonik, David Harvie, Suzanne Lerch, Tadzio Muller, and Hans Widmer.

In spring 2010 I travelled through Ecuador, Peru and Bolivia while on sabbatical leave from the University of East London. Another semester-long sabbatical in 2014 allowed me to finalise a first, very rough and incomplete draft of this book. In both cases, I warmly thank my colleagues for making possible these sabbaticals which, by releasing me temporarily from my teaching responsibilities, allowed me to finish and now publish this book.

During my 2010 travels I visited numerous community associations, absorbed their all-pervasive community spirit, and shared conversations with commons movement participants. I still remember, afterwards, returning to Europe still trying to figure out what the experience had all been about, whether it had to do only with the cultural specificity of the Andean regions or whether it shared important elements with European and generally Western experience, something perhaps that was scarcely visible but still existing and relevant. Too many people contributed to this experience for me to thank them all individually here. However, I must thank Oscar and Marcella Oliveira, who opened to me the possibility of talking to so many members of water associations in Cochabamba and introduced me, with their key insights, to the experience of the water war and Bolivian politics; Carlos Perez, *dirigente* of the Junta de Agua in Cuenca, in southern Ecuador, whose tales of *minga* –

the commoning moments of indigenous movements – filled my heart with the presence of another, much more fulfilling, way of life and confirmed to me that my research was going in the right direction; Antonio Polo, the amazing priest who for forty years stuck with the once over-exploited community of Salinas, Ecuador, and became instrumental in the development of a unique model of solidarity economy: in our long chat in his living room facing the main square of the little town, Antonio taught me the virtues of commons 'entrepreneurs' – facilitators of commoning processes – and the risks if they overdo that role.

I often travel to mainland Europe for conferences and workshops, and since my research on the commons became my daily preoccupation, I have seized the opportunity to visit commons spaces and talk to commoners. I must specifically thank some key people who were instrumental in opening the way for me to gain key insights. In the first place, Haris Tsavdaroglou, Socrates Papazoglou, Lia Yoka and Iria Grammenou took me around Greece in 2013, presenting a book containing some of my writings in Greek for the Éditions des étrangers. During that trip I was asked tremendous questions on the crisis and the possibilities of commons that further pushed my thinking on the commons. I must thank them for giving me that opportunity, and I also want to thank the students and activist communities of Volos and of the 'Hilton' of the European squats, Rosa Negra in Hania, Crete, for sharing their convivial spirit and provoking my thinking with their amazing questions and comments. Thanks also to Antonis Broumas for inviting me to Athens in 2015 and 2016 for different editions of the commons festival, which allowed me to talk to commoners engaged in social movements and commons associations.

I have been struck by the interest in my work on the commons taken by architects in many contexts. I shared a very fortunate interview with Stavros Stavrides with the journal *AnArchitecture* in 2010, and ever since then I have been invited among architects to talk about the commons. Puzzled by such an interest, I later discovered it was due to the fact that many young architects, aware of the problems of the present-day political economy and unwilling to compete for work in big studios designing big shopping malls, instead want to design commons spaces, spaces to facilitate commoning. Some of these might be like the ones designed and developed by R-Urban in Paris to which I was introduced in 2015 by Doina Petrescu, an architect at Sheffield University who lives and works in Paris. The Agrocité (community garden, kitchen, conference space and greenhouse) complex built in the middle of a Paris banlieue (not far from a recycling and refuse centre) – inspired me further with the great possibilities – and challenges – of urban commoning. Thanks to Doina and R-Urban staff for discussing with me aspects of my work and for opening to me their amazing creation.

In recent years, I have also had the opportunity to discuss aspects of my work with postgraduate students and scholars of critical political ecology. In particular, I would like to thank Giacomo D'Alisa (Universitat Autònoma de Barcelona), Marco Armiero (Royal Institute of Technology, Stockholm), and Federica Barca (Universidade de Coimbra), who helped to clarify for me the central role of the commons in environmental struggles and in degrowth theory. Thanks to Andy Hilton for his useful comments on a draft of Chapter 7 on commoning.

Thanks also to George Caffentzis and David Harvey who have read major sections of the book and provided important commentary on my work. I also thank very much Raquel Gutier-rez Aguilar, Lucia Linsalata, Mina Lorena Navarro and other staff and students at the postgraduate centre at the Benemérita Universidad Autónoma de Puebla (BUAP), Mexico, for their constructive, passionate and critical engagement with my ideas during our week-long discussion in October 2016 at the work-shop 'Revolutión social, Reproductión de la vida y de lo comun', held in Puebla. They helped me to recognise both the strengths and the limitations of my arguments, and the large common ground between the framework-like narrative I use in this book and a more directly political-philosophical narrative. I also thank Silvia Federici, who in Puebla and on many other occasions, reminded me of the key role that women play in defending and building the commons.

I must thank Juhana Venäläinen, who did some social network analysis on community farming in Italy when he was visiting the School of Social Sciences at the University of East London, work which resulted in one graph I selected for this book. I also would like to thank Pat Harper, who as an editor has done a magnificent job of cleaning the text of strangely composed sentences. Finally, many thanks to Zed's commissioning editor, Kika Sroka-Miller, for her enthusiasm and patience in getting this book out of me. All the Zed team have been fantastic, and I am very happy that this book and the In Common series hit the shelf with a creative commons licence.

I wish to dedicate my work to all commoners in struggle, for their dedication to reproduce life through value practices obsti-nately opposed to that of normalised capitalist processes, and their efforts to be resilient, open-minded and creative in adverse circumstances.

Introduction: Omnia Sunt Communia

Our time

Our time is a time in which ever-devastating crises combine together to add further sorrow to the already many existing ones. As individuals we sense tremendous powers out there moving things around in directions we do not control, while fear and anxiety, often projected into xenophobia and racism, build in ways that are directly proportional to our dependence on those powers and our precarious status. In such critical conditions there are winners and losers, those who profit from the crises and those who lose out, and most people, as usual, feel they are going to lose out. For example, the ever-faster melting of polar ice, the changing of the seasons, the erratic intensification of extreme atmospheric events, and of the politicians' charade on climate change, are elements of the climate crisis in the sense that some people are working to profit from it while most of the world's population will suffer if they do not have the means to adapt, unless a radical change in the way we (re)produce our lives occurs. Silences and illusions are packaged as progress; there's no cause for alarm after all, we are often told, we will one day hire engineers who will design big vacuum cleaners to suck up all the excess carbon dioxide and store it in old oilfields, and build big walls to protect the richest cities. Their safety will of course be 'assured', just as the nuclear plants of Fukushima were proclaimed safe before it contaminated vast areas of Japan and the Pacific Ocean following an earthquake and tsunami. While some scientists pipe bad news amplified on social networks, other scientists are thinking to blame humans for all the problems thinking we have moved to an unpredictable and life-destroying era dubbed the Anthropocene (Steffen et al. 2015) – although it should be called the Capitalocene (Moore 2014), since it is the profit-driven capitalist mode of production that is destroying pretty much every life system on earth (from biodiversity to fish stocks, from forests to relatively stable climate and water sources) even while many humans are trying to save it through struggles and alternative practices (Armiero and De Angelis 2017). Then again, the paladins of capitalist development tell us the fable that life on earth can be re-engineered in labs, selected to be useful, to be pretty, to substitute the loss of species, at least partially, dependent on the scale of investment in biotechnology research and development (R&D). From the point of view of the reproduction of capital, the environmental crisis is not that bad: by destroying things it allows for the creation of new things at a profit or, in the mythology of the 'weak sustainability approach', human-made capital can perfectly substitute for natural capital, at a profit. Schumpeter, after all, already defined capitalism as 'creative destruction', and now capital is in the business of destroying life with a plan of creating new life in the lab, artificial life more compatible with the needs of accumulation.

Another critical element is the impact of the crisis of 2007–8 and the perpetual austerity that followed with its vicious cuts to the remnants of welfare and the wage, the major intensification of inequalities, the implosion of the 'middle' (working) class, as well as the new wave of enclosures such as land grabs in Asia and

Africa, and neoliberal governments' preservation of the global financial system from mortal collapse, a favour not returned by the banks, which instead insist that austerity should become the permanent regime to enable governments to save enough money to repay their debts to the banks and prevent future collapse. I wrote this book in the midst of a major exodus from war-torn regions, the multiple conflicts in Syria, the repeated bombing of civilians in Gaza, the boats in the Mediterranean Sea that often turn into coffins for the thousands of African and Middle Eastern migrants attempting a journey to safety and hope, where for many there is instead detention camps, xenophobia and the lowest wages. Walls have been built in Europe to regulate the flow of migrants and refugees – women, men and children – or to keep them out entirely, out in the cold, in wretched conditions, in an existential limbo with a destroyed past, no future and a precarious present. Moreover, whatever dimension of social reproduction we look at, precarity, the condition of existence in which there is little or no predictability or security, is everywhere: in the means of life (casual work contracts, low wages, all forms of debt), in the foods we eat (whenever we think of their ingredients and trace their production, interrogate their manipulation by agribusiness or the potential impact on our health), in housing condition and housing rights, in the growing racism and xenophobia, and so on. The capitalist neoliberal plan is no plan for the rest of us who are making social concerns and social reproduction the centre of our collective preoccupations. Under the neoliberal plan, each person must devote her life to sustaining competition, in conditions of ever-increasing resource constraints and corrupted goals, which reproduce the same collective problems.

The only plan is to increasing precariousness of every aspect of life, again at a profit for capital.

The intensification of these critical phenomena, however, also becomes one of the preoccupations of at least a section of the establishment and its institutions. The impossibility of identifying a way out of the current precarious conditions and multi-faceted crises for them is a question of 'risk assessment', that peculiar system of accounting used by military, geopolitical and financial agencies to suggest the chances that conditions will develop in a way that destabilises the profit system. The Pentagon, for example, sees the risk brought by climate change as 'urgent and growing', recognising that climate-related security risks include social impacts, migration and war, as in the case of Syria:

> from 2006–2011, a severe multi-year drought affected Syria and contributed to massive agriculture failures and population displacements. Large movements of rural dwellers to city centres coincided with the presence of large numbers of Iraqi refugees in Syrian cities, effectively overwhelming institutional capacity to respond constructively to the changing service demands. (Department of Defense 2015: 4)

Recognising climate change as a 'present security threat' and 'not strictly a long term security risk', all agencies of the US military are also considering financial and security meltdown, whether brought about by energy crisis, financial crisis or dollar collapse. Consequently they are preparing a new surveillance and security regime also addressed to the threat of global insurrection and radicalisation. Between 2007 and 2013, the US National Security Agency (NSA) obtained access to emails, chat, videos, photos, stored data, VoIP communications, file transfers, video confer-encing, logins, and online social networks from pretty much all data providers. The NSA can also access special targeted commu-nications without having to request them from the service providers (Greenwald and MacAskill 2013). With such a massive amount of available data, past or emerging social movements and waves of radicalisation are researched in multimillion-dollar projects such as the Minerva Initiative, a Department of Defense-sponsored social sciences research programme launched in 2008 'focussing on areas of strategic importance to U.S. national security policy'. This has included studies of social mobilisation in South Asia, the Middle East and North Africa, West Africa and Central Eurasia. One project, by the Pentagon and Cornell University, hoped to determine 'the critical mass (tipping point)' of social contagions by studying 'digital traces', for instance relating to 'the 2011 Egyptian revolution, the 2011 Russian Duma elections, the 2012 Nigerian fuel subsidy crisis and the 2013 Gazi park protests in Turkey.' Another, led by the Pentagon and the universities of St Andrews and King Juan Carlos ponders 'who does not become a terrorist and why?' (Rasmussen, English and Alonso 2013). Yet another, led by University College London with collaborators from Imperial College and the University of East London and the University of Aarhus, studied the life histories of NGO members sympathetic to radical causes to focus on 'The Social Ecology of Radicalisation', capitalising on the knowledge and method of criminology to investigate places, processes and systemic processes promoting radicalisation.[1]

The story that crises are linked to some sort of mobilisation and social conflict is not new. According to the Economist Intel-ligence Unit, 65 countries out of 150 (43 per cent) were at high or very high risk of social unrest in 2014. That is an increase of 19 countries in the high-risk category compared with a report five years earlier (The Economist 2013). But what is more interesting than the effects of anticipated social movements is the fear underlying much of media pronouncement on this. Venture capitalist Nick Hanauer warns his 1% class, with their multimillion-dollar houses and private jet planes, that 'the pitchforks are coming' and that 'revolutions come gradually and then suddenly'. London's *The Telegraph* reports that a 'credit rating agency raised the prospect that future tax rises and spending cuts could trigger social unrest in a number of countries' (Conway 2009). Social unrest poses the chance of real apocalypse for the establishment, and so it is getting ready to repress it: for example, while the police force in Michigan was one of the first in the USA to equip itself with military surplus items, including armoured trucks, grenade launchers and bayonets, in August 2014 in Ferguson, Missouri, heavily armed police and armoured trucks clashed with protesters over the Michael Brown shooting.

Will the suspected growing mobilised energy be able to open a space with the establishment of new institutions, new social norms and a new regime of values, or is the establishment forging sufficient means to confront, limit and absorb their impact? The establishment, or the global 1% as it is called today – replacing with an accounting sign the more 'old school' term *the bourgeoisie* – will definitely not give up easily its position of privilege, and its powers have grown ever more in the years of the crisis. According to Oxfam (2016) the 62 richest people in the world – who would comfortably fit inside a London double-decker bus – have the same total wealth as the bottom half of the world's population, or 3.5 billion people. Global inequality has grown at an astonishing rate since 2010, when 388 of the richest people were required to match the wealth of the bottom half of the world's people. Much of this concentration of wealth has occurred through the neoliberal states' 'licensed larceny' (Hildyard 2016): the process of enclosures, expropriations, looting, financial extraction and tax avoidance (using tax havens) that is impoverishing the Global South and larger and larger areas of the Global North. Moreover, the size of the global wealth in the hands of the richest means that this 1% class has a tremendous capacity to mobilise financial resources to protect themselves, either viciously or subtly, for a long time, reinforcing divisions among the 99% and creating new divisions.

The real problem for most of us is thus our material dependence on this corrupt system aimed at accumulation and profiteering, which shows scant interest in the resilience of ecological processes, in the decline in biodiversity,[2] in the quantity and quality of resources destined for social reproduction, or in the type and rhythms of work that fails to sustain a good quality of human life.

So, this is our time, corresponding to the contemporary phase of the too-long neoliberal era – a plan A of a capitalist regime aiming to develop the most devastating forces of capital by also criminalising as a 'free ride' any instance of redistribution and conviviality, forgetting that redistribution is occurring all the time in neoliberalism, but in favour of the rich (Reich 2014). It could be even worse. If social resistance was not diffused in so many areas, the neoliberal plan A could march on abolishing people's remaining rights, further wiping out environmental regulation in order to reduce capital's costs, tightening up surveillance to develop ever more dystopian means of repression. If you think we are at the bottom, think again, and be glad that many do speak out and struggle on: in doing so they are creating a force of attrition against the neoliberal plan.

So, will growing social movements be able to deliver a new form of capitalism, or even to push towards postcapitalism, or is it more likely that they will be overcome by tanks, pepper spray and old-style bayonets? There is, of course, a section of the estab-lishment that thinks in terms of a plan B for capitalist regimes. This section proposes that the state must reverse the current trend of redistribution, reducing the gap between rich and poor, and reregulate banks and the financial sector, while adopting a more vigorous policy to deal with climate change (most likely with some public investment in megatechnologies). Although some effective policy of redistribution to the poor and the work-ing class would be a central aspect of an alternative agenda – a basic income perhaps – I do not think this would be enough to deal with the capitalist-generated problems from a capitalist perspective, without at the same time promoting capitalist accu-mulation. A plan B won't work for capital, unless perhaps it is preceded (like last time) by a huge devaluation of capital and wages brought about by economic crisis, destruction and massa-cre on a huge scale (not dissimilar to, if not greater than, that of World War Two). This is in order to allow the rate of profit to be high enough for capitalists to start to reinvest again, a rate of profit which today is at a historic low (Roberts 2016). We have to remember something else about plan B. Last time round (1945 to the mid 1970s), the increase in the social wage was accompanied by an increase in productivity brought about by workers' relin-quishing of the control of production to managers, the so-called productivity deals (De Angelis 2000). This enabled capitalist and workers to have the same share of wages/profits within a growing economy. The 'old' new deal was also based on a series of gendered and racialised exclusions from it, and could only work again by producing some people as unwaged and others as waged (De Angelis 2000). A plan B today would not be immune to the need to exclude, reproduce hierarchies, further discipline and control, and deeply securitise. Ultimately, however, for plan B to work for capital, the 'deal' must have a positive effect on profitability and not only on the social wage. This means that there has to be a correspondence between the growth of the social wage rate (i.e. wages per hour) and the growth of productivity (output per hour). This would guarantee that profit per hour also increases at the same level and that the overall wages/profit share remains more or less constant. Today the deal could be this: a basic income to all (indexed to inflation would be great and including non-citizens would be best) plus some key services and rights (health, education, etc.) versus complete, both-ways flexibility of labour. If such a deal with capital would allow strong economic growth (capital's ultimate desire), we would nevertheless still be left to deal with the huge environmental consequences, from biodiversity to global warming and climate change, with their consequences for many communities around the world: it would be difficult if not impossible to square the circle of maintaining a system in which capital accumulation is a priority together with both a huge reduction in materials extraction and carbon gases and an increase in biodiversity. The *homo oeconomicus* dream of an increasing global middle class, still presented in the development manuals, is our collective nightmare.

Perhaps it would be better for the rest of us to start thinking through the problem of alternative system building within the

context of a society in which capitalist, financial and state policies are grabbing so much of our time and common wealth.

Plan C

Is it possible to find a collective path towards an exit from capitalist production and authoritarian and corrupted state systems
through system change? How do we do that?

In my book *The Beginning of History* (De Angelis 2007a), I
began to pose the question of alternatives in terms of commons,
value practices that are alternative to that of capital and that are
interlinked by commons networks. By and large, the commons
imply a plurality of people (a community) sharing resources
and governing them and their own relations and (re)production
processes through horizontal doing in common, commoning.
Although commons are institutions ingrained deep in human
history that are prima facie distinct from social movements, in
the last few years we have witnessed several cases of alignment
of social movements to the commons, a commons turn which
offers great potential. We have witnessed several social movements directly linked with the defence of a commons (the Gezi
Park protests in Istanbul in May 2013, for example), the creation
of new commons to face the Greek crisis (the crisis began in
2010 and solidarity is still ongoing in Greece; see boxes 2 and 3),
and the use of commons as an organisational model of struggle
(the *indignados* in Spain, from May 2011; the Occupy movements in the USA, beginning in September 2011; Box 1). These
are only a few examples. The commons as a political principle
(Dardot and Laval 2015) is extending: from campaigns against
water privatisation in Italy to principles of city administration
(Barcelona, Naples); from the occupation of an old theatre for

a new type of production in commons knowledge (Teatro Valle in Rome) to grassroots movements and struggles against enclosures of land and fisheries by multinational corporations around the world (ejatlas.org) and the self-government of indigenous territories in the Zapatistas-held areas of southeast Mexico.

What is the general sense of these movements? Could their very cultural diversity be the early warning sign that something deeply recomposing is moving within what Bauman (2000) calls liquid modernity, something that even classical ideologies such as anarchism, communism and socialism could not completely grasp? I believe so. I believe there is a social revolution in the making that, if recognised and able to attract more energies from people around the world, could give us a chance to embark on a process of transformation towards postcapitalist society. My underlying conception of revolution (De Angelis 2014a) is aligned to that of Marx which sees social revolutions – that is, the growth of alternative modes of production – as the material condition for any political revolution. A radical transformation of our world implies that people come together into communities that develop these alternatives to the logic of capitalism, multiply them and interconnect them: I understand commons to be such alternatives. In this book, commons are not just resources held in common, or commonwealth, but social systems whose elements are commonwealth, a community of commoners, and the ongoing interactions, phases of decision making and communal labour process that together are called commoning. Like any social systems, they are sites of powers, and in this book I argue that it is these social powers and social forces that, if they develop and are oriented towards expansion and the creation of greater spheres of commons ecologies, could represent a meaningful challenge to capitalist processes and statists' neoliberal policies.

But where are commons? Many commons are already latent within society and channel much of the support and resources through which we reproduce our lives and knowledge. We are generally born into a commons, even if it only consists of interactions with our parents or carers, siblings and friends. As soon as the process of socialisation begins, we reproduce our subjectivities in bodies and spirit through engagement in social cooperation that confronts us with the need to develop values practices and measures that are truly alternative to the subordination of life to profit or that push us to learn to adapt to it while keeping a distinct identity. Values practices, such as loyalty to friends, conviviality, mutual aid, care, and even struggles, are developed in the commons. As soon as these networks of social cooperation develop into systematic patterns in neighbourhood associations, cooperatives, social centres, food networks and social movements (and given the development of communication and information technologies), these commons-based forms of social cooperation have the potential to expand and reshape their boundaries, renew their social compositions, develop multicultures of horizontality, destabilise official science – especially that official science promoted by agribusiness or nuclear engineering – and give rise to commons ecologies, that is, plural and diverse cooperating commons with institutions and arrangements we cannot predict. In this way, commons cannot be reduced to the empirical findings and interpretations of commons theories, and they do not have a glove fit with any model put forward by any romantic or radical versions of what constitute good or socially just systems in the abstract. The very fact that commons have to live in environments that include capitalist and state systems means that their expansion is met by constraints posited by this social environment. It is up to the commons, therefore, to develop their own politics to attempt to shift these constraints, whether this is concerned with fighting laws that prohibit the sharing of commons-produced seeds, or the right to a basic income to guarantee a source of income to put back into the commons, or the rights of communities to decide that a high-speed train track, a new motorway or a dam cannot be built in a given territory.

Although commons exist in the here and now, their further development and interlacing would also enable us to respond to the inevitable crisis of capital and climate disaster in ways that amplify commons autonomy vis-à-vis capital and the top-down logic of states. One broad group of commons activities, I think, needs to have a privileged role to play (without taking anything from the importance of the knowledge commons and peer-to-peer networks in cyberspace), that is, all those activities that serve the immediate purpose of reproducing life, both of human beings and of nature. These commons of reproduction are already being set up spontaneously by many commoners around the world to address lacks and needs or aspirations for accessing healthy food, housing, water, social care and education. But besides their meeting of needs I believe the further development of these and similar commons would be such a crucial strategic asset that they would form the material basis of a new commons renaissance in many spheres, building its foundation on these reproduction commons. This is because not only would they give us the benefit of new communities, new cultures, and new methods of establishing wellbeing, security and trust within complex organisation, they would also protect us from the whims of financial markets, and, especially, increase our security and power to refuse the exploitation of capitalist markets. The more that capital can blackmail us into poorer conditions, higher insecurity and ever-more gruelling work rhythms, the less we have the power to refuse its logic. Conversely, this power grows the more we have alternative means for our reproduction.

In this book I have developed an approach to the commons as variegated social systems operating within an environment in which not only ecological systems but also other, often contrasting or co-opting, social systems, such as state and capital, operate. I discuss critically commons theories and extract some useful elements. I explore commons systemic features, their interactions to shape systems at greater scale, the development of commons ecologies, the strategies of capital to deal with commons, the relation with social movements, and the complex possibility that commons could develop into a hegemonic force to push us into a postcapitalist mode of production. The title of this book, *Omnia Sunt Communia* (All in Common), could have been the battle slogan of the German Protestant reformer priest Thomas Müntzer, an important figure in revolutionary Christianity and the European peasant rebellions of the sixteenth century, as suggested by the novel *Q* (Luther Blisset 2003). But it could also be the 'confession' extracted through torture of what Müntzer's captors most feared, the spectre of communism: 'all things are to be held in common and distribution should be to each according to his need' (Müntzer 1988: 437). Add 'from each according to their capacities' and we have the full definition of modern communism as spelled out by Karl Marx in the *Critique of the Gotha Programme* (Marx 1970): 'to each according to their needs and from each according to their capacities'. But my book is not a book on communist doctrine; it only enunciates a *communist horizon – omnia sunt communia –* and discusses the social forces that are best equipped to embark on the journey: not people, not the multitude of individual subjects, but the diverse multitude of the commons, and within them the individual subjects socialised to the commons, the commoners.

I am a commoner

You should know that I am a commoner, and therefore I see my work as a contribution to a common cause, as much as seeding wheat and harvesting by a convivial collective is a contribution to the common cause of living. Much as we can discuss appropriate food-growing techniques and make collective decisions that lead to actions, my work is a contribution to the discussion of the social and economic postcapitalist transformation of our society. The form of that postcapitalism is not for me to say, since I believe that it will depend on billions of interactions in power fields that we cannot anticipate. But we can work towards the building of those power fields, selecting the most appropriate avenue to do so: strengthening the commons and maximising their autonomy from state and capital, while still interacting with the latter when necessary, even attempting their transformation.

Not long ago I presented a plan, to my association in the Emilian Appenines, for the local production of an antique strain of wheat and for the building of what could be the first local supply chain for the production of bread from that wheat. The plan followed a year of public meetings and conversations on the damage to our intestines and our health in general of modern wheat, which has been selected to have the very high levels of gluten necessary to allow mechanised multinational agro-industry to transform it quickly into bread, pasta, pizza dough, biscuits and children's snacks. We realised also that modern methods of flour milling discard bran and destroy the most nutritious aspect of wheat, wheatgerm, which is then packaged and sold as a supplement in pills or dry food in health shops. We realised that consuming industrial flour-based products is almost like eating chewing gum, and increases the incidence of coeliac disease, allergies and gluten sensitivity. The plan to create a local alternative was discussed, criticised and in the end supported, even if we could have chosen to abandon it. I see my contribution in this book as being in the same vein. The material in this book is not as detailed as a plan, since the complexity of social transformation is, needless to say, much greater than that of producing wheat with limited means, and so I will deal with this complexity at a greater level of abstraction. I will not indulge, as in previous works, on the horrors of capitalist production and state repression, although these are ever-present in my thinking. My focusing on the path that alternatives carve out in the present, and my speculation on the broad dynamics necessary to overcome capitalist production nevertheless share a deep problematic intrinsic to the wheat plan adopted by my small association. The latter plan does not take into account the contingencies of the future – a powerful storm, wild boars or hungry deer can ruin our crop as much as a new world war or deepened and more pervasive forms of repression and regulation can push more commons underground. Disastrous climate change and wars can destroy crops as well as the social relations keeping commons together. Political persecution can further increase the flight of refugees away from their commons which only in time could be reconstructed anew and in new forms. I am aware of all this, as many are, but I am not engaged with scenario building in this book, only with what I think are the foundational principles of social transformation towards a commons-based postcapitalist transformation of our societies.

Moreover, the readership of this book will be, I hope, far larger that the couple of dozen who belong to my association in Italy, and they could generate insights to expand the present work in new directions, or dismiss it as the work of a utopian who does not spell out the utopia, an idealist who does not abandon a preoccupation with conditions and power fields, a romanticist who is the last to romanticise hard work and oppression, and does not desire to replace the old with the new, but only to let the old speak to us in new terms. Mine is the attitude of those specific types of commoners who focus not only on their daily life but also on pushing the boundaries of commons alternatives within broader circuits of society. From the moment I release this book to the public, I am no longer its owner, so I can only make an appeal to consider it part of our commonwealth: just a little dot in our collective swing towards *omnia sunt communia*.

What will follow

There is neither prophecy nor mythology in enunciating a horizon such as *omnia sunt communia*, only a moving principle, a sense of meta-directionality when applying social forces in specific contexts of the here and now. On the other hand, the subjects of this movement, the commons, are not here understood as *individual* subjects, but as already systemic subjects within which individual subjects are already socialised – at least to a certain extent – to life in common. It is for this reason that my opening in Chapter 1 echoes Marx's opening in Chapter 1 of *Capital*, just read from the bottom up. While for Marx the commodity is the elementary form of capitalist wealth, so for me common goods are the elementary form of wealth of a postcapitalist world. But just as Marx's commodity is itself a contradictory form between use value and exchange value opening up to the discussion of capital as a system (De Angelis 2007a), so I posit the common goods, or commonwealth, as a twofold form opening to the discussion of commons as systems. I thus offer an understanding of commons that contrasts with many other contemporary ones.

I continue Chapter 1 with a critical review of some classic and contemporary understandings of common goods and problematise their meanings within a concept of commons as social systems. Notice here that I differentiate between the commons and common goods, or commonwealth. This is crucial to my conception, marking a clear differentiation from the widespread conflating of the two concepts. In this chapter I set out this differentiation by indicating that the common goods (commonwealth) are only one element of the commons while the latter are specific social systems that include also commoners (the social subjects) and the activity of doing in common, or commoning. Notice also that by *commonwealth* I do not understand a general political statement, only one of the conditions of existence of particular commons (the other being commoners, community and commoning). Therefore my use of the term *commonwealth* does not align in this book to the understanding of the term by Hardt and Negri (2009), who regard everything produced as part of the commonwealth since it is produced in common. In their work, the common (singular) is a political principle that interprets the many struggles around us against neoliberalism (Bardot and Laval 2015). My approach is different. Although I share their political stance that, indeed, everything that is produced on earth is produced by social labour and therefore we can claim it as commonwealth, in reality this claim encounters the barrier of property rights enforced by state and capital, which we cannot overcome by social movements alone. Such a barrier also exists in the actual structure and subjectivities of contemporary modes of production, implying that we are not yet at the point of claiming the wealth produced by all social cooperation as commonwealth. To reach that point is the task of the commons (plural) as effective social forces for the construction of alternatives and of struggle. The expansion of the commons systems and their greater integration in commons ecologies is what would allow us, together with social movements, at some point in the future to give *effective force* to such a general commonwealth claim. For this very reason, I should perhaps use *the common* (singular) only as a sense horizon of a commons movement, as in my understanding of *omnia sunt communia*. Strategic thinking, however, requires to be grounded in contexts, and the expansion of the commons needs to capture within them the elements produced outside the commons and thus develop and change their form.

Having posited commons as a system, in Chapter 2 I review my initial basic conceptual toolbox with respect to systems. The conceptual toolbox here is basic to the extent I am using a penknife to dig a hole instead of a shovel. In the definition of power, for example, I refer to a formulation that is little used in my usual radical circles – that of Kurt Lewin – without much reference to the power masters, such as Weber, Foucault, Mann or Lukes. It is not that their writing on power – fundamental for generations – is unimportant for the conception of the commons; in many of my notes and previous publications they are evidently important. But I needed tools that I could use effectively and rapidly to explain my intuitions on how the commons could turn into social forces and move on. Lewin's idea of force field is similar to something my teacher and friend Harry Cleaver of the University of Texas at Austin told me when I was a postgraduate student in the late 1980s, to explain to me that every category of Marx's *Capital* is a category of class struggle. As a Newtonian physicist he drew on a paper towel two arrow lines pushing in different directions, thus representing 'conflicting' social forces, the length of the arrow summarising its force and the orientation of the arrow its direction or objectives, desires or aspirations. The beauty of Kurt Lewin's notion of force field is also that he connects the notion of *values*, *power* and *goals* to that of *force field*, making these key concepts variations, modulations or deviations on the same 'substance'. In subsequent chapters I translate this 'substance' in terms of labour – whether in the social form of commoning for the commons or in that of exploited abstract labour for capital. I use Lewin's conceptualisation as loosely as I can to give this insight a grounding and to understand both capital and the commons as qualitatively and opposed social forces, hence able to construct the world in different ways, often opposing and clashing, other times cutting deals.

In Chapter 3 I briefly discuss the general characteristics of two of the three elements constituting the commons, that is, commonwealth (or common goods) and community, the plurality of commoners and the set of their relations. I leave a fuller discussion of this crucial element, that of commoning, to chapters 6 and 7, that is, until after I disentangle other system properties of the commons.

I do this in chapters 4 and 5, where I discuss the insights on the commons we can obtain from two important but generally unrelated authors, whom I will draw from to illustrate two aspects of my analysis. One, discussed in Chapter 4, is Elinor Ostrom, Nobel prizewinner in economics in 2009 for her life's work on the commons. The other, discussed in Chapter 5, is Karl Marx, the critic and revolutionary, for his work on the capitalist mode of production as a system geared towards accumulation and riddled with class struggle. Since my analysis posits the commons as a system inserted within fields of power relations vis-à-vis capital and state, which in its neoliberal form is only a champion of capitalist interests, by discussing Ostrom and Marx in two successive chapters I am able to review critically what each author leaves out in her or his work. Ostrom lacks a critical stance on the often-threatening environment, including capital and the state, that most commons experience, and the capability of commoners to give rise to commons even when she logically excludes the possibility. Marx leaves out the (re)productive force that the commons constitutes in the very capitalist world that he describes and analyses.

The great work of Elinor Ostrom is foundational to the theory of the commons, much as Adam Smith's and David Ricardo's work were foundational to the theory of the capitalist economy. In Chapter 4 I also develop some further conceptual tools that revise Ostrom's notion of resources and expand the concept of common resources to include what conventional economics calls 'private goods'.

In Chapter 5, on Marx, I derive the formula of the commons
– a system-like stock-and-flow circuit modelled on Marx's
circuit of capital. Here I build on the feminist debates of the
1970s criticising Marx for disregarding the circuit of reproduction of labour power. I reproduce this circuit of reproduction of
labour power and argue that itself it is but a moment of a broader
circuit, that of the (re)production of commons. In this chapter
I reveal the commons popping out of our daily life in which
capitalist production, the anathema of commons, is coupled to
systems that reproduce labour power. In this section I discuss
the system of the 'economy' as the articulation between two
circuits introduced by Marx in the first volume of *Capital*: the
selling-in-order-to-buy system, which we, commoners, do in
order to live with limited means in relation to the powers within
society, and the buying-in-order-to-sell system of capitalist
profit logic. This allows me to introduce the dramatis personae
whose actions and communication loops give rise to the interplay of commoners and capitalists. I then break down the two
circuits to reveal the realities of production behind them. While
the analytical breaking down of the capital circuit does not reveal
anything more than what Marx taught us – that is, exploitation
within a capitalist valorisation system – in breaking down the
selling-in-order-to-buy circuit I discover the variegated world
of commons. This selling-in-order-to-buy circuit is nothing
more than a membrane of interchange between commons and
capital systems, the boundary separating commons from capital.
As a subset of a larger commons circuit, the simple selling-in-
order-to-buy circuit only appears as *contingently* necessary, and
different commons may be distinguished by the degree of their
dependence on capital's monetary circuits.

The question of commons governance is one of self-management horizontality and participation, which is a moment of *commoning*, the doing in common. I devote the next two chapters to commoning. I wrote most of Chapter 6 right after a four-month trip to various areas of Ecuador, Bolivia and Peru in 2010 while on sabbatical leave. It describes techniques of mobilisation of social labour to do commoning. In these areas I discovered that there are two main ways to mobilise social labour for the commons: as a moment in a network of reciprocity (reciprocal labour) or as a call from a recognised node in a network in which all the community participates (communal labour). In each case, a dense cultural, social and affective lattice obviously defines the costs and benefits of participation or absence from the activity. What is remarkable to me, however, is that on the surface, these modalities of mobilisations were and are also operating in European and North American cultures. From this perspective, therefore, *indigeneity* is something that is crucially not an exotic phenomenon of distant societies, but a phenomenon of the commons everywhere, albeit expressed in different cultural forms.

I also use here some of the categories of the cognitive sociologist John Fiske to discuss measuring and valuing processes. I here propose the hypothesis that commoning is the production of the dance of values as opposed to the capitalist imposition of abstract labour as the substance of capitalist value. It is a dance, because in their diversity commoners seeking consensus – whether through collective choice or constitutional decision, or through the praxis of their operations – negotiate among themselves different models of social cooperation in different contexts and conditions they face.

In Chapter 7, I interrogate bottom-up commons histories on autonomy, and I translate the work of evolutionary biologists Maturama and Varela on cells as autonomous and autopoietic systems in terms that give insight on commons systems. I also relate these commons properties of autonomy and autopoiesis to the production of boundary and sense. Commoning thus becomes the foundational source of commons power, it gives forms to autonomy and autopoiesis, and it shapes the types of boundaries of commons systems and the 'sense' of the commoners.

In Chapter 8 commoning becomes the social force that connects, creating larger commons systems. I call this *boundary commoning*, the commoning that exists at the boundaries of commons systems and that creates social forms of any scale, opens up the boundaries, establishes connections, and sustains commons ecologies, or that could reshape existing institutions from the ground up through commonalisation and create new ones. I discuss the case of Genuino Clandestino, a network of small farmers and consumers that has developed an insightful organisation of food sovereignty in Italy; I demonstrate how alternatives could develop through boundary commoning. The development of boundary commoning allows the expansions of commons systems and the creation of commons ecologies, patterned exchanges and interaction among different commons. In this chapter I also discuss my conception of social revolution, which relies on this expansion, and relate it to political revolution and postcapitalist transformation.

In Chapter 9 I discuss some issues linked to the question of commons movements, commons co-optation, and commons and the public. I argue that what system theorists such as Maturama, Varela and Luhmann define as 'structural coupling' among systems allows one system to access and use the complexity of other systems. Thus, even if it is true that capital can co-opt commons, the opposite is also true: the commons can access the complexity of capital systems for their own development. I then discuss the relation between the system of social movements and the commons, and I argue that they are both more effective in social change when they are weaved in virtuous cycles with their own task: the social movement to shift the subjective and objective constraints set in place by state and capital, and the commons to expand in this new space with new commons-based modes of production. I also argue that boundary commoning could be extended to the public realm even if the degree of its commonalisation obviously depends on local conditions and the social force mobilised by commons.

In Chapter 10 I attempt fully to take stock of the complexity of the problematic of social transformation towards postcapitalism. Clearly, in reality, this transformation does not occur in a vacuum, but successes for the development of the commons will depend on the social forces that are deployed and mobilised. I assume a generalised mutation of contemporary social movements into commons movements. I ask here what are the general conditions within which these commons movements could succesfully instigate social change. Such a naïve question becomes more grounded if we raise it in the context of complexity theory and Ashby's Law of Requisite Variety. This law tells us that in order for the regulators (or state and capital, in Marxian language) to be able to regulate society in which also commons exists, they need to match the complexity of society. Failing this, the regulators cannot regulate. State and capital can match the ever-increasing complexity of society only through two means: either by reducing the complexity of society through repression, or by trying to transform it into a form of complexity that is compatible with their processes and the complexity already present within the capital and state regulators. I argue that in this instance elements of complexity science can align to Marx's proposition that social revolution (as revolution of the modes of production) is a prerequisite of political revolutions (taking the 'winter palace'). Through the synchronisation of social movements and commons – or commons movements as defined in Chapter 9 – it would be possible at the same time to increase the complexity that capital and state cannot in the short term manage, and to self-govern this new complexity in new commons ecologies. This is a theoretical proposition certainly, but the 'invisible hand' of Adam Smith was a theoretical proposition that allowed capitalists to orient themselves when replacing the feudal privilege with theirs.

Some parts of this book are simpler than others. I do depend on concepts that are not common currency in social and political science projects. My only disclaimer here is that the difficulty is not only in the joining of these important concepts and theories but, also and more important, in the actual creation and expansion of alternatives to capitalist production. The path of social change is not made of plastic, nor is it plastered with 'conveniences'. In the end, we have only each other, the commonwealth we still have to claim back, and a life of convivial commoning.

Part one

Commons as systems

Chapter 1

Common goods

The twofold character of common goods

The wealth of postcapitalist society as it peeps on the horizon of the many heterogeneous practices of communities, associations, peer-to-peer networks and social movements appears in the first instance as a collection of common goods, a commonwealth. We need therefore to enquire about this elementary form of postcapitalist wealth.

Common goods have a twofold character, revealed in the first place by their own name, which combines a substantive (good) with an adjective (common). They are 'goods' in the sense of being social objects of *value*, use values, objects (whether tangible or not) that satisfy given socially determined needs, desires and aspirations. They are *common* goods, in the sense that they are *use value* to a *plurality*. Thus, in the first instance, *common goods are use value for a plurality*.

However, this is not sufficient to define common goods in the postcapitalist sense. An airport lounge is a use value to a plurality, as is any public space, a city, a train, a park, a school or a street. Also, any mass-produced commodity is a use value to a plurality in the sense that it serves the necessary or acquired needs of a subset of a population, although this cup, this computer, this car is a use value to me. *What is common to all these cases is that the plurality is largely silent; it is only a passive user or consumer of these goods.* To make it a common good, the plurality needs to come alive as a plurality of commoners, by claiming ownership of that good. To claim ownership is not simply a question of defining property rights in the legal sense. A plurality that claims ownership of one or more use values is one that, in different forms, given situations and contexts, not only uses or accesses that use value, but that also governs its production and reproduction, its sustainability and development. In thus doing, the plurality shapes a relationship to that good and to the environment within which it is produced, while the subjects of that plurality govern the relations with one another. This plurality therefore also creates other values besides the use value of the common goods. It creates relational values, by measuring, assessing and giving particular sense to the models of social relations through which the common goods are (re)produced and their use value is distributed among the commoners. In thus doing, and to the extent that the plurality sustains that claim of ownership, the common good is turned into an element of a common system or, briefly, a *commons*:[1] this built space is an element of the self-organised social centre in Milan; these pipes are an element of the water associations in Cochabamba, Bolivia; these garden tools are an element of my community garden in the Modena Apennines; this knowledge and know-how are elements of a peer-to-peer network in cyberspace.

The twofold character of a common good, therefore, is this: on the one hand it is a use value for a plurality; on the other it requires a plurality claiming and sustaining the ownership of the common good, and this can be done only through the creation of relational values, that is, values that select the 'goods and bads' of social action while at the same time sustaining and (re)producing one another, social relations, social practice and the ecology in which social practice is embedded. Thus the initial sentence of this chapter stands now to be corrected. The wealth of postcapitalist society *also* includes this normative and relational wealth.

This implies that the common good coincides with a force field that, if the commons are produced in a contest of capitalist domination, will often be oriented by goals that run opposite to capitalist production. Indeed, the twofold character of the common good is distinctively different from the twofold character of the commodity in a social system dominated by capital, as discussed by Marx (1976) in the first chapter of *Capital*. The commodity is a use value and an exchange value. However the latter is not the result of a plurality taking ownership of the good produced in common (in a factory, an office, through a diffused network of producers held together through competitive markets, etc.), but the result of an individualised plurality divided in wage and wealth hierarchy and set to compete for livelihood against one another and for which their common condition of production is a matter of insignificance, an unproblematised given, a fact of life one does not even try to question or govern in some way, and therefore an alien force. In capitalist commodity production, value presents itself as exchange value, neither good nor bad but a ratio: pounds per carton of milk; euros per smart phone; dollars per hamburger. Values here induce force only within a systemic integration with other capitalist producers who take these ratios as a benchmark to meet or beat in order to reach their own goals of profit. The values of conviviality, social justice and ecological balance as well as the goal of livelihood get squeezed out by this incessant competitive struggle, which instead shows what such a systemic integration really values: growth for growth's sake. This value, this inducement to a social force field that ultimately produces increasingly social injustice, accelerates global warming and establishes the horror of Capitalocene, occurs within capital systemic loops that impose measures, assessments and sense production that are heteronymous to (outside) the producers themselves, thus giving rise to exploitation, widening power hierarchies and environmental catastrophe.[2] This is possible to the extent that social conflict – in the form of class and community conflict – has insufficient direction and force in constituting a balancing feedback mechanism for the definition of commodities' exchange values, and the constitution of the what, the how, the how much, the who and the why of production.

The twofold character of common goods is at the basis of our understanding of commons as specific social systems, very different from capital, which if they develop into a strong enough social force can contrast with and replace capital production. The twofold character of the common good contains two basic elements – one objective (the 'common goods') and one subjective (an ownership claiming a plurality of subjects) – that give us an entry point to understand commons as *social systems*.[3] The potential dynamism and movement of these commons social systems emerges from two *interconnected* processes.

One is internal to the commons itself, and defines the modes in which a plurality of subjects establishes their ownership to the common goods and the forms of the social relations they set in place, negotiate or even contest. For example, in Zapatistas-held areas of Mexico, the indigenous communities together hold the territories and the land as commons, but women therein constitute social movements to question women's subordinate position in the communities. Here commons are also centred on social conflict, but a conflict that is reconciled with itself in the sense that it is not concealed, marginalised and brushed aside as 'deviance' but instead acknowledged as the key expression of democratic vigour.

The other element that give commons dynamism and movement is external to the commons, and given by the way in which the commons in question are articulated or structurally *coupled* to other commons or capitalist circuits of praxis, together with the degree in which they are exposed to destructive social forces such as the enclosing or co-opting force of capital. The nature and effective transformational force of these endogenous and exogenous processes is key to understanding, and they problematise the development of commons systems as a social force that is transformative of the real. Hence it is impossible to understand commons without understanding capital. Even when we deal with the commons in very general and abstract terms to highlight their properties, the commons we deal with are never romantic outsides, but *situated* outsides, social systems that must negotiate their way in an environment in which predator capitalist systems are ready to enclose or subordinate commons. For this reason, I centre this investigation with the question of the relation between commons and capital systems, a relation that has always been crucial, but particularly so in moment of crises, as today. This question will be a constant preoccupation throughout the book, and is acknowledged in the very definition of commons as social systems, having as their environment also other systems such as capital systems. I will deal with this in subsequent chapters.

We need thus to keep an analytical distinction between common goods and commons, as the former defines for us only *some* systems *elements*, but not the types of relations and correspondent systemic processes of the latter. At this stage, we can simply refer to these structural elements as, on one hand, a use value for a plurality and, on the other, a plurality claiming and sustaining ownership of the common good, or, commons resources and *commoners' communities*. It will also become clear in later chapters that there is a third, central element of the commons, its driving force, constituted by the doing in common of the commoners, or commoning.

On common goods

Common goods (as use value for a plurality) and commons (as social systems) are often conflated in the contemporary literature on commons. Even when the rule-setting role of a plurality, or community, is acknowledged in defining the modality of access and governance of common goods, commons often become just another name for what is shared. Thus, since what is shared goes down in history and cuts across contemporary cultures with several variations, it is necessary to start looking at typologies of common goods.

If one types the term 'commons' into a search engine, apart for links to games, websites, the House of Commons and journals, what is found is a series of links to definitions of commons, and the vast majority of these define them as some sort of resources, as things, as common *goods*. In other words, much of the conventional wisdom on commons defines them as goods – resources – that are *shared* among a *plurality*. Our exploratory journey must therefore begin from this very basic general level, which is also relayed in more academic treatments of the commons. Here I explore some contradictions, limitations and strengths of approaching commons as goods when we seek to weave them into a narrative of emancipation.

The economist

A way to start to map commons as types of goods (commons goods) is to use the typology of 'goods' of neoclassical economics. Before briefly reviewing this, we must remind ourselves that when economists speak, they speak assuming big things, very big things. Their first assumption, of course, is their methodological individualism, which see people through the eyes of that social force we call capital, a force that has always driven towards the individualisation and atomisation of people, forging the chains that keep people separated from others. Therefore, for the economists, there cannot be commons in the sense discussed in the previous section, of systems brought about by a plurality. The economists' second assumption is that desires, dreams, needs – or, in short and using the abruptness of economic speech, preferences – could be 'aggregated' through a mathematical function, a social welfare function, ranking social states as less desirable, 'allowing governments to choose alternative complete descriptions of the society' to be ranked in such terms as 'less desirable, more desirable, or indifference for every possible pair of social states. The inputs in such a function include any variables considered to affect the economic welfare of a society'. Clearly, each of these variables is weighted according to particular algorithms and worldviews of powerful elites or raging commoners, since 'there are infinitively many ways to choose the weight[,] [s]o the resulting social preference

relation is arbitrary, in so far as the particular weights are arbitrary' (Feldman 1980: 194).

Social welfare functions have been used to represent prospec-
tive patterns of collective choice between alternative social
states, and in a sense this is precisely what the economist Paul
Samuelson wanted to do when he introduced the distinction between private and collective goods. He was seeking to
represent that social choice as being between capitalism and
socialism – or a definite optimal mixture between the two. Like
many of his colleagues in that pre-neoliberal era, he believed
that societies could find an 'optimum' welfare in the distribution
between collective and private goods, thus providing a historic
compromise, a deal among the two regimes of property and
management. Politically, that would have been like finding the
optimal 'coupling' between capitalism and socialism, an urgent
preoccupation of post-World War Two Western governments,
since after the cycle of working-class struggles that had followed
the Soviet revolution in 1917, elites had to think through how to
provide health, education, roads, pensions, in short welfare and
public goods (collective goods) to the masses, plus recognise
trade unions and increases of wages for core sections of working
class and *at the same time* allow profits for capital accumulation,
for growth. While at the aggregate level the coupling of capitalism and socialism was operationalised through governments'
Keynesian macroeconomc policies (De Angelis 2000), the
economic theory of these policies lacked micro-foundations.
This implies that Keynesian theory applied to the aggregate
macroeconomy, and it formally required to be linked to basic
microeconomic conceptions of choice. Samuelson's classification of goods was part of this enterprise. Thus he introduced the

distinction between private consumption goods and collective consumption goods in terms of whether these goods can be parcelled out among individuals, or whether their consumption can be done collectively 'in the sense that each individual's consumption of such a good leads to no subtraction from any other individual's consumption of that good' (Samuelson 1954: 386). Samuelson therefore introduced the question of rivalry in the use of goods. Goods are rival, if the use by one person subtracts from the total available to others. If it does not, then they are non-rival. For example, a physical formula, a software code, etc., are non-rival goods, as are the law, national security and the safety net. A few years later, taking the same line of enquiry, Musgrave (1959) introduces a different distinction among goods: not so much whether their use subtracts from the uses of others, but whether it is feasible to exclude people from the consumption of goods or not. The contributions of Samuelson and Musgrave have formed the basis for the 2-by-2 matrix in which economic goods are still classified today. Table 1.1 reports a milder and more recent version of this matrix, that introduced by commons scholar Elinor Ostrom (2000) which substitutes binaries with gradients, and rivalry with subtraction. Here exclusion and subtractabilities are not binaries, unlike the categories of Samuelson and Musgrave, but define gradient scales.

A few words are needed here to explain better what subtractability (or rivalry) and exclusion means for the economists. In economic theory, rivalry or a high degree of subtractability is a characteristic of a good, not of the capitalist social relations through which a good is produced. A rival (subtractable) good is a good whose consumption by one consumer prevents simultaneous consumption by other consumers. I am eating this sandwich, not you. On the other hand, it is non-rival (non-subtractable) if the cost of providing it to an additional individual is zero (marginal cost equal to zero). Knowledge is one example, or Internet services, although few goods can be said truly non-subtractable in all conditions. Let us take the Internet: it is non-rival (low subtractability) to the extent that there is enough mainframe and cable capacity to carry sufficient users. Up to this point, everybody can dance in cyberspace. But there is a point of congestion after which an extra user reduces the speed of all: in order to continue to have non-subtractability, more capacity needs to be added. This implies that more energy usage, more materials extraction needs to be considered. As I will argue,

Table 1.1 Commons as a type of good

		Subtractability of use	
		High ('rivalrous' good)	Low ('non-rivalrous' good)
Difficulty of excluding potential beneficiaries	High	Common-pool resources (common goods): groundwater basins, lakes, irrigation systems, fisheries, forests, etc.	Public goods: peace and security of a community, national defence, knowledge, fire protection, weather forecasts, etc.
	Low	Private goods: food, clothing, automobiles, etc.	Toll goods (club goods): theatres, private clubs, daycare centres, cable television

Adapted by De Angelis and Harvie (2014) from Ostrom (2010: fig. 1).

this problem is an important aspect of my criticism of cyber-communism, which regards the peer-to-peer exchanges creating free software or downloading music as an example of the future.

In any case, most tangible goods, both durable and non-durable, are subtractable goods. A hammer is a durable rival/subtractable good. One person's use of the hammer presents a significant barrier to others who desire to use that hammer at the same time. However, the first user does not *use up* the hammer, meaning that some rival goods can still be shared through time. An apple is a nondurable rival good: once an apple is eaten, it is used up and can no longer be eaten by others. Non-tangible goods can also be rivalrous. Examples include the ownership of radio spectra and domain names.

In contrast, non-rival goods may be consumed by one consumer without preventing simultaneous consumption by others. Most examples of non-rival goods are intangible. Broadcast television is an example of a non-rival good; when a consumer turns on a TV set, this does not prevent the TV in another consumer's house from working. The television itself is a rival good, but television broadcasts are non-rival goods. Other examples of non-rival goods include a beautiful scenic view, national defence, clean air, street lights and public safety (police and law courts).

More generally, most intellectual property is non-rival. In fact, certain types of intellectual property become more valuable as more people consume them (anti-rival). For example, the more people use a particular language, the more valuable that language becomes. However, while rival/subtractable goods can be commualised/shared, many of the non-rival goods that could be shared freely without asking anybody could be made scarce by technological and legal (property right) means.

Samuelson's Cold War distinction between public (collective) and private goods are on the diagonal from the upper right corner to the bottom left corner of Table 1.1. Goods that are non-rival are goods that can be enjoyed simultaneously by an unlimited number of consumers. Goods that are both non-rival and non-excludable are called public goods. This leaves two other cells. The one on the bottom left, low substractability and low difficulty to exclude, is what James Buchanan, writing in 1966, called 'club goods' (now, after Ostrom and Ostrom (1977), they are sometimes called toll goods). Club goods are goods that sit in between public and private goods and reveal to the economist an interesting aspect of social cooperation to theorise also along income class levels:

> Everyday experience reveals that there exists some most preferred or 'optimal' membership for almost any activity in which we engage, and that this membership varies in some relation to economic factors. European hotels have more communally shared bathrooms than their American counterparts. Middle and low income communities organise swimming-bathing facilities; high income communities are observed to enjoy privately owned swimming pools. (Buchanan 1965: 1)

To develop his theory, Buchanan sees both private goods and public goods as club goods of different 'optimal' membership: one person (or one family unit) for the former and infinity for the latter. So it is clear that his preoccupation with club goods is 'that of determining the membership margin, so to speak, the size of the most desirable cost consumption and sharing arrangement' (Buchanan 1965: 2).

I do not share this optimising preoccupation in this book, but I cannot avoid noting that Buchanan has opened a can of worms. If, instead of the neoclassical utility and profit-maximising functions, we assume that people *in different contexts* find their 'optimal' way to share goods, whatever their degrees of rivalry and exclusion, using criteria and measurements that are based not only on self-interest but also on valuing mutual aid, solidarity and affects in diverse contexts, then this idea of club goods – goods shared by a group of people of diverse number – is pretty much evoking that of common goods or commonwealth, which I understand as one constituent element of commons systems. Buchanan here sees that people can share all sort of goods, even what we think of as private goods, even 'shoes' or 'haircuts': 'Simultaneous physical sharing may not, of course, be possible; only one person can wear the shoes at each particular moment. However, for any finite period of time, sharing is possible even for such evidently private goods' (Buchanan 1965: 3). Schoolchildren, of course, know this when they pass around their pencils and erasers. But Buchanan also contemplates sharing for services, such as haircuts: 'Sharing here simply means that the individual receives a smaller quantity of the service. Sharing a 'haircut per month' with a second person is the same as consuming 'one-half haircut' per month' (Buchanan 1965: 3), the result of which would be people having longer hair on average. And if a haircut can be shared, why not private jets, luxurious yachts, or most-of-the-time-empty central London penthouses or 30-bedroom California villas. Analyses like Buchanan can be useful for sharing poverty, but why not for sharing wealth?

I am clearly starting off in a different direction from that chosen by commons scholars such as Elinor and Vincent Ostrom

(1977), who constrained the common property resources in one cell of their table.[4] Commons, in this sense, appear as goods that are subtractable and with a low degree of excludability. Fish, forests, water are examples of these goods. I will return to the analysis of Ostrom in Chapter 4. Here suffice it to say that in this mainstream approach, to be a *common* good is *purely a property of the thing, not of the plurality giving social meaning to the thing.* Economic theory has always been such a meagre consolation for those like me who still dream of different worlds.

Box 1 Occupy

The Occupy movement developed from the Occupy Wall Street movement which protested against social and economic inequality around the world and for less hierarchical social and economic relations. Among the movement's prime concerns is the question of how large corporations and the global financial system undemocratically control the world in a way that disproportionally benefits a minority. Hence the slogan adopted by the movement: 'We are the 99 per cent.'

The first Occupy protest to receive widespread attention was Occupy Wall Street in New York City's Zuccotti Park, which began on 17 September 2011. The protests spread to over 600 communities in the USA (Walters 2011) and 951 cities in 82 other countries. By the end of 2011, authorities had cleared most of the major camps, while the high-profile camps in Washington and London finally were dismantled by February 2012 (Quinn and Johnson 2012).

The Occupy movement is part of an anti-austerity/anti-authoritarian movement trend which saw the Arab Spring, the Portuguese and Spanish *indignados* movement, and the protests at the urban development plan for Istanbul's Taksim Gezi Park

Messing up the neat picture

Now, let us take Table 1.1 as a whole and start to deconstruct it without being restricted by the neoclassical assumptions it is based on, but instead being guided by common sense and historical experience. Take, for example, public goods. Let us assume that a public good such as a square is occupied for a time by thousands of people, who in protest at the condition of debt, unemployment, social injustice, or whatever, live in the square for a few weeks, building tents for sleeping, organising large public meetings or even a public library (Box 1). Then a few

(May 2013). All these movements shared a broad method, that is, the occupation of a public space and then the development of horizontal methods of government of that space. By 2015, the Occupy movement was no longer visible, but its DNA, radical in terms both of its style of horizontal self-government and of its methods of direct action, permeated several movements, as exemplified by the numerous defences of home expropriations following foreclosures in Spain, the USA and elsewhere. Occupy not only enabled today's conversation about inequality but also shifted the 'my fault' culture with respect to debt, and allowed people to move from guilt and shame to power and organisation (Azzellini and Sitrin 2014). This was also the case in other protests which, though more subtle, were more sustaining forms of horizontal governance of commons resources. In Detroit, for example, the community garden movement that is taking over the food desert left by Detroit deindustrialisation allows people not only to 'occupy' land to produce food, but also to pursue direct action methods for chasing the water companies out of neighbourhoods to prevent them from cutting the water supply (McCauley 2014).

toilets are brought, a kitchen tent is built and cooking starts with ingredients obtained through donations from passers-by and local family businesses. This square is no longer a public good, but since it is no longer managed by the state, and because of the intensity of relations and of sharing of resources (common-wealth), the square is lived and reproduced (cleaned, guarded, lived) as a common good, in fact being one of the many common goods belonging to this situation. And this common good is neither a club (toll) good nor a *common-pool resource* (CPR). It is not a club good in the sense that the membership is relatively open and not subject to toll. There is no preoccupation with 'optimal' membership: the more people the better in a sense, and if all the people involved can no longer fit in the square, another one can be occupied. It is not a CPR because even if the increase in the number of people 'subtracts' some of the average area available per person (which falls with the increase in people), that square is the condition for the increase in the intensity of commonised experience; up to a certain point it enhances the sense of power that the occupiers perceive by being many, it extends the circulation of 'memes', of alternative values, and of a strong sense that being other than capital is moving some further steps to constitute itself as a social force.

Or take a public good like a health service. Most European health services are public goods in the sense that, at least in principle, it is difficult to exclude people (which means health services are rights or entitlements) and they have low subtractability, in the sense that if you get treatment, I also can get treatment. More recently, though, national health systems have been hit by a wave of cuts, restructuring and rationalisations. In Italy, for example, for few decades now, universal free access has been eroded away and replaced by increasing fees for services, to the point that the private sector has become competitive in relation to the public sector in some services: an electrocardiogram now costs less in the private sector than in the public sector (Burzi 2013). Obviously, what we have been witnessing here is the transformation of a public good into something that has some aspects of private goods and perhaps lies in between public and private.

In the same way, we can imagine a health system as a publicly funded federation of health clinics/cooperatives of different scope, modelled on the many different existing health cooperatives around the world whether they are worker-, consumer- or consumer/worker/community-owned and -governed organisations, or purchasing or shared service cooperatives (Leviten-Reid 2008.) One such example are the clinics developed in Greece to face the deep health crisis that followed the 2011 debt crisis (see Box 2), in the context of a wider movement of solidarity (Box 3).

Indeed, once we relax the strict assumptions of neoclassical economics and instead of its obsession with 'optimisations' follow the habits of social movements and commons, the distinction between public, club and CPR seem to blur, and they all appear as subsets of what we may call common goods. And this is even the case for the antinomy of common goods, that is, private goods. We already saw this when discussing Buchanan's notion of club goods and will discuss this again in Chapter 4 with respect to the distinction made by Ostrom between *resource systems* and *resource units*. Or let us take the realm of what standard classification calls 'private goods'. What is it that prevents toys, food, books, machinery, tools, objects of various kind from being put in a *common pot* for a community to use? The goods may still be excludable and rivalrous in

continued on page 49

Box 2 Greek self-organised clinics

[This is a slightly edited extract from a 2014 conversation between Marina Sitrin and Ilektra Bethymouti, a psychologist, therapist and trainer. The full text may be found at https://zcomm.org/ znetarticle/solidarity-health-clinics-in-greece/2014/. Bethymouti is a member of the Solidarity Social Practice Clinic (www.kiathess. gr), and the Hellenic Observatory for Rights in the Field of Mental Health (http://mentalhealthhellenicobservatory.wordpress.com), in Thessaloniki, Greece.]

Since 2011, people throughout Greece have been forced to fight for and self-organise their health care. Faced with a newly imposed payment for every doctor and hospital visit and in the context of a terrible economic crisis, people found they were no longer able to get treatment or purchase medicine. Some even spoke of having to choose between food and medicine to survive. As with many other areas in Greek life, people came together in assemblies and decided to use both direct action and self-organisation so as to survive. Some neighbourhood assemblies and local communities regularly organise blockades of the cashiers in clinics so that people who need care do not have to pay. Other assemblies, generally initiated by doctors, came together to organise all the volunteer health clinics. There are now over sixty medical clinics through Greece, forty-eight of which are definitely self-organised and called 'solidarity clinics'; the remaining twelve are organised by the Church, and the movements are not clear on the internal forms of organisation. These clinics provide almost all the services people need on a day-to-day basis from general medicine, obstetrics, paediatrics, dental care, psychology and psychiatry, and many other services. They also run free pharmacies, also based on volunteer and donation-based goods and services.

Ilektra Bethymouti spoke with me about the national assembly of solidarity clinics that took place at the end of November 2014:

'According to the new law the people who currently do not have social security are supposed to have access to the public health system ... At the ... national assembly we had last weekend of the 60 solidarity clinics, 26 decided to come together and organised what we named the Observatory. We decided we must discover what is happening with the hospitals, to investigate and see if they are accepting unemployed people and people without social security, and if not, why ... It seems that doctors in the hospitals are not informed of this new law.

'When they passed the law a few months ago, a number of the solidarity clinics began to think together and question whether it was a good idea to continue with our solidarity clinics as a whole or just for immigrants. This was because we had no idea what our identity was going to be if there was access to healthcare for people. We have now all decided to continue since we do not know how the situation is going to resolve itself and there is still need, so we must continue.'

The change in the law with regard to healthcare is incredibly confusing, and intentionally so. On one hand it is presented as a solution to the current crisis, in allegedly creating access to healthcare for all. On the other hand, this new healthcare system is modelled on the German system, so it is not at all free or accessible for all services and needs. As Ilektra explained:

'At the same time they are going to give healthcare for the majority – still not for everyone – but it is going to be a heathcare system that is more expensive, more like the German system. It is going to be privatised in that each type of healthcare will have a cap, so for example if you have surgery and need four days to recuperate, but are only allowed three by the new system for financial reasons, then you only get three days of coverage or the hospital will have a deficit. Imagine – the doctor's salary could depend on these things. At the same time there is "access", they are putting a price on the services and you might not be able to get what you need. ... It seems like they are offering public health but they are taking something back. The government is fixing the prices with the hospitals and private sector ... so whatever need you have is going to have a fixed price and you cannot receive more than that, even if you need it. One of the other challenges that has arisen is around the type of care that is and will be provided. The solidarity clinics are creating a new vision – based on practice – of healthcare and health in general. They are organised by medical professionals, patients and the wider community. The vast majority use horizontal forms of organisation, have regular assemblies where all can participate, and try to break down the division between the professional and the person serviced. They accept no money from the state, and nor do they have a relationship to the state. All money comes from non-affiliated donations. The solidarity clinics are autonomous from all political groups and parties.

'We believe in and want self-organisation because what we are achieving with self-organisation is something more than giving a service, what we are organising amongst ourselves is something new. We self-organise the solidarity clinics with horizontal assemblies – assemblies take place in each specialisation, within the entire clinic and then nationally. This is a new experience and we want to continue with it.

'What self-organisation gives us is the opportunity to achieve what we call a different healthcare, a different sort of health, and that is what we have achieved up until now. For example, in our clinic we have a group for alternative healthcare and we are trying to change the relationship between the medical expert and those who don't know their rights or have the same expertise. We are trying to change these sorts of relationships and are doing so in ways that are very concrete. That is to say, we are finding ways together with self-organisation, and this changes the idea of the expert, of healthcare, and of how we organise amongst doctors and with pharmaceuticals. And we have so many more questions that we have not answered yet, but we want to work on them together and can. This is very different from if you have a public heathcare system only with its pros and cons.'

the strict technical sense, but the community may have found a way to turn the inherent scarcity of their physical limit into the abundance of social relations governing their use – and to make everybody happy. Books are shared in a library, or in a reading group where one reads aloud; tools are 'borrowed' and returned after use; the same for machinery, automobiles and whatever 'private goods' you may think of.

If this is the case, then a thing can be a private or a common good depending on the ways of seeing and relating of a plurality of frames of social actions and relations. Clearly, I would add an extra layer of complexity if I considered also the relations across communities: life is quite complex. What to one plurality are private goods may be common goods for another plurality with deeper relational links, although different rules of access may apply vis-à-vis other communities. Now, as soon as one introduces a plurality, a community, in the analytical radar that tries to come to terms with common goods, one realises that the interplay between 'goods' and 'plurality' mentioned in the first section of this chapter may give rise to commons systems, that is social systems in which a plurality, a 'community', by standing in particular relation to the 'things', the 'goods', also reproduces the social relations among the people. When I move from the *good as commons* to the system that emerges between a claiming plurality and a common good, I am entering the realm of commons systems.

Taxonomies

Nevertheless, let me stick around with these common goods a bit longer, since there are more eclectic classifications and taxonomies that seek to include diverse non-commodified commons

Box 3 Greek solidarity statistics
[Source: Solidarity For All (2014)]

Solidarity health centres 40 (16 in Attica and 24 in the rest of Greece). Volunteers in 16 health centres in Attica: 750 (median 46 per solidarity clinic). Visits per month in 16 health centres in Attica: 2,000 per clinic

Food solidarity structures September 2012, 12; December 2014, 47. Solidarity parcels distributed fortnightly: February 2013, 1,987; March 2014, 3,874; September 2014, 4,318. Participation per solidarity structure: core group 26, plus extra 30 volunteers per action. Solidarity kitchens: 21 (12 in Attica and 9 in the rest of the country).

'Without middlemen' distribution groups 45 (Athens, 26; the rest of Greece, 19). People involved (average per group): 45 (core group 19, plus extra 29 involved in actions). Number of consumers: 655 per distribution group. Households supported in Athens: 2,169. Number of producers that participate: 23 per distribution group. Volume of distributed products (estimate): more than 5,000 tons (2012–2014).

Social and solidarity economy Free-share bazaars, local alternative currencies, and time banks are established as

social spaces into the definition of commons. I found one list, for example, on the P2P Foundation site (p2pfoundation.net), a site devoted to promoting peer-to-peer practices and to extending them from the cyberworld into other realms. Their 'Commons – FAQ' page (accessed in May 2011) provides a long list of commons types. The main classification is done by means of the characteristics of a good or resource, whether it is a material, forms of direct, moneyless exchange of goods and services. About 110 initiatives in this terrain place at the centre of their action the need to meet the needs of the people through collective processes of sharing. Numerous self-managed workers' cooperatives aim to connect solidarity structures and movements. There is one self-managed reclaimed factory.

Solidarity tutorial centres and cultural centres, revitalisation of existing school students', parents' and teachers' associations as collectives As adults came face-to-face with children fainting from malnutrition, or unvaccinated, etc., solidarity activities developed, especially in the poorer neighbourhoods, in order to support the children with food, schooling materials, clothes, etc. This is unmapped solidarity, but integrated into the community.

Workers' solidarity The creation of solidarity structures within workspaces became a necessity both to build support during struggles and also to confront the hardships of wage reductions, austerity and forced redundancies.

Immigrant solidarity networks Solidarity with immigrants, beyond developing the anti-racist movement, consists of Greek-language classes, legal support and recently more and more emergency care for hundreds of refugees who come to the Greek islands or to Athens without shelter, food, etc.

immaterial/social or biological resource. This is of course only one of the possible taxonomies that can be devised following an initial categorisation. In general, however, the physical versus immaterial (knowledge) split offers the first base for designing open-ended lists. So, for example, on a different webpage, 'physical commons' are listed as:

1. Atmosphere Commons; Atmospheric Commons; 2. Food Commons; Food as Common and Community; 3. Hunting Commons; 4. Infrastructure Commons; 5. Land as Commons; 6. Marine Commons; 7. Microbial Commons; 8. Petroleum Commons; 9. Solar Commons; 10. Water Commons. (P2P Foundation 2010b)

On the other hand, examples of knowledge/culture commons include:

1. Aesthetic Commons; 2. Book Commons; 3. Cultural Commons; 4. Digital Commons; 5. Educational Commons; 6. FLOSS Commons: see FLOSS as Commons; 7. Genome Commons; 8. Global Innovation Commons; 9. Global Integral–Spiritual Commons; 10. History Commons; 11. Information Commons; Information as a Common-Pool Resource; 12. Knowledge Commons; Knowledge as a Commons; 13. Learning Commons; 14. Media Commons; 15. Museum as Commons; 16. Music Commons; 17. Open Education Commons; 18. Open Scientific Software Commons; Open Source Science Commons; 19. Patent Commons; Eco-Patent Commons; 20. Psychological Commons. (P2P Foundation 2010b)

The site also adds a list for what it calls 'institutional commons', thus abandoning the physical/nonphysical classification criteria and entering the more precarious terrain of social relations, without, however, engaging in serious scrutiny of the social forces traversing these 'institutions'. Examples of institutional commons provided are:

1. Financial Commons; 2. Global Legal Commons; 3. Household as Commons; 4. Internet Commons; 5. NonProfit Commons; 6. Taxes as Commons; 7. Thing Commons; 8. Urban Commons; 9. Wireless Commons. (P2P Foundation 2010b)

It is unclear to me how such classification could be drawn, i.e. how a 'physical commons' can exist without presupposing some form of 'knowledge/culture commons' and without some rules forged by the knowledgeable and acculturated commoners, i.e. some institution.

There are of course other potential classifications, once we regard commons as goods or resources. We can choose, for example, specific criteria of aggregation, and synergies – based on *classes* of goods types. For example, Sam Rose and Paul Hartzog offer the following typology for commons based on different distributed infrastructures:

1. Energy Commons; 2. Food Commons; 3. Thing Commons; 4. Cultural Commons; 5. Access Commons. (P2P Foundation 2010b)

All these fit the prima facie definition of common goods I am here critically engaging with and I do not subscribe to, namely: 'commons is a general term that refers to a resource shared by a group of people' (Hess and Ostrom 2007: 12).

Yochai Benkler (2003) offers a simple rule to frame taxonomy. Commons can be divided into four types based on two parameters: (1) whether they are open to anyone, or (2) whether a commons system is regulated or unregulated. A simple table can then be derived (Table 1.2).

Table 1.2 Types of commons, following Yochai Benkler's rule

Parameters	Open to everyone	Not open to everyone
Regulated	Sidewalks, streets, roads, and highways that cover our land and form the foundation of our ability to move from one place to another. Air is, however, a regulated commons with regard to outtake. For individual human beings, breathing out is mildly regulated by social convention – you do not breathe too heavily on another human being's face unless forced to. Air is a more extensively regulated commons for industrial exhalation – in the shape of pollution controls, the use of land, and the likely failures that would have to be dealt with in its management. With regard to information, culture, and communications systems, I have explained how resources necessary for information production and communications systems can be managed as commons in ways that are sustainable and desirable.	Traditional pasture arrangements or irrigation regions
Not regulated	Air intake (breathing, feeding a turbine). Also pre-twentieth-century knowledge and culture, most scientific knowledge of the first half of the twentieth century, and much of contemporary science and academic learning	

Source: My elaboration from Benkler's (2003: 6) text.

This rule however can only produce three types of commons as the fourth one cannot be matched by experience: if a commons is not open to everyone, it must be regulated somehow: boundaries are a form of regulation of commons.

Reflecting on these approaches to different types of common goods, I feel that taxonomies of common goods could in principle be generated as a small subset of a far larger taxonomy (indeed, potentially infinite) with a simple grammar rule: add an adjective to the noun, where the latter is fixed as 'commons' and the first word spans over the entire available list of possible adjectives in a human language. When you apply this rule you'll find a potentially infinite list of commons as common goods, ordered by type of resource shared, size, location and even, if you wish, colour (red commons, black commons, green commons, purple commons), useful also if you want to give a common good colour coding in terms of political background. After all, the Fascists in Italy had their 'black shirts' commons.[5]

Selection and strategic horizons

There is, then, a danger of conceptual meaninglessness when types of common goods are listed ad infinitum, as if one was simply using a grammar algorithm. In a sense, this potential infinity aligns to my conception of *omnia sunt communia*, which is a sense horizon that all, in principle, can be turned into a common good. But in a given time, space and context somehow a line in the sand must be drawn, a selection must be made before being operationalised: if everything is a common good then nothing is. I can make this selection in two ways: first, by conceptually *defining* what commons are on the basis of some principles or criteria, while hoping that the historical movement

accepts this definition; second, on the basis of political-strate-
gic considerations and social movement goals within a situated
force field.

For an example of the first case, let us take the International
Association of the Study of the Commons (IASC) definition
of commons. For the IASC, commons are 'resources ... which
people do not have to pay for to exercise their user and access
rights within [the] confine of a set of institutions or rules to
protect the resources from overuse by people who do not respect
the resources' fragility or limits' (Jumbe 2006: 5). Now this definition does definitively bring into evidence some crucial aspects
of commons. The realm of the shared is here pretty much taken
as being a realm beyond the money nexus, and therefore for
different ways to bring social connectivity among the producers.
These ways certainly involve institutional forms, although these
institutions are conceptualised mainly as putting fetters on social
action ('a set of institutions or rules to protect the resources from
overuse') rather than also as promoting social practices that put
constraints on and push back those social practices based on
commodity production and capital accumulation.

But the point here is that, as admitted by the writers of the
IASC, not all commons neatly fit this definition. For example,
knowledge or information, scientific databases, the arts, open-
source software, the electro-magnetic spectrum, do not have
physical limits that need to be managed for their 'sustainability'
as they are 'non-rivalrous' goods (my using the good does not
limit your using the same good).

When limits in the use of these resources are present, they are
entirely socially constructed, embedded in processes of enclosures promoted by state property right policies. Other commons

resources, such as 'global commons' – the atmosphere, deep seas, and outer space – lack an effective planetary community that takes active 'ownership' and responsibility towards their reproduction (unless of course you believe that the existing configuration of states form such a community). Others still, such as city sidewalks, playgrounds and public squares, are 'free access' spaces that are governed by a combination of common-sense 'civil' behaviour and state management, but with very little *active claim of ownership for the (re)production of the common good* (that is, in terms that we will discuss in the following chapters, little doing in common, little *commoning*).

All these cases fall outside the IASC definition of commons, yet when we shift the observing gaze from the commons goods to the plurality relating to those goods, we cannot fail to notice that there are many social practices that *claim* these goods as commons. For example, global commons underpin a variety of communities' struggles against climate change, for example opposing carbon trading and posing instead the question of a limited atmospheric space, requiring the bigger polluters to drastically limit their emissions and pay compensation for climate debt to the people in the Global South who are effectively using a much lower share of the atmospheric space yet are paying a far larger price in terms of the effects of climate change.[6] City spaces are routinely reclaimed as commons in demonstrations and direct action practices. Self-organised community spaces spring up in the middle of city centres reclaiming parking lots as community parks (see Box 7).

Thus one can move to the second way of selecting what are common goods, and this is for political strategic reasons. For example, there is a broad sense in the literature and in some sections of political activism that common goods are some sort of 'special goods' because of their inherent importance for the reproduction of socio-ecological systems: some sort of 'basic goods', which are necessary for the reproduction of everything else (Sraffa 1960). This is for example the case in the very influential work of Peter Barnes (2006).[7] In his *Capitalism 3.0* he provides an argument and a guide for 'upgrading' capitalism to fix its 'disregard for nature, future generations, and the non elderly poor' (Barnes 2006: 11). The current version of capitalism (which is corporation-dominated and globalised) is squandering our shared inheritance, that is the commons understood as 'all the gifts we inherit or create together' or a 'set of assets that have two characteristics: they're all gifts, and they're all shared' (Barnes 2006: 4–5). The other quality that defines 'assets in the commons' is that 'we have a joint obligation to preserve them. That's because future generations will need them to live, and live well, just as we do' (ibid.). These two general criteria then define commons as common goods: in nature (from air, water and DNA to lakes, solar energy and wind energy); in community (from streets, playground and calendar to capital markets, political institutions and flea markets); and in culture (from language, philosophy and religion to mathematics and open source software). The very broad-range eclecticism of this definition is what gives Barnes's approach to commons a currency as a method to *preserve* capitalism, rather than as an entry point to its overcoming. After all, including capital markets as *the* common good is precisely what is in the mind of the current financial crisis managers who saved major banks at the cost of everything else because they were too important and too big to fail. Without entering into discussion of Peter Barnes proposals at this point, it suffices here to say that the gist of this proposal is protecting the commons against the predation of the corporate sector by giving it property rights and strong institutional managers. His major innovation is the commons trust – an entity with the power to limit use of scarce commons, charge rent to polluters, and pay dividends to everyone to compensate for the higher cost of energy in the case of an increase cap in emission. The objective is to bring capitalism and the commons into balance, so that in the end 'private corporations and organized commons enhance and constrain each other' (Barnes 2006: 76).

Whereas for Barnes the strategic horizon is clear (the preservation of life *and* of capitalism), in other, more radical quarters where the notion of commons as 'special goods' is used, the line in the sand in the definition of common goods is seen as contingent to strategic proprieties of emerging urgencies. For example, in the Italian debate about *bene comune* the idea prevails that common goods are *special* goods:

> There are in the world some 'special resources', some particular categories of goods and services: they are neither shoes nor hamburgers, neither TV programs, nor investment funds … They are not 'produced', they are not objects that are made and unmade, that are bought or sold. They are primary goods, basic, in the sense that they are at the origin of everything. They are natural wealth and cultural patrimony accumulated by the generations that have preceded us. They are systems of resources, relational goods that are indispensable to maintain connected the living system. They are those things that, simply, make us live. (Cacciari 2010: 12)

The first characteristics of these 'special goods' include, again, gifts of nature and society, that is, all those goods that nobody can claim to have produced on their own: the atmosphere and climate, solar and fossil energy, water, mineral deposits, animals and wild plants, seeds 'and every other form of life capable of spontaneous reproduction' (Cacciari 2010: 12). All the same, 'knowledge, cultures, languages, codes, the scientific discoveries, artists' goods' (ibid.) are the result of social creation as the former are the results of natural creation. The second characteristic is that they are 'necessary goods, indispensable and irreplaceable for the life of every individual' (Cacciari 2010: 13; my translation).

Unfortunately, when we enter the specifics of these 'special goods', we find that indeed there is the possibility of buying and selling them, and often, even if not for making, definitely for unmaking them. Private ownership of land is not new, and the recent emergence of carbon markets has shown that there is a case for buying and selling the atmosphere, paradoxically, in the name of saving it as a commons, and, in thus doing, contributing to its 'unmaking'. Human labour power is bought and sold even in postmodern capitalism, yet labour power is also a social creation emerging from a variety of situated dimensions of commoning reproducing different aspects of life. The lives of the bearers of the commodity labour power are made increasingly precarious: they are lives unmade by anxieties, fear and poverty, because of the way and condition through which their labour power is socially reproduced. Cultures are social like food, the Internet, and toilets, and to earn a living as a cultural worker in a condition of increasing market dependence and precarity, you need to put a price on a cultural artefact you can claim to have produced. With increasing competition and rent seeking by big publishers and producers, this price produces an average earning which is far lower than many other conventional jobs.

Thus there is no 'special character' inherent in these goods (e.g. the cultural artefact) in conditions of capitalism. Rather, it is for us to claim the specialness of goods that we know are central to the building of alternatives, and the mechanisms of sustaining our lives through them: culture, but also food; ecosystems, but also housing; and so on as we think suited. But if every good is social, how do we decide which are special? It is a political and strategic question and a question of situated values. This is acknowledged:

> Because everything – in the end – is connected to everything else, and everything is sustained reciprocally (living and non-living, material and spiritual, past and future) everything can be correctly defined as a common good. With the risk, however, of falling into a sort of abstract and idealised vision of the world, in which only a fully communist society will be able to resolve the question of the sharing and responsible management of every thing. This risk can be avoided by identifying and practising concrete themes of collective action linked to urgent social and environmental questions. (Rete@sinistra 2010: 21; my translation)

If in principle everything is a common good, and what is here and now claimed as a common good depends on strategic priorities, then on what basis do we derive strategic principles of selection? The urgent social and environmental issues are many, and not only those caused by the 'mismanagement' of the 'special goods' that are defined above as common goods. Indeed, the furthering of the crises should make the need to expand the list of 'special goods' clear, and every struggle in defence of a right or of entitlements, whether these are pensions, universal basic income or jobs, is in a sense a struggle that requires us to do so. The financial crisis has threatened the livelihoods of millions of people around the world, hence what better opportunity to list banks and money as a type of 'special goods' to be claimed as common goods? The economic crisis hitting many factories and workplaces is powerful evidence that these livelihood-giving places should also be considered as 'special goods' and that a community of workers can legitimately reclaim them as common goods, perhaps reformulating the Argentinian experiment of 2001 or the experiments now emerging also in Italy and Greece. The urgent crisis of social reproduction – for example, in the case of care work for the elderly, children or the sick – would require a redistribution of social resources towards this aim, in recognition of the struggles that care workers (mostly women, but also men) are making in response to the new conditions of reproductive labour. The planet's gigantic environmental crises would require recognition of the soil, land, water, the atmosphere, food production, transport and social reproduction in general as common goods. Wow, where do we start? While any principle for selecting what constitutes a common good should be founded on strategic grounds, this claim cannot be made on the basis of some inherent character of the good in question. Rather, it must be made on the basis of the meaning that a plurality has given to that good, and the social force that a plurality of commoners is able to put on the ground in different circumstances, a social force that is willing to take responsibility not only for making a claim, but also for commoning and governing the commons.

Common goods therefore have the potential to provide a sense orientation to frame solutions to real problems independently from states and markets. To claim something as a common good in the context of a social struggle 'give[s] awareness to people, produces active citizenship, and therefore overcomes the passive consumerist model'. It has a civilising function. In other words, 'to put the common goods centre stage implies the view that another world is possible' (Mattei 2010; my translation), but this is so only if common goods become part of commons systems.

The limit to what can be considered a common good is entirely contextual and political, depending on the political boundaries, imaginative capability and involvement in doing in commons that a community can give itself. In this context, the grammar algorithm embedded in the taxonomic approach, although theoretically weak, offers when read politically an endless array of situated opportunities. In short, the taxonomic approach reflects the great potential of the commons' neo-civilising mission. When one speaks of common goods, people in different contexts and involved in very diverse struggles seem to respond: in favour of those who have lost jobs, the precariat, those who queue up for health treatment, those who are asked to pay a high fee for education, those whose houses are foreclosed, those whose land and water are polluted, those who vote for the right and those who vote for the left. The endless list embedded in taxonomies of these types really reflects this powerful character of common goods, and allows me to say *omnia sunt communia* knowing that if I dig enough I will find a different case or a different method where a particular common goods has been turned into an element of a commons by a commoning plurality of commoners.

Material basis

There is, however, a fundamental problem in regarding commons simply as 'goods'. The nature of a good, whether it is material or immaterial, whether it is homogeneous, like a heap of corn, or complex, like a water system or an industrial complex, represents only a substrate of commons; it does not tell us whether, how and to what extent an associated plurality can reproduce or expand that good, and in what conditions, or whether the plurality's governance is environmentally and socially sustainable and just. Goods all presuppose a path of development, they do not give it pulse, conatus and direction on their own.

In other words, the nature of a good, or systems of goods, does not give us movement, that is, for example, *how* a commons system (in other words, the interplay of plurality and object) strives to reproduce itself *in the face of opposing social forces*, externally defined, with their own different and clashing logics and senses. The view of commons as 'goods' does not frame the analysis of commons in an analysis of power. It does not tell us, and does not frame, the question of how reproduction of the commons occurs in spite of and through struggle, through the problematisation of gender roles, through racist and xenophobic discourses or through their overcoming, through the challenge to capital's dominated circuit of praxis, and through ecologically sound paths. *The problematising of commons within a project of emancipation thus must not simply rely on lists of isolated objects, but must open up to the internal relations among the components of these lists and the respective commoning pluralities, as well as the relations that commons have to their plural environments.*

Therefore, I am not only talking about 'corrupted' commons (Hardt and Negri 2009), that is, commons in which oppressive power relations operate internally, but also great contemporary innovative commons predicated on a horizontal and innovative activity of sharing, which however do not problematise sufficiently the relation of this activity of sharing to its environment.

Take for example the ecological aspects of the commons environment from the point of view of the operations of a peer-to-peer (P2P) network in cyberspace, one of the more innovative commons of recent times. In the words of Michael Bauwens, one of the main proponents of peer-to-peer organisation and the founder of the p2pfoundation.net, this is a 'form of human network-based organisation which rests upon the free participation of equipotent partners, engaged in the production of common resources, without recourse to monetary compensation as key motivating factor, and not organized according to hierarchical methods of command and control' (Bauwens 2015: 1). I have always listened in wonder to the arguments of their supporters, to the promises of open software development and more recently to the claims made for P2P money such as bitcoin. A computing or networking distributed application architecture is P2P when it partitions tasks or workloads among peers. The term is not restricted to technology, but covers every social process with a peer-to-peer dynamic, whether these peers are humans or computers. I am here referring only to the first case, when computing is the crucial medium for the P2P processes. Open and free software are part of this story, as are peer-to-peer web hosting systems that use peer-to-peer networking to distribute access to webpages, or P2P file sharing, allowing users to access media files such as books, music, movies and games using a P2P software program that searches for other connected computers on a P2P network in order to locate the desired content, and even P2P money, in which transactions take place between users directly over a computer networks, without an intermediary or central bank emission.

The nodes (peers) of such networks are end-user computer systems that are interconnected via the Internet.

> P2P processes are not structureless, but are characterised by dynamic and changing structures which adapt themselves to phase changes. [The P2P process's] rules are not derived from an external authority, as in hierarchical systems, but generated from within. It does not deny 'authority', but only fixed forced hierarchy, and therefore accepts authority based on expertise, initiation of the project, etc. ... P2P may be the first true meritocracy. The threshold for participation is kept as low as possible. Equipotency means that there is no prior formal filtering for participation, but rather that it is the immediate practice of cooperation which determines the expertise and level of participation. Communication is not top-down and based on strictly defined reporting rules, but feedback is systemic, integrated in the protocol of the cooperative system. Techniques of 'participation capture' and other social accounting make automatic cooperation the default scheme of the project. Personal identity becomes partly generated by the contribution to the common project. (P2P Foundation 2006)

Decentralised communication and communication models founded on P2P dynamics springing out of cyberspace have greatly empowered communities around the world in accessing music, videos, cultures and software programs. I can listen to a music file downloaded on BitTorrent – a communications protocol for the practice of peer-to-peer file sharing that is used to distribute large amounts of data over the Internet: about 3.35 per cent of worldwide bandwidth and more than half of the 6 per cent of the total bandwidth dedicated to file sharing. I can read about BitTorrent on the English Wikipedia, which with its 27,136,077 registered users and roughly 120k monthly editors (February 2015), represents a peer-to-peer publishing community present in our daily lives.

P2P activity in cyberspace create use values that go back to the commons sphere and nullify the cost of accessing music and videos, or of software programs – machines, as Paul Mason (Mason 2015: 164) calls them, that could have lasted for thousands of years if they were not already becoming obsolete: the marginal cost of producing an extra bit of information is minimal with P2P, and the cost of accessing it is virtually zero.

However, we should also remember that these P2P information machines (as well as all types of decentralised communication and collaboration, even the one between me and my boss) depend on the laws of physics, and have in turn an ecological impact. As IBM engineer Rolf Landauer stated in 1961 (Mason 2015: 165) and elaborated in 1996:

> Information is not a disembodied abstract entity; it is always tied to a physical representation. It is represented by engraving on a stone tablet, a spin, a charge, a hole in a punched card, a

mark on paper, or some other equivalent. This ties the handling of information to all the possibilities and restrictions of our real physical word, its laws of physics and its storehouse of available parts. (Landauer 1996: 188)

If this is the case, producing or erasing information creates … heat. When we scale up from this physical property I shudder in the awareness that doing the simplest operation online has environmental costs that we take for granted. Not only decentralised communication in cyberspace, but any operation within it, or any form of computing, whether P2P or not, feels virtual, immaterial or intangible. Nevertheless accessing on a screen the cultures of the world by means of a few words in a search engine is very material.

The distinction between the material and the immaterial type of common resource, is what Maretz (2010) refers to as the constitution of the commons good. Simply put, '*material goods* have a physical shape, they can be used up or crushed out. Purpose and physical constitution are linked with each other, material goods perform their purpose only by their physical constitution.' On the other hand, '*non-material goods* are completely decoupled from a specific physical shape'. The two are discussed in terms of their different properties, especially in relation to the object. So, a computer is a physical good, while software is not. Computers are subject to the constraints of rivalry and exclusivity, while software is not necessarily. This type of classification enables us to make some important distinctions, but it leaves out the *structural dependence* of the 'intangible' on the 'tangible' as noted by Landauer, a crucial element when we want to conceive of commons in the broader context of transformational politics.

By structural dependence here I mean to say the obvious, that is, that for the 'intangible', such as software, knowledge and culture, to be what it is, it must be given material body, that is, it must be coupled with material processes. Software needs computers and mainframes somewhere, and computer and mainframes need water, energy and minerals for their industrial production. Also, software programmers need to eat, rest and allow their psychophysical systems to reproduce in health and equilibrium. In turn, all the 'materials' necessary for these purposes need to be dug and poured out of the earth, and hence social processes are coupled to (currently overpolluted) ecological processes and (currently exploitative) economic processes.

We may experience social change driven by the intangible and immaterial (like P2P networks), but until social change has reached the realm of the tangible, we haven't had any radical change, or any change has not been translated into a change in the material conditions of existence.

Our paradigms of transformation must address the social stratification and division of powers that are immanent products of capitalist development and these paradigms must also question how a system of continuous growth such as the capitalist mode of production necessarily relies on increasing absolute levels of energy consumption, greenhouse gas emissions, and mineral mining; and it must recognise that no quest for energy efficiency (change in the ratio between flows of outputs and resource units) can solve the problems posed by these absolute increases (Sarkel 1999; Princen 2005).

Others have identified more specifically the dependence of the 'intangible' on the 'tangible', namely the dependence of our peer-to-peer cyber-practices on hardware, and hence on oil, land and enclosures. So, for example, it is estimated that every day about 200 million people around the world use the Internet, most of whom will make use of web searches. In 2007, Gartner Research estimated the 'global information and communications technology (ICT) industry accounts for approximately 2 percent of global carbon dioxide (CO_2) emissions, a figure equivalent to aviation' (Gartner 2007). Gartner did not include in this estimate consumer electronics other than cellphones and PCs, only global commercial and governmental IT and telecommunications infrastructure. Alexander Wissner-Gross, a physicist and environmental fellow at Harvard University, has estimated that 'Even simple online activities take a toll on the environment. Google does not divulge its energy use or carbon footprint but, based on publicly available information, we have calculated that each Google search generates an estimated 5–10g of CO_2, in part because Google's unique infrastructure replicates queries across multiple servers, which then compete to provide the fastest answer to your query. On the other hand, just browsing a basic website generates about 20 mg of CO_2 for every second you view it' (Wissner-Gross 2009). The figure for the carbon dioxide generated by a single web search refers to a 'Google search that may involve several attempts to find the object being sought and that may last for several minutes' (Leake and Woods 2009). Two of these web searches are roughly equivalent to boiling a kettle, or about 7g of CO_2 per search.

More complex animation and websites require far more energy and correspondent emissions. Second Life is an open-source virtual reality world developed and managed by Linden Lab, in which participants maintain a character (known as an *avatar*) for playing, exploring, interacting and building worlds.

We could say that Second Life does not have an objective-driven, gaming focus, but offers a virtual platform for user-created, community-driven peer-to-peer collaborative and creative projects. In January 2008, on average, 38,000 residents were logged in at any particular moment. The maximum concurrency (number of avatars inworld) recorded is 88,200 in the first quarter of 2009 (Second Life 2009). Nicholas Carr (2008), the author of *The Big Switch: Rewiring the World*, calculated that maintaining an avatar in the Second Life virtual reality game requires 1,752 kilowatt hours of electricity per year. This is far above the per-capita consumption of electricity in a country in the Global South (which is 1,015 kWh) and about the amount consumed by the average Brazilian. If we convert this into CO_2 emissions this corresponds to about 1.17 tons of CO_2, or the equivalent of driving an SUV around 2,300 miles. There is of course a P2P case for reducing the energy impact of these applications.[8]

This of course does not account for other 'externalities' that the 'material' element of ICT requires. According to Silicon Valley Toxics Coalition, a non-profit organisation engaged in research, advocacy and grassroots organising around issues of social and environmental justices emerging with the rapid growth of the high-tech industry, e-waste is not only the fastest growing part of the waste stream, but is also dumped across communities in the Global South in countries such as Nigeria, India, China and elsewhere (http://svtc.org/our-work/e-waste/).

And what about cryptocurrencies, the digital currencies in which encryption techniques are used to regulate the generation of units of currency and verify the transfer of funds, operating independently of a central bank and through P2P networks. There are about forty of them, subjected to up-and-down movement in their value due to speculative pressures as investors hold them expecting increases in their value. According to *The Economist*, bitcoin is the most important of such cryptocurrencies. And as Giannelli and Fumagalli (2012) put it:

> the capacity of elaboration expressed by the 'peer-to-peer' network that extracts bitcoin currency is ... superior to any similar network ever put in operation. The natural question to ask is whether such a power of calculation could have been obtained for the reaching of a collective objective, for example research on the cure of a disease. In other words, would the individuals who are cooperating to produce bitcoins to keep in their computers with the expectation of a growth in their value in dollars have made available their resources for an objective not directly to their own advantage?

There is more to this though. While some believe bitcoin is ready to supersede currencies in time of crisis – offering especially a Plan B to countries in deep crisis such as Greece (http://imgur.com/euaovbu), if one looks at the issue from the ecological point of view the reality is startling: the cost of making one bitcoin transaction is tremendous. According to Malmo's (2015) calculations, a single bitcoin transaction uses roughly enough electricity to power 1.57 US households for a day (compared to one Visa transaction, which is equivalent to the electricity use of 0.0003 households). It is quite something that this innovation in monetary technology is not just less energy efficient, but so energy inefficient, hence not a commons tool to counter or even adapt to climate change. Maybe this is because cryptocurrency transactions are just a small fraction compared to world banking system capitalisation, 'which in 2010 alone was over 1,889 times bigger than today's' (Malmo 2015). Still, envisaging a speedy increase in cryptocurrency transactions would skyrocket the total environmental cost of doing peer-to-peer monetary transactions. It is an impossible alternative.

Within a profit-driven global regime of capitalist production, peer-to-peer in cyberspace does not only have an ecological cost. It also means social hierarchical division across producers. Thus, for example, peer-to-peer in cyberspace, that is, in the realm of immaterial commons, does not resonate with the experience of commoners who depend on material resources for their reproduction, and who often see these resources enclosed and privatised so that industrial-scale extraction of raw materials, fossil fuels and water can continue because they are required also for the building of electronic and IT equipment for the energy generation upon which cyberspace depends, and for the buildings in which P2P commoners may continue their commoning. Richard Pithouse (an activist and researcher involved in the community struggles of the poor in Durban, South Africa) puts it in this way:

> My first concern about all the P2P stuff ... is ... the fact that it depends on both other modes of labour and extraction (like digging coltan in the Eastern Congo) and other modes of enforced and very material (guns, fences, guards, borders etc.) social division within and between societies. (Pithouse 2010; private correspondence)

The neat distinction between immaterial and material, therefore, becomes meaningful only from the perspective of relatively *isolated* and privileged spheres of practices. By this I mean to emphasise the fact that these spheres are 'operationally closed', that is, the social practices in these spheres occur as if there is no relation between the different spheres. Thus, for example, although my web searching depends on very physical and very energy-sucking mainframes and correspondent exploitative relations through which mainframes and energy are provided through capitalist commodity chains, this is not a problem of mine in the very moment I type the word 'Anthropocene' into a search engine or P2P. Also, it is not a problem of ours as peer-to-peer commoner sharers of film, knowledge, or software codes. All this occurs and can occur in forms and modalities that are operationally closed to these issues. Just as in my daily reproduction the meta system of structural dependence is given to me at all levels of social life, from food, to health services and so on, so it is for Google or participation in peer-to-peer cyberspace networks. From the perspective of a radical paradigm and a possible political recomposition, I think this is an isolation that must be overcome, and it can only be overcome if and to the extent that some forms of constituent commoning across 'material' and 'immaterial' circuits become a reality and a social force at the basis of transformative politics. There is no panacea, no new invention operating as a silver bullet, only the expansion, multiplication and interlacing of commons systems, especially those that reproduce life (food, care, housing, biodiversity, …). But what are systems anyway?

Chapter 2

Systems

Restarting from the ordinary: social systems and daily life
It is a very cold January night and I go to a local bar in the tiny
village 3 kilometres from where I live. A friend of mine has
organised a tournament of *briscola*, a trick-taking card game
very popular throughout Italy. She organised the tournament
as a way to collect funds for the association we have set up, an
association that aims to promote a variety of cultural, social and
ecological reproductive activities in the area. The *briscola* tournament in a sense is both an end in itself and a means to get some
money. I enter the bar, where people have already started playing. Several groups of four players are disposed at tables, all busy
concealing their cards and making signs to their teammate at the
opposite side of the table, subtly communicating whether they
have good cards or not, and making decisions on what card to
play next. Entering the bar felt like entering an observation point
for a controlled experiment on micro social systems. Here I am,
surrounded by people playing cards, communicating through
particular codes, selecting their action often as a result of a quick
exchange among mates, acting by throwing down the selected
card, collectively and consensually measuring the values of the
cards on the table, estimating the winner of the hand, and in
so doing giving rise to the next communication event, the next
selection of card and action, and so on, until the end of the game

announces the winning and losing pair. In other words, the tables are occupied by micro social systems.

Then I say hello to my friend, who organised the game. We enter into a brief conversation about the evening, how great it has turned out, how successful the call for a tournament ended up, we evaluate, we 'measure', (re)produce the sense we have been co-creating. Indeed, together with a few other villagers around, Loretta and I have been working together for the past few years. We have worked in a theatre group, we have set up an association, we have organised a summer festival for kids, we have taught through the problems of the local volunteer-run ambulance services, we have set up a community garden, and we have many projects still in their infancy. My greeting with Loretta therefore is a punctuated moment of a social relationship in which communication and action are articulated. Here we are in the presence of another social system.

With the approval of the association, Loretta charged €15 per playing couple and bought two whole prosciutti as a first prize, then two whole mortadelle for the second price and Parmesan and Pecorino cheeses for the third prize. Needless to say, apart from the Pecorino which comes from Tuscany – the other side of the mountain – all the prizes are local products, and are produced by small cooperatives. Needless to say also, these products were the outputs of social systems (whether cheese or prosciutto factory) and were bought, that is accessed via money on the market, another social system. The goods were all displayed in a large basket with red ribbons laid on the billiard table, itself covered with a large green cloth. Incidentally, this is the one and only pool table left within a range of 100 kilometres, because the state now taxes their possession; hence local bars generally prefer now to install slot and poker machines rather than billiard tables. So we are in the presence of another occasion of promotion of individualised entertainment, and another encounter with other social systems somehow showing their presence in this situation: the state, its taxes and regulations and the feedback processes that give rise to them; the old family running the bar and the processes that have led them to decide to keep the pool table as well as hosting the *briscola* game. But then, really, just look around and think of all the people playing cards who will be going home at the end of the evening. The majority will go back to the domestic micro social systems we call families, with their feedback processes, their routines, their habitus, their conflicts, their decisions, the conditions they face, their actions. And all the players and observers here at the bar will also couple with their social systems at work. We have farmers here, who 365 days a year work in their cowsheds and produce milk for the Parmesan cheese cooperative. Yet this local small production system is also coupled with a global production system, from which they purchase fodder (mostly containing GM soya and corn), and on which they depend to compensate for the increasingly low price of milk. We have factory workers, who alternate weeks of morning, day and night shifts in the remaining tile factories, that is, other social systems with their tight accounting measures of life rhythms, their micro conflicts – social systems also tied into global (market) systems through prices and profits that define the likelihood that the tile workers will have a job tomorrow. And then there are students – trying to tie their life rhythms to the curricula and exam schedules of their 'educators'; the precarious workers – not really knowing whether they'll get a job tomorrow, so they have intermittent systemic links to their employers' systems. And there are the self-employed artisans (often struggling to hide as much as possible of their declining income from the tax office), and the moneyless unemployed, kicked out of work by the invisible hand of the market but helped out by the invisible hand of social cooperation, mostly unknown to the majority. The lives of each of them, actually of each of us, is articulated into not one, but several social systems and often in more than one at a time. And when we meet here in this bar, this social space we created to raise funds for our small local association, we do it by articulating two small social systems – the micro business of the bar owner and our association – into a temporary new one, limited in space and time, through the creation of other social systems: a cards tournament (it could have been a dance; a conference, an event of any type).

And this is really a first general conclusion that I want to make as a starting point. Take any moment in your daily life, try to think through your patterned connections with others, whether in formal organisations or informal social relations, and you will see some sorts of social systems popping up, often related to one another, social systems which are certainly very different in nature, but without which your daily life, for good or bad, would not be what it is.

Subjects and systems

To illustrate this first point, let us look at Figure 2.1. Each ellipsis represents a social system disposed in such a way as to give a sense of temporal path, from the near past (greater ellipsis), to the near future or present (small ellipsis). By living their postmodern, rushed and globalised lives, the subject – illustrated by the dots making up the arrow – passes through, participates in to different degrees and forms different social systems, through direct, indirect or virtual relations. We often do this on a daily basis, without actually being aware of it, although we experience these different systems as a different environment to our own psycho-physical system. Systems in fact are not visible like heaps of things, since we are *inside* systems. Since systems are made not only of things but also of the relations and practices of these things, in the last three decades, the increasingly flexible conditions of production and reproduction as well as the explosion of communication technologies and network forms of social cooperation (Castells 1996) have increased enormously the potential points of contacts with different systems, especially if we consider potential contacts in cyberspace. The systems have become more complex. So Figure 2.1 will look different for a typical person today compared with a version representing someone living fifty or one hundred years ago. If your life is all work, church and family in a small rural village in nineteenth-century Europe, you will have a regular alternation of three interrelated systems in your daily life: a pattern of

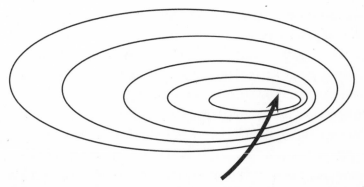

Figure 2.1 Temporal subject (body) path through the commons

social systems quite different from that of a precarious student worker in twenty-first-century London, alternating jobs and having a very lively social life in a global city, where even if you'd like to keep your emotional life confined to a set of relations and affects, the city will make it very difficult to sustain a productive involvement with your circle of affects. This is not just because of the sheer accelerated temporality of the global city needed to sustain your life economically but also because of the high turnover of people arriving in and leaving London.

In Figure 2.1, the subject relates to any particular system from a subject position. Indeed, every moment of her life is located within a system, whether she is aware of it or not. Any space is a space constituted by one or more systems at a time, but for simplicity in this illustration I assume it is constituted by just one. Whether the dynamic of this system creates a smooth or a striated space is not for us to say at this moment. The subject's diary, life scheduling or mood gives her direction: from the home to the street, from the street to the bus, from the bus to the school, from the school to the job, from the job to the home, from the home to the pub, from the pub back to the home. And then of course, at any given point, she enters the virtual space of cyberspace, connects, laughs and 'likes', watches, messages, downloads and ... smoothly shares.

Looking more closely, however, whether I am in a smooth or in a striated space matters. According to Karatzogianni and Robinson's take on Deleuze and Guattari, 'Smooth space refers to a figure of a desert or plateau on which flows move freely, forming a patchwork or a web of rhizomes, whereas striated space is crisscrossed with lines which make movement across it difficult, confining flows to particular parts of the space' (Karatzogianni and Robinson 2010: 22). Empirically, smooth space and striated spaces complement one another. A student enters the university system and a line filters her access to staff, but no lines come between her and the student body, unless of course racial and other types of division exist. When she boards the bus, she interacts with the city transport system either as a ticket-buying passenger or as a worker: driver, inspector, or owner or shareholder of the bus company. In each subject position, she will face a smooth and a striated space as a condition of her doing, of entering and creating systemic patterns with others.

Figure 2.1 illustrates different systems indistinctively, without specifying what systems are in general and how different systems distinguish themselves. In their daily life, subjects follow their temporal paths across systems. At this point, what I want to emphasise is the presence of social systems in the plural, with their lines and specificities, but also with their commonality, the fact that, for good or bad, they are systems. This is of course a methodological point that is required to create a smooth space in our understanding before we begin drawing lines and make distinctions. Actually, distinctions are made by themselves, since each system, to be a system, has a boundary dividing itself from an environment. Smooth spaces, where communications can flow freely, are not spaces without boundaries, but spaces in which boundaries interact freely. The nature of the boundary is truly variegated and really depends on the type of system at hand, but at this stage it is important to point out straightaway that boundaries are common features of all social systems, indeed all systems, and that this indicates the fact that certain criteria have to be met if a number of social relations are to constitute a system. One of these is a boundary: without boundaries, there is no defined social space, whether striated or smooth, within which the specific operation of the system can occur, hence no relation between system and its environment. So social practices oriented by certain values, codes, beliefs and goals constitute companies, schools, sports centres, households, neighbourhoods, communities, community centres, churches, offices, economies, friends' networks, states, social movements, armies, transnational corporations and financial centres; moreover, all these systems are systems precisely because they are operationally bounded. 'Operationally bounded' means that the operations occurring in these 'sites' bind them as systems and thus give them the specific unity that allows us to call them by their names.

Several systems may actually be environments to one another, something that Figure 2.1 does not show, since in this figure I followed the temporal line of a subject rather than the structural composition of a social object such as a system. From an observation point situated within the operating of each system, whatever is outside the system's operations constitutes its environment. Each social system (integrative function systems such as the economy or politics, or organisations such as a household, a company, an association) has other social systems as its environment. Crucially, though, social systems also have non-social environments, upon which they depend. Social systems have as constituting elements the bodies of people, that is physical and psychic systems, and they are part of larger ecological systems. In turn, psychic and living systems have each other and social systems as their environment. This implies that what constitutes an 'environment' is always relative to the system, hence there is no single environment. To put it in the words of the anthropologist Tim Ingold: '"environment" is a relative term – relative, that is, to the being whose environment it is. Just as there can be no organism without environment, so also there can be no environment without an organism'. Substitute 'organism' for 'social system' and you get the point. Incidentally, this also means that sense and meaning are constituted within the relations of a 'system–environment unit': 'Thus my environment is the world as it exists and takes on meaning in relation to me, and in that sense it came to existence and undergoes development with me and around me' (Ingold 2000: 20).

In Figure 2.2. I follow the symbolism that biologists Maturana and Varela (1998: 74) use for biological units – cells – to describe a social system unit. In Figure 2.2, I take any one of the ellipses in Figure 2.1 symbolising social systems and observe it in such a way as to reveal its environment: here the circle symbolises a social system while the wave at the bottom represents its environment. The two lines linking the circle to the wave symbolise any type of interaction between system and environment.

Since the environment of a system is itself made of social or ecological systems outside the system one is investigating,

Figure 2.2 An illustration of the system-environment relation

those interactions are interactions among systems, something that if repeated with a certain regularity we understand as *structural coupling* among systems, a property I will investigate in Chapter 8 on boundary commoning and Chapter 9 on the relation between capital and the commons. The interaction between system and environment may well be at the origin of the system's structural change, either as a change triggered by interactions coming from its environment or as a result of its internal dynamics.

Capitalists, politicians of all persuasions and bankers all like social change understood as structural change. The implementation of a big project such as a new tunnel under the Alps in order to build a new high-speed train line that speeds the path of commodity circulation while externalising the environmental and social costs onto local communities in Val di Susa, where the gallery is located, is a type of structural change. Also, to call for an increase the number of women or minorities into the realm of command, whether in companies or in government, is to demand structural change. Structural change implies that a given system changes some of its components but not the fundamental relations among these components that allow that system to operate as a unity. If on my bicycle I replace the hard seat with a super-padded saddle that makes me feel like I am sitting on a soft cushion, I have structurally changed the bicycle, which remains nevertheless a bicycle by virtue of the relations among its components. It is these relations that constitute the bicycle as a unity.

The social change that I personally would like to see, like many in social movements, is not one in which a component is replaced, like replacing a board of directors or a brand, or a numerically controlled machine with a robot. I want to see social change that is change not only in terms of the components of social systems but also in terms of the set of social relations and social practices constituting social systems as a unity. Change to the relations and practices that constitute the capitalist system as a unity would be one example: a social change whereby profit and accumulation are no longer the overarching motive of social practice, but rather it is care, solidarity, conviviality, community and ecology, and social wealth is no longer in the hand of the few but accessible to the many. In this changed system, fear for lack of work-related income, or the threat and actual life of destitution would be simply impossible because the society of the commons would make it impossible.

This question of system change is, of course, a very big question, and I am not going to provide big answers, only to suggest a method for its framing. In order to do so, I need first to be aware of the properties of any systems. I need to integrate our systems thinking with traditional formulations of force, power, values and goals.

Basic properties of all systems

According to basic social system and cybernetics literature (Meadows 2008; Capra 1982, 1997; Skytter 1996), all systems whether natural or socio-economic have the following properties.

1. They have elements or nodes. For example, in a market system, the elements are competing entities, whether people or firms; in a forest system, the elements are trees and living organisms; in a commons or a company they are a set of people and 'things'. In this sense systems have structure, defined by parts and their composition.

2. Systems have interconnectivity, that is, the different nodes relate to one another in particular ways. The relationships among the different parts reproduce the system's structure and structural components as well as the articulation of functions. Interconnectivity also differentiates systems. Thus in relation to point 1 above, there was no difference between commons and multinational businesses (they both were assemblages of people and 'things'), but if we now look at the social relations making up their practices – their interconnections as well as their horizons – we can start to distinguish them.

3. These relationships are constituted through patterned feedbacks among nodes/components of the systems. Feedback loops are the causal paths that lead from the initial generation of a signal to the subsequent modification of an event. Feedbacks are always value-ridden (re)actions (De Angelis 2007a) and are not only communication loops. Instead they are an ecology of bodily, cognitive and affective circuits and action loops, although in given power contexts some of these circuits are just shut down.

Take, for example, an owner of a small factory reacting to a loss in profit opportunities consisting of closing that factory and firing its workers. This (re)action may be consistent with the economic value of a management decision trying to maximising profit in view of a lower cost of production in a country nearby. The economic environment has fed back on the factory system. This decision, however, constitutes a feedback to the population of workers: the material condition of their job is going to change. This provokes not only various emotional and affective responses when workers are among their kind, but often also a range of performances in order to maintain negotiation with management or the state along the code of 'proper', 'professional' or 'civil' communication. In this latter particular instance, some circuits are shut, that is, not communicated. Bordieu's habitus[1] here plays a role in restraining workers within traditional mechanisms of representation and therefore of ultimate acceptance of economic logic within the given increasingly poor safety-net compensation mechanisms. There seems to be no alternative. Economic logic permeates the 'symbolic capital' of workers as well, or at least the institutions representing them. Ultimately, what matters is not to question this logic in practice, but, rather, to constitute some bare mechanisms of welfare to enable the fired workers to survive for a while. The massive presence of poverty acting as an ever-present threat will tell them they are relatively lucky.

This is of course the story of thousands of restructured or closed-up factories, restructurings and closures being a process that has accelerated in Europe through the post-2007 crisis. It is also something that happens regularly in capitalist production, with a different measure of destitution as a result of restructuring. When this happens, following this feedback, workers' relation to capital changes as does the relation among workers themselves and their communities: they are unemployed. Reflexivity and organisation may change things, however, and prevent that habitus from dominating workers' responses. If workers are open to consider other options and to evaluate them strategically, the the type of feedback they give to the factory owner and the state, the habitus of individualised subjectivities, is no longer only to accept the inevitable. There are also synergies, creativity, new horizons and situated emergence. For example, in Argentina through the early 2000s (Sitrin 2012) and in southern Europe in recent years, factories have been 'reclaimed', that is, workers have seized the means of production, and not simply managed the factories but governed them in horizontal ways, involving decisions to change the production processes, redefining the role of those factories from places of capitalist production to places of conviviality and commoning, spaces to be shared with communities, (re)producing affective relations and ecologies, and engaging in virtuous networks of solidarity economy with other reclaimed factories.

4. Because of property 3, the individuals within systems and the systems themselves have 'behaviour', that is, patterned movement, which involves throughput sequences (inputs, processing and outputs of material) and hence expenditure of energy (whether human – such as labour – or not) or information. However they also have strategy, understood as selection of meaning and action path at any given moment in given contexts. They therefore could have power to disrupt and/or change the patterned behaviour of the system if a sufficient social force is applied. In this sense, patterned movement can fork out along clashing values, as in the example above. Social change occurs when resources are distributed from one system to another allowing differential power to emerge favouring one system or another. Clearly, when they do so, their meaning changes. In the hand of capital, resources are capital. In the hand of the commons, resources are commonwealth: two completely different social forms.

5. Systems have boundaries and one composite environment. The nature of the boundary, its porosity vis-à-vis the outside world, and the nature of its interchange with it, are crucial in identifying the nature of the system. Smaller systems with tight boundaries – such as commons – can hide oppression such as

patriarchy or corruption. No boundary implies no governance, and therefore no resilience and no reproduction (P.M. 2014). The boundary of a commons is constituted by its practices, by the values it is founded on and those that develop through its doing, by the sense it makes of itself and the surrounding world, and by the challenges it receives from the outside, whether from other commons or from state and capital. We may think here of the double face of Janus, the Etruscan divinity adopted by the ancient Romans, at the boundary, with one face looking to the outside and one to the inside of the boundary. Janus, the god of doors, has one mind and two perspectives, a very schizophrenic position. At the boundary, the practices, codes, values and sense underpin a oscillation of liminal investment between two poles: one paranoiac, reactionary or fascisising pole and one that escapes, make connections open to a line of flight, mestizising subjectivities, and redeveloping the relation between the inside and the outside (see Deleuze and Guattari 1984: 366).

The environment of any social system is constituted by two main domains: (a) other social systems which interact with it, whether of the same nature or not and (b) the natural environment, the land, air, water and biosphere with which any system interacts. Looking at social systems therefore necessarily involves looking at ecological relations.

6. Systems have scale, in that systems can be nested into one another: a household commons within a neighbourhood commons, the latter in turn nested into a citywide association and so on. In the case of the water associations in Cochabamba (see Box 4) nesting is clear between first-order (neighbourhood) and second-order (all participating neighbourhoods) associations. Moreover, the capitalist system comprises among other

elements companies, which can be regarded as systems on their own terms. In turn, companies have among other elements factories, which are systems in their own right. Furthermore, factories comprise among other things people working in them. Finally, people themselves are complex systemic entities made of interacting organic material. Nesting means there are institutions or social systems connected to one another through rules or cultural norms. As Ostrom (2005: 11) reminds us, 'what is a whole system at one level is a part of a system at another level'. Arthur Koestler (1973) refers to such nested subassemblies of part–whole units in complex adaptive systems as holons. 'The term holon may be applied to any stable sub-whole in an organismic or social hierarchy, which displays rule-governed behaviour and/or structural Gestalt constancy' (Koestler 1973: 291).

7. Finally systems exhibit adaptive, dynamic, self-preserving and evolutionary behaviour, involving impasse, collapse and the overcoming of impasses; this is because systems are more than the sum of their parts and therefore prone to unanticipated, emergent characteristics.

Commons systems

Starting from the position that we should not confuse the commons with resources held in common, I approach commons as social systems in which resources are pooled by a community of subjects who also govern these resources to guarantee the sustainability of the resources (if they are natural resources) and the reproduction of the community, and who engage in commoning, that is, doing in commons that has a direct relation to the needs, desires and aspirations of the commoners. Through commoning, subjects create conditions of resilience

continued on page 98

Box 4 Water commons

In April 2010 I attended the third Feira del Agua in Cochabamba, Bolivia. If anybody had any doubts about the existence and relevance of commons to people's lives and livelihoods, a fair like this should help dispel any such doubt. Spread along the four sides of a large football pitch and beyond, dozens of community water associations and cooperatives, such as that of Flores Rancho which I had visited some days before (Box 6), were making their own showcases, with the help of hand-made posters and polystyrene models, to mark their presence and to exchange information, knowledge and technology.

The fair coincided with the tenth anniversary of the water war that forced the then Bolivian government to repeal its water privatisation law (see Chapter 9). Notable presences at this fair – besides some international development NGOs, some associations proposing waterless bio-toilets and some documentation centres – were Semapa, the municipal water company, highly controversial because of allegations of corruption and ineffectiveness in providing water, and Misicuni, a consortium of national and international companies building a large dam in the mountains north of Cochabamba that promises to remedy the water deficit of the region.

Cochabamba is indeed a region with a water deficit. In spite of all the amazing self-organisation efforts that community groups are making, they cannot offer water to all the local communities. The area of Cochabamba most affected is the south, the vast suburban area where about 200,000 people live and where water provision is poor. In the 1980s and 1990s, substantial migration from rural and mining regions into cities like Cochabamba occurred, putting pressure on water provision. The subjects living in these areas face three distinct realities with respect to access to water. First, there is the market reality. This is the reality of those who lack access to water, don't organise and thus depend on private providers. Their provision generally occurs in unsafe and unregulated forms. Private suppliers driving cistern trucks deliver the water to homes, where it is poured into 'turril', large, 200-litre open canisters generally kept outdoors. Not only is the water astronomically expensive (up to 30 bolivianos, £3, for a turril, and not just for drinking water, but for the household's entire water usage), it is also vulnerable to contamination as a result of storage in old, rusty containers and exposure to the elements. The individual here is hooked into the alien grand scheme of the market that externalises to them the health cost of water.

The second reality is of those who self-organise themselves and are lucky enough to live in areas where water is present and community wells can be dug. The work being done here is impressive: communities build from scratch entire water systems, dig wells up to 100 metres deep, construct water storage facilities such as large raised cisterns, connect pumps, lay the pipes for home distribution, monitor water quality (which in this region is always threatened by waste contamination), and manage the entire system. All this is not bad as a form of commoning and mobilising circuits of praxis. Interestingly, it is generally recognised that the initiative to dig for water emerges in a population that has recently migrated from the countryside, and therefore has a memory of self-reliance and a relation to nature that is empowering. Rural people always settle close to water sources and and find ways to extract it from the ground and use it. This is not a trivial fact, and I now consider that a crucial aspect of the countryside subjectivity everywhere in the world is such self-reliance and autonomous spirit, a spirit that is lost through successive waves of urbanisation which add mediations between people and nature in the form of money and bureaucratic and legal codes.

The third reality is of those who self-organise but are not lucky enough to live in areas with water. The commons self-organisation in this case occurs through a system of water collection by cistern trucks. The water is generally purchased from the municipal water company Semapa at far less than the market price and distributed in the community. Generally, the community associations also establish systems of distribution based on water storage facilities from which water is piped into the houses. In one case (the Asociation de Produccion y Administracion de Agua y Saneamiento APAAS, a community-based organisation set up in 1990), water is fetched from 7 kilometres away; to get the water the community has set up pipes, pumps and storage facilities along the crest of a mountain down to their suburban neighbourhood.

Both the second and third types of water provision in Cochabamba are examples of circuits of praxis based on some type of commoning, in which the individuals are part of a community that gives itself organisational form as an association. The different community organisations seem to function in different ways according to different conditions, but all rely heavily on community labour in addition to self-funding and some access to external funding. The need for a degree of socialisation of production in some functions – and therefore for greater scale – is met by a further level of organisational structure, that is, associations of associations.

One such second-level association is Asica-Sur (www.asica-sur.org/index.php), one of the main organisers of the 2010 Feira del Agua. Asica-Sur pulls together about ninety community organisations of the second and third categories discussed above, roughly split in half between those which have access to a well and those that do not. Asica-Sur offers four types of services to their members: it provides community associations with a platform of organisation and negotiating power vis-à-vis the state and municipal water authorities; it strengthens the capacity of the water systems by facilitating information sharing; it provides technical assistance and services, for example, through its cistern trucks which it provides to those communities without wells, but also through enabling smaller community groups to access government and NGO funds; and it offers help in the management of water resources, infrastructure and equipment. It also seems increasingly to mediate and find political solutions to problems encountered by larger community water systems.

For example, APAAS encountered some problems due to human settlement along the 7-km pipeline, problems unknown when it was established more than two decades ago. The new dwellers pretended that APAAS gave them water for free as payment for allowing the pipes to pass through their territory. Obviously, any solution for this water war among the poor depends on a political processes among different commons, rather than abstract recipes. Access to a resource like water is never limited here to a given community; nevertheless, although appeal is made to traditional forms of administration or forms of *convivir* (living together) 'based on ancient cultural rules and customs where the prevailing collective work and active participation in deliberation and decision making on the assets and affairs concerning the community takes place according to the principles of reciprocity, solidarity, justice, fairness and transparency' (Asica-Sur pamphlet), these forms have to deal with a reality in progress and a web of bottom-up and bottom–bottom situations of conflict that continually challenge the forms in which these basic principles apply. Here we have a major challenge facing commons and commoning as a political paradigm. The reality is one in which the commons and the commoning perspective must embrace the new and the challenges of the times, while at the same time valorising and reclaiming the old and the ancient. The solution is not inscribed in written handbooks of given knowledge, but in the art of negotiation and in the political and organisational inventiveness of communities. In a seminar I attended I heard a Columbian activist referring not only to *mingas* (community collective work; see Box 5) to build and maintain water systems, but also to *mingas* of social resistance. To this we may add the need for *mingas* of intercommunity relations and solidarity. The many associations and their collective organisations, such as Asica-Sur, all want to do more – whether to extend access to water to more members of the community, or to improve sanitation and water quality. They want, that is, to increase the organisational reach of their commoning. This implies, however, that they all need more commonwealth, that is, they need to mobilise more social power. But scaling up necessarily raises the question of the construction of commons in relation to markets and states.

From what I saw, an increase in the commonwealth of water commons in Cochabamba can occur in one or a combination of the following ways (leaving out robbery of peers from other communities): (1) members of the community all chip in from their own material or financial savings; (2) donors (such as NGOs) are found; (3) the community takes on a debt; (4) the state pours resources into the community; (5) the community expropriates the property of the wealthy or of the state, or occupies or squats it (like the Brazilian landless movement, MST).

Each of these methods represent challenges and limits from the perspective of scale and social justice, because they themselves need to have 'sources', and in particular sources of power. Also, each has risks. The first method is of course limited by the degree of material wealth of the community, and complicated by the division of wealth within the community and the degree of cohesion despite differences in wealth. Here the question is how does a community govern its own structural division of economic power? The second method, as well as being limited by the money available and the work and know-how necessary to bid for the money, also may require the local project to align itself to the priorities of the international NGOs. The third ties the local community to repayment plans and therefore to markets. The fourth brings with it the alignment of local communities to the priorities of the state and, in given conditions, may favour their co-optation. The fifth brings the threat of repression.

Talking to people from different water associations present at this fair, I gained the impression that all these options have been used, except debt. For example, APAAS participated in a competition and won money from the World Bank to fund the purchase of its pipeline. Some community organisations pool savings and buy the land upon which they dig a well partially funded by an NGO. In another case, the state pours in money for a community water store as part of the Bolivia Cambia Evo Cumple campaign. However I was told by some community associations activists that while the government has given some money directly to grassroots associations and not to local authorities, this has happened significantly more in areas where there is greatest opposition to the government – such as Santa Cruz – while in Cochabamba – the stronghold of MAS, the party in government – there have been only timid disbursements. Finally, in other cases foreign development funds are channelled into community organisations.

Thus, it seems that in order to grow, commons cannot escape development, whether we are talking about transfers from states or supranational institutions such as the World Bank or NGOs, or the need to access money from the market in order to pool savings. In principle, we could of course imagine an alternative process that makes no use of state or markets, that is, one based entirely on method 5 above. But this would require the abilities of commoners to sustain the consequent repression by the state. In the end, which of the five options are taken, or their mix, depends on strategies in the given conditions of power relations.

If we scale up to reach higher levels of association, there are other ways to extend the social power of commoners. One is posed by Asica-Sur with the question of *cogestión* – or co-management. The question of co-management with Semeca is not yet clearly defined, and some community activists are afraid that involvement with the organisational forms of the municipal company would irreversibly contaminate community organisational values. But the rationale is obvious: to have access to resources now available to the ineffective and corrupt structure of Semapa. The problem is really to find a form that articulates community forms of organisation with this greater, urban-scale organisation.

Another issue, perhaps linked to the question of co-management, is the demand that the state should allow large companies to make available their means of production and equipment to smaller associations which have little equipment. This is perhaps a mild form of temporary 'expropriation' that does not damage anybody really (aside from clashing with capitalist values and preventing private companies from recovering the depreciation of their capital), but would give community associations access to fundamental resources and increase the scale of their operations. It is also evidence for a conception that sees the need for private and public property to be commonalised (see Chapter 9) not so much in terms of formal ownership status, but rather in terms of the forms of its access and management (see Chapter 7), allowing us in certain contexts to move beyond old dichotomies.

But big corporate mega-projects are also on the horizon and bring new challenges. There has been controversy surrounding the Misicuni project – whether a project on this scale was really necessary and whether alternatives could not be found – but in general all the association representatives I talked to in 2010 were happy with the water availability promised by Misicuni. I asked Carlos Oropeza, a technician with Asica-Sur, if this project would reduce the need for grassroots associations, but he did not seem to be concerned. 'Local co-ops will buy water and distribute it themselves,' he told me. Asica-Sur was already building the storage facilities and strengthening the infrastructure for local distribution. The water produced by the business consortium would eventually be hooked up to the infrastructure built and administered by the grassroots communities. On whose terms? Who will co-opt whom? It is still too early to say. Meanwhile in 2013 the project was halted by contract disputes.

and self-organisation and may develop from grassroots into more all-encompassing systems. Thus, commons come in many shapes and sizes even if their organisational unit can be represented by an image like that in Figure 2.3.

Figure 2.3 highlights two important aspects of the future of commons systems. In the first place, the arrow in the circle indicates the ongoing praxis and (re)production of social relations necessary to reproduce the commons, or commoning, an activity which is social, bodily and intelligent. It also indicates the sense of directions, that is, goals and values that are able to translate the power fields within the commons into an effective social force field (see below). Also, and crucially, as systems commons are defined not only by their own internal relations – from which, for example, Elinor Ostrom (1990) derived her principles of sustainability of commons (discussed in Chapter 4) – but also in relation to their environment. The commons environment includes other systems. In the first place, this means ecosystems. All commons have a relation to

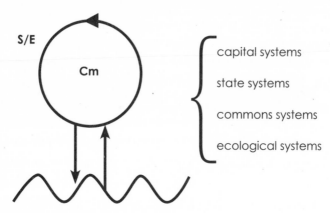

Figure 2.3 Commons as a social system

ecosystems, and thus have responsibilities regarding the earth's natural processes (even if not all commons act responsibly from an ecological perspective). In principle, therefore, there is no special essential relation of commons to ecosystems, although many commons rely on the natural environment for their resilience, and so have a special interest in developing ecologically sustainable practices and in struggling against the 'externalities' of other systems, especially capital's system. Others develop this interest and frame it in particular cosmologies that integrate the whole of earth's ecosystem inside the commons themselves. So, for example, indigenous cultures pretty much everywhere represent the 'spirit of the planet' through their rituals, their sensibility to ecological conditions as those of 'mother earth' as in the case of the people of the Andes, and through their consequent resilient practices.

Commons, then, have relations to capital and the state and to other commons. Think, to make a simple case, of a household micro-commons. Its members pay council taxes for collection of their rubbish and pay income taxes or collect unemployment benefits. This is a day-to-day relation to the state. But the police, traffic laws, civil and criminal laws regulating certain behaviour, etc. are also in relation to the state. The members of the household micro-commons also relate to the state as recipients of what remain of welfare services: education or health. They relate to capital when they face consumeristic advertisements and have to deal with the threat of their internalisation; they pay with increasing work rhythms or lower wages and more precarious conditions; they do not control the means of life and are exposed to norms of production that they cannot control when they are the subject of expropriation and accumulation, when the commons' wealth and labour are co-opted to reduce the costs of capitalist production (as when volunteer workers dominate a corporate project or reduce the cost of capitalist production).[2] Commons also relate to other commons, and in the strength, kind and scale of these relations resides the possibility of emancipation. (I will discuss in detail the basic framework for these relations in Chapter 8.) Finally, in commons environments we also find hybrid forms: social systems that are a bit of all three types, commons, state and capital. In reality most social systems are hybrid, with a dominant factor. So, I enter a semi-privatised hospital for a visit (state), and I can interrogate a doctor or a nurse about the effects of the recent wave of private investment (capital) while I have a glimpse of a junior doctor holding the hand of a dying woman (commons).

Clearly, all these relations are in turn interrelated. If the state and a multinational are taking away the land used by communities for generations (Daniel and Mittal 2009), this will probably make different households relate to one another and start a process of political recomposition enlarging the boundaries of their household micro-commons. This has happened, for example, in the case of Val di Susa, in northern Italy, where communities of struggle have been formed contesting for the past thirty years the development of high-speed trains. Similar examples are numerous and can be found in every part of the world. The ecological justice atlas (https://ejatlas.org/) is a great document, allowing access to information about the most diverse enclosures, including land grabs and in many cases the struggles against them. For every struggle, there is a community of struggle being formed and sharing resources.

The typology of commons

It must be remarked that at this preliminary stage, the commons seem to have an ontological equivalence to social systems such as state and capital. To the extent that they are all social systems this is correct, but as soon as one begins to investigate their distinctive processes, key ontological differences begin to become clear.

The phenomenology of commons is grounded in daily life. Households are one example of commons – at least, they are when claustrophobic boundaries and patriarchal hierarchies do not turn them into micro-states, or corrupt commons, to use the term of Hardt and Negri (2009), or, in the vernacular and from the perspective of subaltern subjects, 'fucked up' commons. Networks of supporting friends are another example of commons, consisting of lifelong connections or ephemeral relationships: temporary commons are still commons, with very loose boundaries but very little direction. Community organisations, housing co-ops and social centres, self-managed workshops, community gardens and water associations all are forms of commons systems, as are peer-to-peer (P2P) networks in cyberspace for sharing music, codes, files and books and generally promoting all forms of digital cooperation. As the listing of friendship and virtual networks implies, commons may occupy a social space rather than a physical place; they need not be situated in a particular locality, although those that are have the additional strategic task of claiming a territory.

It is important, I argue, that we do not think of commons as a third sector, beyond state and market. This influential view among commoners was recently echoed by Weston and Bollier (2013: 350).

the overall goal must be to reconceptualize the neoliberal State/
Market as a 'triarchy' with the Commons – the State/Market/
Commons – to realign authority and provisioning in new, more
beneficial ways. The State would maintain its commitments to
representative governance and management of public property just as private enterprise would continue to own capital to
produce saleable goods and services in the Market sector.

This repartition presupposes a deal among three social forces
with clear boundaries and big conflicts of interests. A deal can
be an outcome of a conflict, not an assumption to prove how
effective a policy would be. Furthermore, the idea of sectors
as discrete divisions operating alongside, in parallel with, one
another does not take into account the most difficult aspect of
commons: their current entanglement with capital and the state.
Commons exist both outside and inside states and capital, and,
to the extent that states and capital influence the subjectivities
of commoners reproducing commons, states and capital are
inside commons even if their systemic patterns and logics are
outside them. Thus, for example, we find commons not only in
neighbourhood associations, care networks or reclaimed factories, but also in private enterprise, on the shop floor of factories
and in the canteens of offices among co-workers supporting one
another, sharing their lunch and developing forms of solidarity
and mutual aid; and we find commons inside state schools and
universities, often divided on hierarchical lines: the management commons, the teachers' commons, the students' commons.
Commons are therefore often entangled within class relations
and exclusive relations, such as library commons in universities
in the UK, which are only for those who are willing to pay £9,000

annual fee for a degree. And, as I will discuss in Chapter 10, to be 'entangled with' is the essence of complexity, a word derived from the Latin *complexus*, the past participle of *complectī* ('to entwine, encircle, compass, enfold'), from *com-* ('together') and *plectere* ('to weave, braid').

Not only, therefore, are the commons related to pooled resources governing rivers, coastlines, forests and rivers and their ecosystems as studied by Ostrom and her associates; and nor, moreover, are they only found outside and in opposition to capital (and state), as in unemployed people squatting empty houses and sharing tricks on how to fool the benefits office; but also within and at the heart even of capital, such as among the rich and privileged. Bill Gates, for example, becomes a commoner with respect to his family and his class, even though his peculiar family commons is part of that 1 per cent of society that concentrates 50 per cent of the world's wealth (Oxfam, 2014) and the physical siting of his commons systems is most likely protected by barbed wire and security cameras that warn armed security guards – transforming a commons boundary into a border that keeps the poor and their commons systems out. Indeed, politically, the relation among commons is not a given; it must be politically constructed through boundary commoning (discussed in Chapter 8) and a clear sense of the class enemy.

Commons and capital

Commons and capital are two distinct, autonomous social systems; that is, they both struggle to 'take things into their own hands' and self-govern on the basis of their different and often clashing, internally generated codes, measures and values. They also struggle to be distinct autopoietic social systems, in that they aim to reproduce not only their interrelations but also the preproduction of their components through their internally generated codes and values. They do this of course, in a clear, distinctive way. Capital can reproduce itself only through profit and its accumulation, which ultimately imply the exploitation of labour, the creation of divisions among the working class, and the trashing of nature. Commons can reproduce through commoning, doing in common, which is a social process embedded in particular values that defines a sharing culture in a given time and context, through which they reproduce resources and the community that comprises them. Both commons and capital may employ high or low tech, make use of oil or not, have functions that require a certain level of authority. Commons are generated in so far as subjects become commoners, in so far as their social being is enacted with others, at different levels of social organisation, through a social practice, commoning, that is essentially horizontal and may embrace a variety of forms depending on circumstances (implying the broad typology), but ultimately is grounded on community sharing. Capital, by contrast, tends to objectify, instrumentalise and impose hierarchical order.

When we consider commons, we are not (should not be) indicating utopia, and nor are we (should we be) pointing to dystopia with capital. It may appear manifest that capital cannot bring us to utopia, since its own *conatus of self-preservation* (De Angelis 2007a) is boundless accumulation, and the processes for realising this are not only environmentally destructive but also socially divisive and exploitative. It is equally the case, however, that we cannot claim (should not imagine) either that commons will lead us to utopia, since utopias are not made of concrete structures contingent on particular situations. What we can claim, though, is that commons and capital have distinct and conflicting characters and that each, if left to develop without the constraints that the *other poses on* its development, would lead to a completely different social form.

As I will argue in Chapter 4, the commons and capital/state are often linked, coupled through the buying-and-selling site of the market, that is, the 'economy'. Both capital and the commons buy and sell, although with different priorities and as parts of different movements (although both defined and regulated by state laws of contract, its violations protected by the state police, and with production structured by health and safety regulations, unless they do these practices 'underground'). Capital buys in order to sell at a profit – in the case of commercial capital – or as means of production, to turn resources into commodities (add value). Commons, on the other hand, tend to sell commodities in order to buy means of sustenance and reproduction. For example, some members of a household sell their labour power to gain an income in order to be able to purchase the goods necessary for the process of reproduction of that household; or an association engages in petty trade to fund itself; or a social centre sells beer at a concert to purchase the materials to build a kitchen. Buying in order to sell and selling in order to buy are two opposite praxes, as they have been since the time of Aristotle, the former governed and limited by a life activity ultimately wasted in accumulation and the latter governed by the needs and desires of reproduction (subject to market constraints). In other words, as I argue in Chapter 4, while reproduction of labour power is a feature of the commons production of the commodity labour-power sold to capital, capital does not necessarily control (or controls only in part through the state and the education system) the labour of reproduction which is fundamental to the commons. The constitution of the selling-in-order-to-buy circuit which is typical of the labour-power circuit is only the market moment of a commons social system. It is certainly here that labour power is reproduced ... but not only labour power.

I began Chapter 1 with a simple genealogy of commons systems: a plurality establishing relations to each other and use values. At any moment of their development, commons systems have interconnected sets of elements (commoners or commons wealth) that are organised in a way that achieves, if nothing else, the reproduction of those elements. Commons systems differ from all other social systems – neoliberally governed schools, cities, factories, capitalist economies, corporations, politics and armies – in the particular form taken by three of the factors they have in commons with all these other social systems: namely the forms of their elements (material, psychophysical, and immaterial), the interconnections or social and material relations, and their purpose or function.

Common resources and their associated plurality (community of commoners) develop forms of social interactions and relations through the praxis of commoning, and not, for example, via exploitation with the aim of profit.

Like any system, commons systems are prone to adaptive, dynamic, self-preserving and evolutionary behaviour, impasses, collapse and the overcoming of impasses, since they are more than the sum of their parts and therefore prone to unanticipated, emergent characteristics. A commons may exhibit adaptive, dynamic, goal-seeking, self-preserving, and sometimes evolutionary behaviour (Meadows 2008).

Also its basic elements continuously change: subjectivities evolve, change, die out and are renewed; materials decay, technologies change, ideas spread, and their environment – with which the commons is interacting continuously – changes too. Furthermore, the environment of present-day commons is dominated by capital loops, the circuits of capital that all wish to enclose and all wish to turn into a profitable enterprise and overwork or destitution for others. If we were to take the large, bird's-eye view of history, of the original accumulations of the sixteenth to eighteenth centuries in South America, Africa, Asia and Europe up to the most recent transition from the post-1945 Keynesian deal to neoliberalism, several books could be written about the *co-evolution* of capital and the commons, about how commons sustained the enclosures of the former by regenerating newer forms in different areas, and how capital has regenerated itself under the impulse of commoner struggles on the shop floor, in neighbourhoods, in bread or antiracist riots or women's sex strikes. Many books indeed have been written: what I am suggesting here is the overarching interpretative grid of capital and the commons as two opposite social forms each manifesting itself in diverse historically specific cultural ways.

Commons = S/E = power = enacted social force

Why is it important to look at commons in terms of social systems? Is this an academic exercise? Where is the politics in this? There are several reasons. In the first place, to interpret commons as social systems is to observe social productive and reproductive activities as a whole set of social relations, practices and wealth, and this allows us to problematise this whole as the basis of social power generated and *therefore* of social force of transformation. This because a social force does not emerge and sustain itself without social systems that are able to generate it and reproduce it. A molar social force, in other words, emerges out of the web of interactions that are molecular social forces. In this sense, I understand a *social force* as a particular expression of a social system that – seeking its own reproduction through its operations at whatever scale of social action – influences, clashes, contaminates, subsumes, couples with, transforms, or destroys other social systems, making them the means of its own development. A social system is thus the coagulation or composition of a plurality of social powers around particular types of value practices, that is, social practices and correspondent relations that, in so far as their social reproduction is concerned, articulate social subjects and ecologies through value-specific and coordinating operations. This articulation is produced by individual singularities discursively selecting what is 'good' and what is 'bad' within a value system they themselves create through their common engagement and actually acting upon this selection (De Angelis 2007a).

This way of looking at a social force in its broad sense as an expanding social system vis-à-vis other social systems, as circuits of praxis (re)producing value and sense, organisational reach and social power vis-à-vis other social forces, is at the basis of an organic bottom-up conception of social transformation in which social change is not only *structural* change, that is, change in the material and immaterial components of systems, but also change in organisation, in social relations, in modes of production and distribution, modes of making sense, giving meaning and valuing, change in modes of accessing socially, not individually, produced wealth.

But this way of looking is one that also puts ourselves into the picture and therefore demands that we be self-reflective. To clarify this, let us make the distinction that system theorists make between first-order and second-order observations. When I consider objects out there I often look at them as 'things' outside myself. This type of relation with the object works on daily life: as I drive off passing a small fire at the edge of a forest without worrying about its possible consequences, or as the onlooker watches the farmer's crop, or as redundant factory workers look at the tools and equipment for the last time before their factory's closure, or as the passers-by look at the abandoned warehouse, the field turned into wasteland. In these cases, we look at objects we do not relate to. This is first-order observation, when the object is outside ourselves. But I could call up the forest authorities or the fire department, or even, if it is a small fire, put it out with the old blanket in the boot thus preventing a big fire from developping (while having my children watch from the car at a safe distance). The ecological farmer relates to the crop in attending to its nutritional needs. Some among the factory workers who are about to leave the factory after its closure begin to think and discuss how they could actually use the equipment for other purposes. The passers-by can begin to reflect on whether they could find ways to use the wasteland and turn it into community gardens, and the old warehouse into a community centre. All these latter cases are cases of second-order observation that require us to take a step back and observe ourselves observing and interacting with the object and the other people. This second-order observation is when we see objects no longer as 'things' outside ourselves, but as element of social systems which include ourselves as subjects within them.

From this second-order observation standpoint, the common goods are nothing other than an elements of the commons, and we can scream and shout about wanting common goods, but until we invest our time and energy in their (re)production and the (re)production of the relations among each other there are no common goods and there are no commons. But when there are commons, then it is because there is an 'us' in communication and relational practice with one another and with the common goods through commoning. (This is my take on Krippendorff 1995 and 1996.)

Power-force/values-goals

At the most general level, there are two main parts that govern the structure and organisation of systems when considered dynamically, and these are their stocks and their flows. Stocks are the reservoir of 'things' – both material and immaterial – that a social subject (individual or collective) has available. The flow is what moves in and out of this stock, or the social life activity that constitutes it. So a river may be said to flow in and out of a lake, as water flows in and out of a bathtub (Meadows 2008).

Modern economists and social scientists such as Bordieau (1986) call the reservoir of material and immaterial things 'capital'; this 'capital' might be a collection of machines in a factory or of money in a bank, but also the connections one subject has, the network one can bring to bear for a particular action and objective (social capital), the skills one has available (human capital) or the type of culture of signs and symbols (symbolic capital), the type of culture one has been exposed to in life (cultural capital), different types of biomass and ecologies (natural capital). Now, all these notions of stocks are called capital because the hegemony of the capitalist mode of production urges us to see them in terms of their possible contribution to make money, to accumulation. Even people promoting commons transition consider these things 'capital' and point to the need for 'cooperative accumulation'.[3] I want to escape from this temptation here. With reference to the commons, the term I will use to denote all elements of stocks that are available in the commons as wealth – to the extent that this wealth is not used for private monetary enrichment, whether individual or collective – and mediates and is reproduced by commoning activities – is 'commonwealth'. Unlike capital, it is a wealth that is available to all who seek it, through encounters, friendships, networks or organisations that pool it more effectively, or social movements that claim it. Like capital, commonwealth is thus a stock, but unlike capital the flows it generates possess different goals and it is enacted through different practices. However, like any other systems including capital, its flows aim at going back to stocks, reproduce them, replenish them and enrich them, although enrichment for commonwealth does not necessarily imply a monetary value – it could be a spiritual, cultural, natural or symbolic value.

The task now is to begin investigation of some aspects of the stock-flows nature of social systems and translate it to some key categories of social sciences. In the first place, let us look at flows and our relations to flows.

In our daily journey through systems as in Figure 2.4 geared up with our instrumental first-order observation, it is more likely that we experience flows than systems in their complexity. Flows hit people and nature like forces of different intensity and qualities. Flows are manifestation of social forces. These social forces move us along, pushing us in different directions, and we find our path only if we find a inherent force adapting or resisting or pushing in a particular, maybe different, direction. Foucault got it right when he hailed the art of governance as a crucial art of survival in a sea of opposing forces. In his now seminal book *The Rise of the Network Society* (1996), Manuel Castells reflected on global society as the societies of global flows: finance, migrants, commodities, and social movements. Flows are social forces since they have direction and impact. Often at any given moment we experience a multiplicity of social forces, internal desires and needs and aspirations, the constraints from the outside – the directive that we need to observe by a given deadline otherwise it seems the world will fall apart, and so on. Thus social forces are constituents of force fields. A force field is a distribution of forces in space. Everything in daily life is constituted by multiple forces of different strengths acting in different directions and generated by the internal processes of different systems, and moving social objects according to the resulting net balance of forces. Equilibrium is an example not of the absence of forces but of a social 'conflict' between at least two force fields moving in opposite directions which have the net result of zero. This implies that stasis is not absence of conflict, but also that conflict of some type is always constituent of reality. Figure 2.4 illustrates this, using the notation of the classic social psychologist Kurt Lewin (1997).

In Figure 2.4 whether the forces to the right or the left of the diagram will be able to 'move' or change the social object will depend on their relative strength at a given time. By social object here I mean any aspect of social life – norms, rules, uses, practices, relations, institutions, values, systems, property regimes, contracts, resources, etc. – whose specification (characteristics,

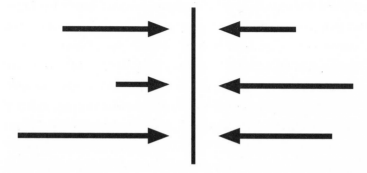

Figure 2.4 Force field

requirements, modalities), topology (disposition in physical, conceptual or discursive space), order (sequence, types of relations, degree of hierarchy) or constitution (boundary, selection, values) in time is the result of contrasting forces. By 'move' I refer to figurative locomotion in the social space, an abstract concept that is generally clear when applied to people who come together in social movements (here understood in a very broad sense including contrasting aims) pushing for social change of any social object.

But social forces are only one aspect of social systems. Social systems also include stock variables, not only flows. Power is a stock as well as power fields, while social forces and field of forces are different concepts and have different dimensions than social power and field of powers. Kurt Lewin (1997: 198) puts in this way with regard to psychological power: 'power does not have the same dimension as psychological force. That the power of A is greater than the power of B does not imply that A actually exerts pressure on B. The concept of power refers to a "possibility of inducing forces" of a certain magnitude on another person.'

This can be translated at the level of social systems. The concept of power refers to a possibility of inducing forces of a certain magnitude on another social system; this possibility is akin to a 'reservoir', a stock.

This possibility is not yet actualisation. Take the Marxian concept of labour power, the name for the capacities that the workers sell to capitalists for a given period in a day. Labour power cannot be compared to the concept of labour, with which conventional economists wrongly define both the activity and the commodity bought and sold in exchange for wages. And one important reason why for Marx the two notions are separated is that the capacity to work (labour power) is translated into actual labour activity of the workers, labour that applies a force (rhythms of work, quality, etc.) through expenditure of life energies as opposed to, that is vis-à-vis, the counter force that a foreman, a managerial system and, ultimately, the system of competing capitals impose on workers. The capitalist has purchased labour power, but the workers who expend their labour do so not always in proportion to their capacities or powers to labour, but, rather, also in proportion to *their* life rhythms, needs and desires – in terms of their ability to common in adverse circumstances, and therefore to build a counterforce to the capitalist pressure to intensify work. The end result in terms of rhythms of work, wages and all that is not a given, but a result of two opposing social forces playing cat and mouse.

One of the ways in which the US military establishes its military power is through a network of military bases, radar installations, army depots, etc. The human and equipment resources belonging to these are powers in the sense that they are part of the capacity to act in case of war of the US military.

However, within specific allied hosting territories the bases act as force: they occupy a particular territory delimiting its space, they contribute to economic life, or pollute a territory with harmful radiation, and so on. Within a country that is not allied, the military installation still acts as a force, but in this particular case a hostile force. In either case, power and force are linked, in the sense that the former is an accumulation of forces.

If power is the possibility to induce force, through what mechanisms are forces *actualised?* This is predicated on two other features, and these are goals and values and their derivatives. Goals have the conceptual dimension of a force field, that is:

> of a distribution of forces in space. [A g]oal ... is a force field of a special structure, namely, a force field where all forces point toward the same region. To conceive of a goal in this way gives it a definite place within the totality of possible patterns of force fields. (Lewin 1997: loc 4498)

Interestingly, the counterpart of goal is not resistance (as in the terms used by Lewin: 'difficulty' or 'barrier'), but aversion, the distribution of forces away from the region specified by a goal. To translate this into political economic language, emancipation from capital is not (only) resistance to it (making it difficult for capital or constructing barriers to its mad development based on dams and land grabs), but constructing systems that actualise an aversion for its goals, that have alternative goals.

Values are distinct from goals. While goals can be reached – even as suboptimal positions – people never reach or try to reach values, even if they say they do. Social movements that fight for social justice should rather say that social justice guides their actions. Companies that say they are moved by the value of sustainability as well as profit will never reach this as a goal, since the pursuit of profit for profit's sake is an 'aversion' to the goal of ecological sustainability, since companies value profit before ecologies. Thus 'values determine which types of activity have a positive and which have a negative valence for an individual [or system] in a given situation' (Lewin 1997: 197). This means that 'values are not force fields but they "induce" force fields'.

Thus, while goals define force fields in which forces point toward the same region, values induce forces to be applied or not in a particular region. This means, as for Deleuze, that 'concrete morals and political goals sought as an end are constituted by our seeking them. Thus the process of seeking freedom or justice is a process of eternal movement, change, becoming, possibility, and novelty which simultaneously demands eternal vigilance, and endurance' (Jun 2013: 104).

Individuals who operate within social systems as in Figure 2.1 are both constituent elements of force fields and subjects of a multiplicity of forces that bind and constrain some expression of their value selections (specifically emerged through the process of their socialisation) and give space to others, values that are often contradictory from one system to another. These contrasting forces as well as their history as marked in memory, in objects and in the built environment, in the first place constitute the individuals as subjects. Individuals are in turn coupled to different social systems. To be structurally coupled to a social system – as in the famous first part of the *Matrix* trilogy – is often to act as a reserve of energy that systems can use to put us in a position of producing a flow of labour activity. The matrix is capital. This of course occurs because each and every one of us is ultimately dependent on others for food, clothing, energy and culture, and the means to access these – money – is scarce only to the extent that it is concentrated in few hands. But it also means that – depending on our observational stance – filtered by our cultural and symbolic wealth, we can detach from capital-matrix and see the system for what it is for the great majority of us, a life-sucking machine powered by work for profit. Once we take the red pill, we can make a decision: either go back and take the blue pill and choose to run the rat race; or we fight. But unlike the *Matrix* movie, obviously, we do not simply 'fight', but also construct with others alternative systems and conversations, which also means contributing to shared goals that are averse to that of capital-matrix, and with our activity-flows induced by values that are utterly different from that of capital. Thus we build our dependence on others in different forms, in communal forms rather than competitive forms. Enter a second-order observation, the commons and us, a power – commonwealth – a force – daily reproduction in commons and social movement – a goal, the next objective in the expansion and governance of our commons, the next conversation, the next friend of a friend, the next friend, the next constitution of value, an inducement to action, conviviality, social justice, and a horizon: *omnia sunt communia.*

Chapter 3

Elements

Pillars

At a general organisational level, in order to have commons systems of whatever type we need to have at least three constituent elements, which I present here as the dry specification of a life-enhancing, socio-ecological, metabolic process in which cultures of sharing are (re)produced:

- pooled material/immaterial resources or commonwealth;
- a community of commoners, that is, subjects willing to share, pool, claim, commonwealth;
- commoning, or doing in common, that is a specific multi-faceted social labour (activity, praxis), through which commonwealth and the community of commoners are (re) produced together with the (re)production of stuff, social relations, affects, decisions, cultures.

Fundamental to all systems as the basis of their dynamics, the concepts of stocks and flows apply to this listing also. The first element here, the (material and immaterial) resources, is a stock category, that with which any commons begins its reproduction, while the third, commoning, is a flow category, allowing the transformation of the resources and social relations into new or renewed forms.

Before discussing each of these elements, I would like to highlight that it is the diversity in the material and immaterial aspect of these elements across different commons that specify their diverse phenomenology. These three elements are general in the sense that the specific form in which they are constituted and find expression is very much contingent on cultural, geographical and historical specificity. A commons in which a community shares some water sources at high altitude in the Andes, is different from a commons organised around the need to manage fisheries' access to sea water. A commons among communities cultivating 1,500 types of potatoes in an Andean region of north Peru is different from a commons developed to manage and sustain a public park created by a local community after squatting a car park in the centre of Athens. A commons created to care for children in a neighbourhood in London is different from a commons created to care for children in a neighbourhood in La Paz. A commons founded as a consumer co-op among waged workers in an Italian city is different from a commons founded as a producer co-op in a village in Kurdistan. The differences are not just 'technically' determined by the type of resources that are pooled together (land, water wells, sea water, toys or urban space and the tools and instrument of reproduction). They are also very much a function of cultural specificity, history, subjectivities and types of formal and informal rules of doing that the commoners – the subjects involved in commons – give themselves or that they implicitly or explicitly accept as stratified heritage of their past doing: skills, symbols, myths, knowledge, perspectives. They are also very different in terms of the relation of social forces they are inserted into, their relative 'distance' from the frontline of value struggles vis-à-vis capital.

The commoners in these different situations have found different ranges of opportunities in the correspondent arenas of institutional development, opportunities that they seized on the basis of the specific knowledge and social powers they have been able to mobilise. How we judge these differences politically and how we think these different forms can be part of a process of political recomposition are crucial theoretical and political questions but go beyond my preoccupations in this analytical chapter.

I will take these elements of the commons in reverse order, and discuss commoning first, as this is the basic driving energy of any commons system whatever its level of commonwealth.

Commoning briefly explained

This explanation is brief because this book has three other chapters on commoning. At the most intuitive level, commoning is *doing* in common (Holloway 2002). Commoning is the form of social doing (social labour) occurring within the domain of the commons, and thus is characterised by modes of production, distribution and governance of the commons that are participatory and non-hierarchical, motivated by the values of the commons (re)production, of the (re)production of commoners' commonwealth and of the affective, material, immaterial and cultural (re)production of the commoners and their relations. In relation to the commons environment, commoning produces effects that could range from new commoners joining in the commons and maintaining relations to them, to the spread of memes, cultures, techniques, goals and values of the commons in a territory or a social network. When commoning bridges two commons systems creating interrelations among them, I call it boundary commoning, discussed in Chapter 8.

Commoning has the power to articulate a diversity of values expressed by the different commoners – thus inducing a social force – to produce a common goal – a force field oriented in one direction (Lewin 1997); the way this direction occurs is through a process of doing, which includes common decision making, networking, application to task and projects, and coordination among them. In commoning, the two elements (diversity of values and common goals) are not aligned through top-down discipline as in centralised organisation and political systems associated with capital and the state. Rather, the series of stock–flow relations necessary to (re)produce anything are regulated in both goals and methods through reinforcing and balancing feedbacks produced by commoners during consensus proce-dures, swarming, assemblies, intermediation, conflict resolution procedures, or even walking out. The term *commoning* captures the labour and interaction that are necessary to reproduce the commons system. Commoning is an activity that develops relations preoccupied by their reproduction and therefore – to use ecological terms – the 'sustainability' of the commons and its 'resilience' vis-à-vis external shocks. In our formulation, commoning is the activity that has as main goals the (re)produc-tion both of whatever the associated commoners consider to be commonwealth, and the bodies, the affective and social rela-tions that comprise the community, that all together give rise to the commons. Thus commoning life practices are at once predicated on and give rise to the operational norms and rules that the community of commoners must establish to turn their commons into resilient systems. There are two main moments that commoning takes on. One is the plural activity of doing, understood simply generally as social labour taking the form of commoning. The other is the decision-making process, the definition of rules for the collective governance of the commons, another form of doing in the form of self-reflective collective orienting of the commons towards the next step, the next event, a plan, a collective problematisation of an issue faced by some commoners, or embedded in the nature of the commonwealth, or a particular event, shock, opportunity emerging in the commons environment. Commoning is therefore the plural social doing that can reproduce all the aspects of life in common, the participatory social force to mobilise for a change in the mode of production.

Community briefly explained

The idea of belonging has always been associated with that of community, whether that be a community of cognitive and symbolic structures underpinned by lived spaces and social processes, or a community that is 'imagined' (Anderson 2006). If one attempts to understand commons' communities against the large number of definitions and conceptualisations of 'community' (Wikipedia reports ninety-four discrete definitions of the term by the mid 1950s) the meaning of 'community' gets a bit complicated. In general

for sociologists community has traditionally designated a particular form of social organization based on small groups, such as neighbourhoods, the small town, or a spatially bounded locality. Anthropologists have applied it to culturally defined groups. In other usages, community refers to political community, where the emphasis is on citizenship, self-government, civil society and collective identity. Philosophical and historical studies have focused more on the idea of community as an ideology or utopia. (Delanty 2003: 198)

Often this utopian character of community is real, as when journalists and politicians refer to the London community, the neighbourhood urban community, and so on, while often the people living in these urban sprawls have only alien or indifferent relations to one another. How often have I heard that an old man or woman has died alone in a flat and months have passed before the corpse was discovered. How often have I seen indifference to poverty and destitution in the busy commuting crowds rushing along to the next urban train. In so many moments in our urbanised life, communities are absent and if we evoke them it is only in an imagined sense.

However, I am instead referring to the term *community* as applied to commons systems, and this identifies the plurality of commoners and their affective and social relations. These communities are not utopian, but their real characters emerge in the many moments of commoning.

At one level, the term *community* is straightforward, referring to the group of commoners involved in sustained social interaction through commoning to (re)produce their commons. The group could also be a community of struggle, that is, a plurality that constitutes itself in the moment it claims a resource for the many vis-à-vis a claim for the few. For this purpose, a 'community' is not necessarily predicated on a common location (the inclusion of peer-to-peer networks as commons demands this, for example, but also sustained global networks of solidarity), thus disposing of a substantial chunk of definitions. Nor is it necessarily predicated on a common cultural, political or ideological affinity, since the reproduction of bodies, affective and social relations (the main 'function' of commons) does not necessarily require people to like the same bands or share the same political ideologies. Finally, nor is community necessarily predicated on shared class strata – understood as income or group – since the reproduction of commons also occurs inter-class (in a sociological sense, that is, in terms of the coming together of social strata with differential income, wealth and social power). It goes without saying that this inter-class element of commons may be problematic – as can be any other differences within the commons, differences that by their nature may be the source of frictions and hegemonic stirrings of the commons to meet the interest of some group rather than others. But these risks are unavoidable if we want to conceive the commons as a plural space and an opportunity actually to turn the commons into complex institutions whose benefits are shared with some sense of social justice.

Commons thus are not the place for imaginary communities (Anderson 2006), for those who feel they belong to the same nation, race, or foodball club without even leaving their private living rooms. Commons are instead made of real communities, in the sense that their practices reproduce not only a networks of relations, but also a web of recognisable faces, names and characters and dispositions; the accidents of life also shape the web of affects, the mutual aid and the networks of reciprocity that constitute the web of solidarities and friendship. These communities come together for a variety of reasons. It may be because there is some type of affinity among the subjects, for example, they all share an interest, or the same job, or the same school. Or it is a networks of friends, and mutual affection is their glue.

Or what brings them together could be needs of reproduction of any kind – for domestic help, care or a community garden. Or perhaps they are of the same family or they live in proximity. In all these and many other cases, when communities are formed they start to share common resources, and not only their skills, world views and meals.

In the epistemology of the commons, communities are thus the collection of subjects and their interrelations as commoners, that is, as sharers, carers, developers, creators and recreators of those resources, participating together in their reproduction and governance. This presupposes a particular culture, a set of inter-related meanings and values that are shared, understandable, performable or evocative – in short, some common ground. This common ground is then the object of ongoing redefinition by the commoners themselves, who in the process of commoning also redevelop the character of their common ground as well as the orientation of their doing in common. The community in this sense, together with their cognitive apprehension of the commonwealth, is the repository of commons power – the possibility that a given collective has of inducing a social force (following Lewin 1997).

Commonwealth

Commonwealth is the set of all material and immaterial 'things' available in the commons. While material resources include anything material (from food, houses, warehouses and transport to tools, IT, DNA and energy) – however obtained (purchased or donated, loaned, pooled or occupied) – the immaterial resources are the skills, qualities, expertise, knowledge and dispositions of the subjects involved in the commons, the commoners – again, however they have obtained these through their life histories. This definition may seem similar to Bourdieu's (1986) definition of symbolic, social and cultural capital. I disagree: I would call them social, symbolic, cultural wealth, since the purpose of sharing these, unlike for capital, is not accumulation of a monetary value for its own sake.

The meaning of the term 'commonwealth' is at one level obvious: it refers to the 'things', the material and immaterial 'objects' that are pooled, shared, in different contexts and temporalities. I emphasise four distinctions that need to be made to help recognise the role of commonwealth in the constitution of commons.

Resource pools and resource units

In the first place, commonwealth is of two types. First, they may be *common resource systems* that is, ecosystems (water systems, forests, and so on, as well as their integration); second, they may exist as *pools of resource units*, as when a community pools together financial, technical, human, knowledge, symbolic, cultural or mythological resources in a 'common pot'. These two types really exhaust pretty much the spectrum of what is possible to pool together as commonwealth. When we have the first type of commonwealth, a common resource pool, it is often necessary to have elements of the second, pools of resource units, since commoning of a forest (sustainable logging practices) or on a water system (e.g. irrigation systems from a river) requires at least some human-made tools and skills. The converse is also true: a common pool of resource units (books, food items or the many codes elaborated in a peer-to-peer commons) requires some resource systems from which the units are drawn, even if these resource systems are not necessarily part of a commons.

These observations point at a strategic problem of the commons. The very fact that we can commonalise resource units that come from some resource systems outside of the commons requires that commoners look beyond the boundaries of their commons, if their preoccupations include ecological sustainability and social justice issues. So, for example, a pool of resource units of a cooperative of labourers involved in manufacturing and exposed to the pressure of competition, that is, cost minimisation, puts pressures onto them to externalise costs to the environment and wages as for any corporate sector. The strategic problem faced by postcapitalist commons is here how to extend the boundaries of their operations, through development, boundary commons and commons ecologies, to include the ecological and capitalist systems with which they interrelate.

Biophysical or immaterial?

A second way to understand commonwealths is from the perspective of their nature, which we can divide along the main general lines of biophysical and immaterial. The rationale for this division has already been discussed in Chapter 2, the main aspect of which concerns the fact that biophysical types of commons resources are rivalrous (if using the good by one person prevents its use by other people) while immaterial ones are not (a usage is non-rival if it does not prevent others from using the same good). We find ourselves with the same issue as before, but spelled out from a different angle. Material and immaterial are of course never distinguishable in so far as the separations of body/mind and reason/emotion are not. A material resource – whether commons or not – requires immaterial processes of social knowledge and, vice versa, the latter require several material resources. But the distinction is important to point out because postcapitalist commons aim at overcoming the separations between these two realms reproduced by the capitalist social division of labour, and the distinction in separate realms is a barrier that needs to be strategically and organisationally overcome in all contexts of social practice. This overcoming can find inspiration in traditional and indigenous practices that do not recognise such separations, or at least not to such a degree. Herders can share a field, and its bio-reproductive capacity limits the number of grazing animals that can be pulled together. However, the encounter of herders on the field may generate endless ideas in commons for how to set up different joint projects. In my conversations with members of water associations in Ecuador and Bolivia, I discovered that one of the repeated strengths of community systems of management of water had to do not with water (a physically restricted resource), but with the fact that the regular encounters for the purpose of governing water led to exchanges of ideas and the development of collective government in other areas of the community's life as well as of the cultural richness of circuits of affect and friendship of the community.

The realm of the 'immaterial' commonwealth also constitutes the given shared formal and informal rules that present themselves as stratified norms – in the same manner that resources are shared – within a community of commoners. Here again, to problematise the given relation between the 'material' and the 'immaterial' is crucial, as the current 'immaterial' set of norms qua resources can clash with the current material 'needs' or the sense horizons of a community or a section within it, possibly giving rise to new 'immaterial' norms reshaping the character of

continued on page 133

Box 5 The meaning of *minga*

On 3 April 2010, I meet Carlos Perez in the city of Cuenca, in southern Ecuador. He is a *dirigente* of the Junta de Agua of the area, the organisation for the community administration of water. Carlos is a lawyer, and I meet him in his small office on the first floor of a building in the centre of the city. On the walls, there are two small posters each containing an eclectic collection of maxims: one concerning the profession of solicitor (the one that struck me said: as a solicitor you have to defend rights, but if you see that rights conflict with justice, then fight for justice), and one listing some Buddhist maxims of good living (the one that hit me was: every year visit a place you have not seen before).

The Junta de Agua had been involved in a long struggle to defend community water rights. In 1996, a municipal law threatened traditional communal rights on water. The *municipio* of Cuenca sought to usurp the right of communities greater than 150 families to self-manage their water provision. Its argument was based on rationales such as these: people are incapable of administering water provision, they cannot make sufficient investment, they are ignorant, they are inefficient. In 2003 a national law was discussed that attempted to nationalise community water as a first step towards privatisation. The bills sparked a long season of struggles, large mobilisations, and civil disobedience that in the end succeeded in winning a U-turn from the government.

Instead of the law expropriating communities of their water commons (and water commoning), the Junta de Agua managed to draft and push through a law in which community autonomy is fully recognised.

As Carlos proudly shows me, article 2 of the 2003 ordinance of the canton of Cuenca acknowledges the right of community systems to participate in the planning, construction and administration of water systems, while article 3 states that by community systems is meant self-managed community systems as well as those in which the community co-participates with other institutions.

But the troubles are not finished. Today the struggles are not only for the defence of water and water self-management, but also against mines, as the two issues are increasingly linked. Carlos shows me a coloured map of the area around Cuenca, where large areas of mining concessions signed by the government are clearly indicated. The threat posed by mining to water commons and water commoning is increasingly urgent and controversial. This is not only because mines need a lot of water for their operations and also pollute water sources, but also because they are responsible for 20 per cent of climate change.

The struggle against new mining therefore is a struggle to defend not just local commons, but also global commons. Struggles against mining are on the rise in the region. In northern Ecuador, there has been a series of successful struggles against mining and in defence of community forests, among other commons, in the region of Intag. In northern Peru, in the regions of Ayabaca and Huancabamba, there are strong struggles against mines and in defence of water commons.

In relation to water, Carlos insists that what people want is administrative autonomy with no external interference, where it is community assemblies and not some manager or bureaucrat who decides what to do with the water and how. He also makes an economic case: 'In community management,' he says, 'each family pays $2 a month for water in order to collect the funds necessary for the maintenance of the supply. In cities like Cuenca one pays $10 a month. Why? Because of the highly paid bureaucracy. In the community, instead, the president of the water committee earns nothing. In Cuenca the managers get $3,000 a month.'

The payoffs for communities in keeping control over their water commons are not simply monetary. Water here is a commons not just in an ideal, principled sense. The water commons Carlos is talking about is a commons because it is a resource truly pooled by a community who must engage in commoning for its administration and utilisation. Hence, here, saying that water is a commons is saying that it is an organic expression of the life of the community. If you take away their right to administrate water, you take away some important aspects of the life of the community. This can be better understood by comparing this struggle with the struggle going on at the same time in Italy against the water privatisation promoted by the Berlusconi government. Here too the movement argues that water must remain a common good. But in this case, water commons are identified with the 'public', that is, with the right of the local councils – not directly of the communities – to administrate them. The difference is fundamental. [The Italian referendum against water privatisation was won in June 2011. Since then, little has been done to respect the popular will and return water services to the hands of local councils. The current centre-left government has made clear that it is not interested in ratifying the result of the 2011 referendum. – MD]When I naïvely ask Carlos to help me to understand what 'administering water' involves, he explains that water management does not only serve the functional objective of administrating water; instead, it is a crucial moment of commoning within the community. In administrating water, the individuals may well get a monetary payoff (say, the $2 they pay instead of $10), but the community also exercises power and autonomy, and this is a value on its own terms with consequent benefits.

It is a value that cannot be captured by the models of rational choice theory. For some of these theories, especially those influenced by Elinor Ostrom (see Chapter 4), commons are justified only in terms of their greater efficiency and payoffs, and there is little or no study of the value created by commoning. For example, *mingas* – a Quechua word used by various ethnic groups throughout the Andes to refer to unwaged community work– are traditionally used to take care of the maintenance of infrastructure. Children, women and men, young and old, all participate in the water *mingas* which, as Carlos reminds me, 'are also *mingas* of ideas, of desires and imagination'. Hence, not only are pipes laid, stones moved, not only is metal bent, food shared by the entire community, but also through the administration of water people meet and discuss other important things relevant to the community. 'There is no hierarchy in *mingas*,' says Carlos. 'Children, women and men all participate in *mingas*.' And the things that the managers of capitalist companies will not understand is that there is another sense of measure going on in *mingas*. The search for efficiency is not an absolute value. To dig a hole and put up a pole could be heavy work if only a few people have to do it so as to minimise costs and maximise productivity. But if the entire community is involved, you do not feel it (although the 'efficiency' obtained in this case is quite small). 'In the *minga* you do not feel the work because everything is cheerfulness (*alegria*) and distraction, and in the end it is participation. In the *minga*, as you are sharing (*compartir*), you are also living together (*convivir*).' The 'law of Ayni' – this phrase refers to a system of work and family reciprocity within the members of the extended family network (*ayllu*) – 'is reciprocity'. (See Chapter 7.) While he is saying this, he crosses his arms and shows me the Andes Cross, one in which one hand gives and the other receives.

commonwealth. But the division between material and immaterial begins to shake when we start to problematise the term 'resource' as a category that reproduces a Western-centric conception that neatly separates the object of work from the subjects. In indigenous cultures around the globe for example, in Africa, the Americas, Asia and Australia, animals, water and earth are regarded as expressing a type of subjectivity, as part of a living being to which one has to relate in a proportionate and equitable manner. We are talking here about cosmologies that

consider the reproduction of social systems as part of the reproduction of ecosystems, or, in the famous words of Chief Seattle:

> How can you buy or sell the sky, the warmth of the land? The idea
> is strange to us. If we do not own the freshness of the air and the
> sparkle of the water, how can you buy them?
>
> Every part of this earth is sacred to my people. Every shining
> pine needle, every sandy shore, every mist in the dark woods,
> every clearing and humming insect is holy in the memory and
> experience of my people. The sap which courses through the
> trees carries the memories of the red man.
>
> This we know; the earth does not belong to man; man belongs
> to the earth. This we know. All things are connected like the
> blood which unites our family. All things are connected. (Chief
> Seattle of the Suquamish people, 1848)

This cosmology is captured by the term 'Mother Earth', used
in many indigenous cultures. Mother Earth is not a 'resource'
because we humans are not separated from it, in the same way
that 'commonwealth' is not separated from commoners and
their commoning activity, but part of the same system. For our
purpose, it is important to point out that Mother Earth is an
expression also fundamentally different from expressions such
as 'earth' or 'environment' for at least three interrelated reasons.
First, it defines a common genealogy shared among all living
beings (as well as a common *telos*, in so far as our bodies will
all dissolve into earth's basic elements and will be re-articulated
into its processes when we die). Second, it defines a set of relations and processes (ecologies) that comprise humans and other
species, but also water, mountains, seas. In this sense, Chief

Seattle's dictum is well pointed to problematise 'earth' as resource: 'the earth does not belong to humans, humans belong to the earth'. Third, it defines a relational field and a set of processes at a scale that comprises and bounds pretty much everything, including the human processes that go under the name of capitalism. If this boundary is not accepted, if we do not socially enforce it, if we do not give it the character of a taboo, then this is it, 'mummy gets angry', and fights back. The planet will exist after us, as it existed for millions of years before, but there will be nobody to call it 'mother' or anything else. If we needed to find a limit to the capitalist mode of production, we don't need to look further than our own condition of existence and (re)production, namely what is called in the Andes Mother Earth! We have now simply to become its voice, as another slogan I have encountered in Cochabamba puts it.

Where does commonwealth come from?

This is the question of the *source* of commonwealth. Where does commonwealth come from? What are the mechanisms through which commoners can access it? My approach here is this: just think how commonwealth has been formed by a plurality of people through history and across cultures, and you have it. Probably, these can be exhausted in four main categories. At a given present time in some cultures things are turned into commonwealth because it has always been done that way, that is, it is custom to do so. Or commonwealth emerges because a plurality actively pools together resource units, say when a plurality puts money in a common pot in order to buy land, or equipment, or simply to have a common fund to ensure against the unforeseens of life. In other cases, there may be entitlements to common resources, that is, a plurality has rights to resources vis-à-vis the state. In this case things get a bit tricky. As I have argued, in terms of my framework, commonwealth is what it is because a plurality claims it, which implies that a plurality makes a commitment to its (re)production and development and that of the community of commoners. A plurality may be 'entitled' to resources when it has won the right to common from the state, as for example in the case of the 'lobster commons' in Maine, which is an ecosystem in which fishers have won the right to govern their lobster fishing following decades of struggle (Caffentzis 2012). In the case of an entitlement of a system of social security and education the plurality's 'claim' has often occurred in past struggles, and the plurality's commitment to the preservation of this rights of access and entitlement occurs in current struggles against enclosures, that is, cuts in social spending. Yet, even in this case, entitlements of these types are part of distorted or 'corrupted' commons systems to the extent that the 'investment' of attention, care and energy in the preservation and development of the commons is structured, managed and measured by a state bureaucracy. Often the latter does not only have in mind the preservation of the commonwealth per se, but must continuously mediate the demands of capital, for which social security and education must have the role of reproducing labour power as a commodity at the lowest possible cost, and of maintaining to the maximum the structure of carrot-and-stick-type mechanisms necessary to capitalist accumulation. Health and education therefore are cases of 'public goods', that is commons that are distorted in proportion to the degree of bureacratisation and managerialism of these systems (see Chapter 9). To reduce the degree of their distortion and turn them into proper commons one has to democratise their governance, that is push to the limit principle 3 of Ostrom's (1990: 90) sets of principles for commons sustainability: 'allow most resource appropriators to participate in the decision-making process' (see Chapter 4).

Finally, the last source for constituting commonwealth is their seizure by pluralities of have-nots. History is full of examples: pirates, heretic movements, factory workers, slaves, women, the wretched of the earth. The world today is not less full of examples: landless farmers in Brazil, homeless squatters in Europe, the democracyless in the USA and Egypt who seize squares in which to practise new forms of democracy, and all those who struggle to protect their existing commons, their territory, their lands, their rivers, their sea, their hospitals from capital's enclosures.

Commonwealth: what do we use it for?

What is commonwealth used for? Obviously, given the potentially endless types of things entering into the commonwealth definition, the answer would be, potentially everything: for playing music, for raising children, for making ships, for fishing, for making video games, for cooking, for caring for the elders, for growing potatoes, and for travelling to the moon. In Chapter 2 I argued that the list of common goods can be quite large: just add the adjective 'common' to any 'good' you see listed in a dictionary.

To gain direction in this open horizon, the question must be framed in slightly different ways, one that is fully aware of the contextual location of the commons into specific force and power fields. And the question then becomes: How can commonwealth be used to create a new commons system, one that increases the incidence of alternative modes of production, and increases the independence of commoners from capitalist systems? How can this commonwealth be used to address, even in a small fashion, the challenges of the times, that is environmental catastrophe, capitalist crisis, and social and economic injustice? And to put it even more bluntly given the nature of the social force – capital – that is at the basis of these challenges, the question becomes: How can commonwealth be used in order to increase the power of the commons vis-à-vis capital? When put in this way, the answer become clearer. Capital can reproduce itself only by putting to work the physical, mental, and affective energies of people for its own systemic purpose: accumulation. The catastrophic effects that its systemic operations have on people, communities and the environment is well known and does not need to be repeated here as I am writing in the midst of the most serious global economic, social and environmental crisis in the history of humanity. Capital can mobilise social labour and subject it to its measure, to its valuing of things, through different means: channelling desires through advertising, misinformation, open repression and use of force, or corrupt systems of political representation that value the advice of big money concentrated in a few hands far more than the needs of the people. But the one thing upon which the power of capital is ultimately based, the one thing that enables it to deploy all the other means of power, is its withdrawal of the means of existence, its ability to control, manage, distribute and shape the meaning of resources that are directly responsible for sustaining human and social life: water, land, food, energy, health, housing, care and education and their interrelated cultures in the first place. An increased ability to govern collectively these resources, to democratise their reproduction, to commonalise them by keeping state and market at bay, are conditions for emancipation for all in all other spheres of life and for make these spheres of life into a type of commonwealth that is enabled to feel a distance from capital. Although I do not advocate particular models of low-tech subsistence economies, I advocate for finding collective strategies on how to turn these basic resources into common-wealth inserted into corresponding commons systems. To have access to these resources would allow people and communities not only to grow more resilient, to share conviviality and enjoy life, but to build a common social force to expand their power vis-à-vis capital.

Acknowledging this use – that commonwealth is necessary for the production of every commons – requires that a political discourse is developed that connects the many already existing ones: on food sovereignty, on housing rights, on the purpose of education, on the right to care, and so on. Only in this way can the commons become a social force. This, is of course is already happening, although often as a constellation of scattered 'single-issue' interventions. For example, food is turned into a commons through relocalisation of food production and the embedding of food into local territories (making imports – and exports – only the exception for particular types of food items), through the struggle against seed privatisation, through the multiplication of seed banks preserving our heritage against enclosures and reducing dependence on large corporate chains, or through the setting up of biological production outside the state definition of 'organic' (see Chapter 8).

In summary, commons that make use of the commonwealth more directly linked to (re)production of bodies and the earth is a condition for the expansion of commoners' empowerment vis-à-vis capital, and a condition of the reduction of the degree of dependence on capitalist markets and capital's devastating effects on ecologies and the production of social injustice. It corresponds to the development of a sphere of autonomy from capital that can develop measures of things independently of the ups and down of impersonal markets, that allows movements to construct a powerful ground upon which all sorts of other struggles can be waged for all sorts of other commonwealth uses.

Part two

From Elinor Ostrom
to Karl Marx

Chapter 4

Commons governance

There is no doubt that Elinor Ostrom is a giant among the authors who have written about the commons. When in 2009 she received the Nobel Prize in economics for her study of the commons – the only woman to have been awarded this and barely two years after the major financial crisis in our times – I kind of hoped something different was happening among the high spheres of the ruling classes, that this was maybe a hint that something was beginning to move away from neoliberalism. I draw an analogy with Friedrich Hayek and Milton Friedman, awarded the Nobel Prize in economics respectively in 1974 and 1976, that is, five and three years before Margaret Thatcher moved to Downing Street with Hayek's book *The Road to Serfdom* at her bedside and in 1981 began, together with US president Ronald Reagan, the neoliberal counter-revolution we are still living today. Unfortunately, Ostrom's award did not herald a move away from neoliberalism, but it is nevertheless relevant that this public acknowledgment occurred: Elinor Ostrom's award was a blow of fresh air that all commoners should have celebrated. In this chapter, I discuss some of her work, with the sense that she was a giant in the same way that Adam Smith or David Ricardo were for classical political economy in the nineteenth century. These authors made many discoveries which were subsequently used, corrected and refined by radical political economists of the calibre of the Ricardian Utopians or even Karl Marx. I read Ostrom in the same vein, drawing the consequences of her conclusions, and correct her assumptions when I think she leaves out important aspects that need to be considered in relation to a postcapitalist transformation.

Commons and open access

I open my discussion of Ostrom's work with her now classic critique of Garrett Hardin's 'tragedy of the commons' thesis. In his seminal article, Garrett Hardin (1968) assumed a group of herders sharing a common grassland, to which each of the herders had open and free access. He argued that since each herder wanted to maximise the fodder for his/her cattle, or the number of animals feeding, this would inevitably lead to a problem of resource depletion. He argued that in order to avoid this, commons rights should be replaced by individual property rights or direct state management.

Ostrom (1990) had no difficulty in pointing out that the case made by Hardin was not a case of commons, but of open access. If the grazing land was a commons, she argued, communities would have set up rules of access and governance to maintain the sustainability of the land resource. For Ostrom, commons are 'where the members of a clearly demarked group have a legal right to exclude nonmembers of that group from using a resource. Open access regimes (*res nullius*) – including the classic cases of the open seas and the atmosphere – have long been considered in legal doctrine as involving no limits on who is authorized to use a resource' (Ostrom 2000: 335–6).

By analytically distinguishing between open access and commons, Ostrom was able to argue that Hardin's parable assumed open access, while commons always imply some form of communal governance of the shared resource with corresponding systems of monitoring and enforcement of the communal rules so as to avoid resource depletion. With this distinction, Ostrom begins her journey of conceptualisation of commons as social systems.

However, Ostrom's analytical distinction between commons and open access does not completely wash when measured against the dynamics of current social movements transformative of social reality. Let us look at this more closely.

There is a distinction between common-pool resources, such as a fishery, a forest or a river, and 'immaterial' goods, such as knowledge of a physical law or an open source code or living in a just and peaceful society. These latter resources share the characteristic that it is difficult to exclude people enjoying them and who live within their scope. But they also differ from a common-pool resource, say a forestry: this is reduced when resource units of value – such as particular trees – are withdrawn from it, while a public good such as knowledge of differential calculus is not diminished when still another person uses it to calculate a share value trend, or construct a new engine, or plot the tendency of the rate of profit to fall. Notwithstanding questions of articulating material with immaterial commons (discussed in Chapter 1), the open access movement is one that with differing nuances is founded on the refusal of enclosures of non-rivalrous goods such as information and knowledge. In academia and in cyberspace, it is a social movement dedicated to the principles of information sharing, open source, copyleft and anti-privatised knowledge commons. In this case, the mutual exclusion between open access and commons does not apply, since there are no issues of sustainability of immaterial resources *within* this realm (putting aside for a moment what we say about the interrelations between the structural dependency between the immaterial and the material in Chapter 1). To put it in economic terms, the marginal cost of an extra download on top of the 32 million pirated in one week of season 5 of *Game of Thrones* is pretty much close to zero (although there is an absolute cost in terms of expenditure of energy and emissions in downloading 32,000,001 times). As in the classification proposed by Yochai Benkler (discussed in Chapter 1), open access of information and knowledge is for many a form of commons.

Also, in cases in which the resource base of the commons is a material or biophysical entity, the analytical distinction between commons and open access may not indicate an analytical and categorical *mutual exclusion*, rather a type of possible, although non-inevitable, *interrelation*: a commons is a system, and free access can be one of its subsystems. The free access has open boundaries, everybody can come in and out, use those resources, maybe a tool library, a lab, a music room, but in order for this free access to (re)produce, to be what it is through time, it has to be part of a commons, and has to be taken care of and governed by a specific bunch of commoners, the maximum number of which could be all the users of the free access space. So, commons and free access are not always opposed, as Ostrom indicated in her enlightening critique of Hardin. There are many cases in which free access spaces are a subset of a commons system. Take a village party in the Appenines near Modena.[1] Every summer a long table is set up along the main village road spanning about 50 or 60 metres, and about twenty people are involved in cooking and serving food and drinks for up to two hundred guests. Clearly, if we all help to dispose of the tables and clean up afterwards, the work per head will be less. But then, another village could organise another party, and the cooks would become dinner guests. Free lunches may not exist in capitalist economies (a fact we are reminded of by Milton Friedman), but they often do in the commons, if we accept responsibility for them, and understand that the gains in conviviality, community cohesiveness and boundaries opening to the outside, to other commoners, are worthy goals!

An abundant quantity of food is shared on such occasions, but then is distributed as a free access. If the organisers of the party find that the donations required to cover the expenses are sufficiently generous to sustain free-access village parties, then the party may be repeated or improved on. Otherwise, alternative resources must be drawn from other activities or fundraising events, or the food available at such parties must be scaled down. Alternatively, the commoners may decide to commodify the space, by selling food instead of putting it in a common pot, something that would clearly change the nature of the event.

If we scale up and zoom out by a large amount, we can recognise a certain commons rationality for free access also in relation to much of the redistributive function of the state, especially in relation to social services that can and ought to be free access and paid out of general taxation. It goes without saying that in the neoliberal period such proto-commons are disappearing, as subsequent cuts in the welfare state have undermined free access for vast sections of the population.

Commons and free access can also be two opposing social forces, two ways to conceive, act and stake claims on the same space, or resource. This opposition may also be the manifestation of a clash of meanings and values between opposing social forces such as capital and the commons around the *meaning* and *form* of governance of commons. For example, as I have argued in Chapter 1, it has become a truism to define the atmospheric space as a common good, since all life depends on it. However, within this shared space, both carbon trading and ecological debt present themselves as two clashing narratives and strategies defining how to share what must be shared. The former is based on the idea that the atmosphere managers (the system of states) decree a cap on greenhouse gases, and then allow markets to redistribute the cost of adaptation through carbon credits. This option does not actually work. Since 2005, the year when carbon trading was adopted following the Kyoto agreements, global carbon emissions have continued to increase, from around 375 parts per million to almost 400 parts per million in 2015. In practice, the atmosphere is a free access resource in the Hardin sense, with effects pointing at major depletion of many life forms and ecosystems on earth. The second strategy is that the system of states not only enforces a cap on greenhouse gases but makes those (the 'Global North') who are most responsible for the occupation of the commons 'atmospheric space' to pay a compensatory debt to the others (the 'Global South') who are suffering most the effects of climate change brought about by carbon accumulation in the atmosphere. Within this narrative, there are also many, like I do, who argue that a drastic change in the way we produce and reproduce life in common is necessary, that is, that we must move to a postcapitalist mode of production.

I must make a final observation regarding the distinction between open access and commons. Just as it is not possible to dismiss open access as utopia from the point of view of sustainability and resilience (once we link it to commons systems), we cannot not identify 'open access' as somehow politically progressive as compared to other forms of commons. A struggle for more 'open access' can be a struggle for democratisation of education and correspondent redistribution of resources at a larger social level, or for access to agricultural land by local communities, land now closed off behind wire fences by agribusiness monocultures, or for access to buildings closed up in order to wait for a speculative opportunity, opened up by commoners who reclaim them and make them available to all. In these cases, 'open access' refers to a claim for the extension and redrawing of the boundaries defining the community of commoners vis-à-vis the state and capital. But the commoners can find themselves on the other side of the analytical split between commons and free access, and fight against free access. For example, the struggle over the definition of the atmosphere – as a sink for greenhouse gases – is an example of this. It is an 'open access' for those big capitalist social forces that regard the setting of enforceable global limits on emissions, or the radical overcoming of the capitalist mode of production as a taboo, while it is *and must be* a commons for those social forces which consider the establishment of these limits a social and environmental necessity. Here Benkler's (2003) classification in Table 1.1 is again useful.

Common-pool resources and resource units
Ostrom also talks about systems in a double sense. One constitutes the governance praxis linking a property regime and a common-pool resource (CPR). The other defines the latter as an 'ecology'. Indeed, the 'resources' themselves within the definition of common-pool resources (CPRs) are understood in

terms of systems such as 'fishing grounds, groundwater basis, grazing areas, irrigation canals, bridges, parking garages, mainframe computers, and streams, lakes, oceans, and other bodies of water'. To be clear, note that Ostrom focuses on the resources as systems, not the resources, and on people forming a social system, as in what I am putting forward.

Ostrom makes an important distinction between the *resource system* and the flow of *resource units* that the system produces. This is the same distinction I made in Chapter 3, when I argued that these were the two different types of commonwealth. While resource systems are stock variables, resource units are flow variables, that is, what individuals appropriate from the resource system. Resource systems have the capability of producing a maximum resource unit flow, without harming the stock and therefore allowing its *sustainability*. Resource units are 'typified by the tons of fish harvested from a fishing ground, the acre-feet or cubic meters of water withdrawn from a groundwater basin or an irrigation canal, the tons of fodder consumed by animals from a grazing area, the number of bridge crossings used by year by a bridge, the parking spaces filled, the central processing units consumed by those sharing a computer system, and the quantity of biological waste absorbed per year by a stream or other waterway' (Ostrom 1990: 30). As 'access to a CPR can be limited to a single individual or firm or to multiple individuals or teams of individuals who use the resource system at the same time' (ibid.), the notion of resource systems can be applied at different scales.

So for example, a resource unit could be the unit of measurement of the amount of greenhouse gases emitted in a year by a country, while the atmosphere, acting as greenhouse sink, is the commons resource. Obviously, the amount (stock) of greenhouse gases emitted into the atmospheric commons will be decisive in establishing the atmospheric commons' capacity to regenerate in such a way as to maintain adequate equilibrium for life processes to continue. Too much greenhouse gas emissions implies depletion of the atmospheric common good in this sense. It is precisely this notion of atmospheric common good that allows countries in the Global South to claim payment of an 'ecological debt' on the grounds that countries in the Global North are occupying 80 per cent of the atmospheric space with their greenhouse gas emissions with only 20 per cent of the world's population.

This characterisation of the commons as CPR thus makes an important distinction: it is the resource system that is a common good, not the individual resource unit, since the latter is 'not subject to joint use or appropriation'.

> The fish harvested by one boat are not there for someone else. The water spread on one farmer's fields cannot be spread onto someone else's fields. Thus, the resource units are not jointly used, but the resource system is subject to joint use. Once multiple appropriators rely on a given resource system, improvements to the system are simultaneously available to all appropriators. It is costly (and in some cases infeasible) to exclude one appropriator of a resource system from improvements made to the resource system itself. All appropriators benefit from maintenance performed on an irrigation canal, a bridge, or a computer system whether they contribute or not. (Ostrom 1990: 31)

It is important to reflect on this distinction. In Chapter 3 I defined commonwealth to include both resource systems à la Ostrom, and the pool of resource units. I did this in spite of the fact that even in the most communal forms of distributing the products of a commons enterprise – say when the food is commonalised in a common pot and everybody is free to access what they want – the resource unit is not subject to joint use or appropriation. The food I eat, whether I bought it ready-made from a corporate supermarket or I pick it from a common pot in a communal kitchen or from a table at a village party, is always *individually* appropriated and processed by an individual digestive system. The key distinction between resource system and resource unit makes sense because it underpins the passage of a 'thing' – a resource unit – from one operationally closed system (an ecological system) to another operationally closed system (say, a digestive system, at the level of an individual appropriator – or a production system, at the level of a collective appropriator). In both cases it can do so however *only* through the *mediation* of a social system (whether, say, a commons or a capitalist market) that works out the *mode* of appropriation of resource units by the individual or the collective participants. This is another way to reiterate the classic insight that a social metabolism, in the form of social systems or of particular types or *modes* of production, is what allows social individuals to withdraw resources from their natural environment to fulfil their needs, desires and aspirations.

Yet, both in history and contemporary life, there are myriad examples in which communities communalise resource units into a 'common pot' and then establish rules or customs for its appropriation. If we look at the history of common property regimes it become obvious that 'many have been based on non-common-pool resources ... On the basis of the history of common property regimes,' Caffentzis (2004: 22) concludes, 'it is difficult to decide what types of goods are "conducive" to private property and what kinds of goods are "conducive" to common property'.

The same is true in contemporary life. In the fall of 2015, I and my friends of the association in the Appenines sowed a rare old strain of wheat, in an attempt to revive its production. This strain of wheat has less gluten and is more nutritious. We pooled the few handfuls of seeds we had in order to have a common crop that we would be able to sow again the following year and have a proper common crop to run to flower. Or I visit a social centre in Modena, and I enter a library (resource system) containing books (resource units) brought by the different participants in the library project. Tool libraries are based on the same principle. Shared food items brought together by different participants and commonalised on a picnic blanket, or the resources used together in a household, a neighbourhood association, or a social centre are all intuitive cases of pooling of resource units.

Another example is P2P production systems in cyberspace, in which individual software developers, with their own computer hardware and their own labour time, contribute to the development of a program, or build the platform through which P2P file sharing occurs so as to commonalise the files for all. Pooling money to buy needed stuff – whether pooling among friends or even fundraising – is a form of aggregating resource units and turning the aggregation into a common pool. For example, members of a community of Mexican migrants collect money in upstate New York and fund social projects in their hometown of Boqueron, Mexico. Projects include ambulances, sports facilities, a well. In this way, the community reduces their dependence on corrupt governments, strengthens their cohesion and creates the conditions for a dignified return for those who so desire (Rivera 2003). In the United States there are about one thousand groups like this one, all pooling resource units to give rise to a new resource system in their home towns. Every 'resource unit', or 'private good', could in principle be commonalised, if it is sensible to do so. Even children are commonalised when they live in a 'community' with 'many eyes', as in the aboriginal collective community, favouring child autonomy and security while at the same time minimising reproduction work (Lohoar, Butears and Kennedy 2014).

In my approach I want thus to generalise the resource base of commons and include in our understanding of commons resources different types of genealogical principles of pooling; we can understand common resources as either a resource system or a pool of resource units previously appropriated by individuals and now commonalised. These two cases of resource systems and pool of resource units seem to cover all the types of commonwealth needed to commons. The resource system, apart from coinciding with an ecological system (a water system, a forest, etc.) can also include an infrastructure such as a water distribution system, or a road system, and from this analytical point of view only, whether these are actually constructed by commoners or whether they are first appropriated in commons by them and then managed together, there is no difference. The pool of resource units covers all examples in which individuals commonalise some of their resources, fundraise or initiate crowdfunding and put all resources into a common pot, and then, by means of old cultural practices, new ideas or negotiated and consensus settlements, establish methods and rules of access or consumption (including methods based on a particular understanding of equity or a particular understanding of community sharing).

Common-pool resources and property regimes

While the distinction between commons and open access originates from Ostrom's critique of Hardin, the distinction between CPR (common-pool resources) and property regimes is all-internal to Ostrom's approach. As I have discussed, common-pool resource 'refers to a natural or man made resource system that is sufficiently large as to make it costly (but not impossible) to exclude potential beneficiaries from obtaining benefits from its use.' (Ostrom 1990: 30) These are for example 'fishing grounds, groundwater basis, grazing areas, irrigation canals, bridges, parking garages, mainframe computers, and streams, lakes, oceans, and other bodies of water' (ibid.).

Any of these resource systems (CPRs) can be coupled to a variety of different property regimes (Hess and Meinzen-Dick 2006: 2), that is, the structure of the enforceable rights defining actions that individuals can take in relation to other individuals regarding some 'thing' (Ostrom 2000: 339).

Thus, 'common-pool resources may be owned by national, regional, or local governments; by communal groups; by private individuals or corporations; or used as open access resources by whomever can gain access' (Ostrom 2000: 338), as there are examples of 'both successful and unsuccessful efforts to govern and manage common-pool resources by governments, communal groups, cooperatives, voluntary associations, and private individuals or firms' (ibid.).

Hence, much of the work of Ostrom and her associates has been to study what attributes of common-pool resources 'are

conducive to the use of communal proprietorship or ownership'
and what attributes of common-pool resources 'are conducive
to individual rights to withdrawal, management, exclusion and
alienation' (Ostrom 2000: 332). In both cases, the requirement
of a CPR is that the plurality drawing resource units from them
employs some method that makes this CPR sustainable, that is,
that allows them to reproduce themselves, so as not to overdraw
resources, otherwise Hardin's 'tragedy of the commons' kicks
in. Much of Ostrom's work is dedicated to demonstrating that
commons property regimes are often more suited to manage
sustainably CPRs. Ostrom therefore is not taking a political
stance, but an economist's stance that, without problematising
the historical relation between commons and capital, conceives
the cohabitation of these different forms as unproblematic, *pace*
enclosures, exploitation and social injustice.

Design principles, rules and commons regimes

Ostrom is truly a champion of the commons, or commons
regimes, when she highlights the design principles that a
commons regime should have in order not to fail. The many
instances of commons systems that Ostrom analyses in her
work, and the many others that we could add and that are outside
the preoccupation of her investigation, apply a large range of
rules for their operation. Indeed, part of her analytical effort
is to account for the fact that 'the specific rules' in each case of
commons systems 'differ markedly from one another' (Ostrom
1990: 89), and therefore 'cannot be the basis for an explanation
across settings.'[2] The explanation offered by Ostrom regarding
the sustainability of commons in time, however, is partially
based on the fact that situated specific rules differ across cases.

'The differences in the particular rules take into account specific attributes of the related physical systems, cultural views of the world, and economic and political relationships that exist in the setting. Without different rules, appropriators could not take advantage of the positive features of local CPR or avoid potential pitfalls that might be encountered in one setting but not others' (Ostrom 1990: 89).

Ostrom's main task is indeed that of *distilling* the design principles of commons sustainability out of the study of hundreds of empirical cases of survived commons. A design principle is an 'essential element or condition that helps to account for the success of these institutions in sustaining the CPRs and gaining the compliance of generation after generation of appropriators to the rules in use' (Ostrom 1990: 90). Ostrom does not claim this is an exhaustive list, but she is willing to speculate that further scholarly work would at least take her proposed principles as core.

These are the basic commonsense governance principles that a plurality (a community of commoners) must follow in their design of commons regimes in order to avoid commons meltdown. How communities are going to do this, is not in Ostrom's radar, but the principles are there, an extremely useful tool for commons building and diagnosis.

These eight design principles are as follows:

1. boundaries are clearly defined (effective exclusion of external unentitled parties);
2. rules regarding the appropriation and provision of common resources are adapted to local conditions;
3. collective-choice arrangements allow most resource appropriators to participate in the decision-making process;

4. effective monitoring is carried out by monitors who are part of or accountable to the appropriators;
5. there is a scale of graduated sanctions for resource appropriators who violate community rules;
6. mechanisms of conflict resolution are cheap and easy to access;
7. the self-determination of the community is recognised by higher-level authorities;
8. in the case of larger common-pool resources, organisation takes the form of multiple layers of nested enterprises, with small local CPRs at the base level. (Ostrom 1990: 90)

In boxes 6 and 7, some of these principles come alive in the case of the water association in Flores Rancho, a village near Cochabamba, Bolivia, and a community park in central Athens. Box 8 (see page 248) is a case of spontaneous development of principles 4 and 5 within the water anti-privatisation movement in South Africa.

All these governance principles are the minimum required for a commons to sustain itself, *if external forces are not deployed to influence, destroy, enclose or co-opt the commons*. Clearly the number of formal or informal rules could vary, and cannot be reduced to a particular model fitting the normative claim of a particular political ideology, whether this is anarchism, communism, socialism, or, more recently, 'peer-to-peer-ism'. A political ideological frame of reference, to the extent that it is not intoxicated with its own image, may however have a value, *together with others*, in contributing to an overall arching framework for commoners to set or re-specify rules that account for excluded or marginalised voices *within* the commons. The voices of communists are useful to

continued on page 162

Box 6 Flores Rancho, 19 April 2010

Flores Rancho is about fifty minutes' drive southeast of Cochabamba. It is a rural community where 120 families (about 480 people) live and manage their common water system. This community was at the forefront of the water war of 1999–2000, when in a few months of street battles, the protestors forced the then Bolivian government to make a U-turn and repeal the new water privatisation laws (see Chapter 9). In this way they also began the political process that led to Evo Morales becoming the first indigenous president of a South American country.

I meet people from the Flores Rancho community during a visit organised by a network of organisations preparing for the third Feira del Agua (see Box 4), a few days of demonstrations, seminars and workshops (as well as an exhibition) set up to enable discussion about the many problems still afflicting water systems in Bolivia ten years after the victorious water war, and to share information and commoning practices. We meet with men and women in the middle of a half-built house, which is to be the Escuela de l'Agua.

While we sit around the open walls, workers are busy on what will be the roof doing their shift of community work. The building is partially funded by Yaku, an Italian NGO, and its purpose, according to different people, seems to be a mixture of community centre, clothes washing centre, education centre, dorms, place to host public meetings, and node in the future tourist infrastructural network of the area. But the general point of having this building seems the need to have some structural reference point in an international network that aims at valorising the 'Andean vision on water'. The building is being constructed using a mixture of traditional (mud bricks) and modern materials (cement and bricks), as evidence of a compromise within the community between those who prefer tradition and those who would like to leave traditions in the past. It is built on common land, purchased by the community, next to the other piece of common land on which the community has its water well. (For a short video see www.youtube.com/watch?v=HeLyMLISODY.)

Don Abdon is an articulate and proud man, and he has reasons to be proud. His name is written next to the well that he wanted the community to dig to find water. Before the community well, each family had its own small well, which was sufficient for human consumption, very few animals, but no irrigation. Don Abdon returned from Argentina with a degree in agronomy and in 1982 convinced the community to pool their few savings, purchase some land and pay for the drilling of an 84-metres deep well. It cost 18,000 bolivianos (£1,800), but they found abundant water. Three years later, in 1985, at a cost of 45,000 bolivianos (£4,500) they built a 20-metres high tank to store drinking water. They spent a further 18,000 bolivianos to bring in electricity (cabling, erecting an electricity pole, etc.). With the help of a Spanish NGO they paid for the pipes and the *bombas* ('bombs' – the nickname for the water storage cisterns mounted on platforms 30 metres above the ground). When the community water well was installed and started working, because of its depth all the private family wells ran dry. But the community's choice offered a good payoff. All families now have access to more water than before, allowing them to increase the number of animals they keep as well as the quantity and variety of their crops, thus improving both their income and the quality of food available to families and the community.

Except for the very specialised work such as drilling, all the construction and maintenance work has been and is carried out by the community itself through what here is called *umaraqa* (what in other regions of the Andes is called *minga* or *minka*, that is, non-waged community work). The water tank is cleaned regularly, water is piped into the houses, and problems are fixed by a group of ten people drawn from the community. Actually, there are ten such groups, and each year one group takes over responsibility for the administration and maintenance of the system: in other words, everyone works a shift of one year every ten years (see the example of a cooking rota in Chapter 6).

Don Abdon stresses that those like him who have expertise – and different forms of expertise are always available in a networked community such as this – help those who work a shift but lack knowledge. The work of each team is all unpaid, which helps to keep the price of water very low. Each community member pays 1 boliviano (£0.10) for each cubic metre of water, that is, eight times less than the price paid by consumers of municipal water in Cochabamba. The community meets on the 5th of every month to discuss all matters to do with the water system. However, as it is generally the case with these community meetings, water becomes only an occasion to discuss and organise around all types of issues. Participation is taken seriously. If a family representative does not show up at a meeting without an acceptable justification, they have to pay a fine: one day's work for the community. Conflict, I was told, is generally dealt with within the community, and very rarely is resolved outside it by appeals to the police or the state courts. I also discover that indeed there is a system of penalties for what are regarded as offences against the community (see Ostrom's commons design principle number 5). With respect to water, for example, one receives a 3 days' water cut if found 'wasting' water, that is, using water in measures and forms that run counter to those decided by the community itself. Other penalties are issued if one is found selling the community water to people outside the community (which, given the relative scarcity of water in the Cochabamba region, especially in the south, I suspect is quite tempting to do). Many of the communities in the area have had experiences similar to Flores Rancho, building their own community water systems. So it is easy to understand why, in 2000, people in such communities got really upset at the government (see the section on the water wars in Chapter 9). For years they had pooled resources, managed their water, organised their work together to get water and distribute it, and then comes a law that allows a multinational company to put its own meters next to the infrastructures that the community had built and maintained – in order to charge its members for the water. The threatened water enclosures were truly robbery of a form of property – of community property. I also learn that from the perspective of a grassroots association like this, the need for external funding by NGOs and the like and for some degree of access to markets – whether for specialised services such as drilling or for access to income for families – is obvious (I have not heard of any funding by the Bolivian state in this case). But it is also clear that the practices of community work and commoning reduce dependency on markets and represents a substantial loosening of the knot tying the community to the necessity of money for its own reproduction. The question becomes not only what communities like these will do with the freedom they have gained, but also in what form they will be able to increase the scale of their commonwealth.

remind the commons of some of the risks embedded in its environment (capital and the state) and some useful principles of sharing. The voices of anarchists remind us about grassroots forms of direct democracy. The voices of environmentalists remind us of our relation to the environment and ecologies. The voices of women and black people remind us of deep divisions in society and therefore the risk if we reproduce them in the commons. The voices of indigenous peoples remind us that struggle and the commons are never separated, since capital expropriations and violence are always a possibility. The voices of spiritual people of various faiths humble us in front of the mystery of it all, the Earth, the cosmos, you and I, and encourage us to find ways out of our internal conflict, ways to discover our common ground in the midst of complexity and diversity. The list could continue with any *ism*: add your own preferences, ideology, experiences, knowledges and flags, to enrich the commons with sensible rules and cultures and measure them against the framework of Ostrom's principles for commons sustainability. For example, would this rule be a specifics of principle 5 or 2? In which cultural specific ways are we defining boundaries or establishing sanctions? Do we actually need sanctions? Why not? And how? Is our commons' autonomy sufficiently recognised by the state? Are we sufficiently defending it in the given circumstances?

The key thing in concrete situations is to understand the type of social relations that give shape to a commons system, both in terms of their operations *inside* the commons, and in relation to other systems outside it. How are decisions with respect to the commons' resource system taken, how are the commons boundaries decided, how are norms reproduced and institutionalised, who are the excluded and why, and how are these rules contested and challenged, and, I may add, how is 'the ever present temptation to free-ride that exists in regard to both CPRs and public goods' (Ostrom 1990: 33) dealt with? Or, indeed, does it always exist to a degree that is damaging to the commons? These are some of the questions that may continuously emerge in commons regimes. In Box 7 I give an account of the difficulty of dealing with subjects that break pretty much all of Ostrom's rules and yet use a common space as a place of free access: Greek youths in an occupied park self-managed by others.

Exogenous or endogenous forces?

Ostrom's work and that of the people working in her tradition[3] recognises that '[o]rganizing appropriators for collective action

continued on page 167

Box 7 Their parking, our park

[In 2010 I made the first of a series of visits to Greece in an attempt to document the crisis and the patterns of resistance and constitution of alternatives. The following case is one that impressed me for the clear recognition of different forces at play in the theatre of an occupied square turned by residents into a park. Here is my account, written in April 2010.]

On 7 December 2008, a fifteen-year-old boy called Alexis Grigoropoulos was killed by a bullet fired by the police during a demonstration on the streets of Exarchia, a lively central district in Athens. The murder sparked a highly impressive wave of public outrage with subsequent mass demonstrations taking to the streets, the burning of Christmas trees, attacks by schoolchildren on police stations, and local neighbours turning parking lots into parks.

About a hundred metres away from where Alexis Grigoropoulos was killed, on Navarinu Street, a parking lot cut a grey and empty space amid the urban environment. It belonged to the powerful professional organisation of engineers, the Technical Chamber, which was just starting to enquire to the council about the possibility of building another building on this spot, after the council, for years, failed to act on the possibility of turning the area into a public park.

On 7 March the local community decided to take things into their own hands, that is, to do some commoning. It started as a symbolic act of space reclaiming of the urban guerrilla type – in which people plant trees and vegetables in places where you would expect tarmac and then go home after having made a point. And indeed this time too they went home, but the next day they returned, and the next day and the next day. In the first few weeks, about a thousand people got involved, with about five hundred people a day frenetically tearing tarmac out, planting trees, building low walls with the stones taken from beneath the tarmac, creating a children's playground with swings and wood structures, and setting up benches. Teams of designers made up of young architects, artists, engineers, folk musicians, hippies and housewives marked with white chalk where the tarmac had to be removed; team of removers, made up of the designers themselves plus others who joined the collective effort in the days ahead, removed the tarmac, though not always according to 'design' specifications. 'The end result is a hybrid combination of design and work,' I was told by a young woman, a commons organiser who I found at the site. My impression was that when intellectual conception and manual operationalisation are not rigidly separated, the moment of designing also occurs at the moment of manual labour, which is not only the doing but also the great pleasure of removing the tarmac and finding a hearth beneath.

Many people took many initiatives: some painted the walls with 'tribal' drawings, someone else decided that the park could also turn into an open-air cinema and hence set up a screen on the wall, theatre performances were organised, music was played, a kiosk with leaflets on migrant rights and other political literature was set up under a large plastic raincover. 'People were just turning up with initiatives and ideas.'

Debates on 'how to' and 'what to' run wild in the general assembly held twice a week, which decides matters of aesthetics, material to be used, and politics. The assembly is open to everyone, and indeed this may be tricky since new people come all the time, not aware of older debates and decisions, which always risks causing some frustration in the regulars. Often debates run wild: 'We should not use capitalist technology,' said one strict-principled school of thought. 'They only wanted to use bare hands.' a young engineer told me, 'but when it was time to work, they never showed up.' When I arrived one late morning on 3 June, a bulldozer was there moving soil around to make a small hill. The service was hired, together with many other tools. Capital's commodities can, therefore, come from capital's circuit, leave momentarily its monetary loop after payment of an exchange value, enter the realm of the commons for its use values to help create things that remain in the not-for-sale commons (another example one could add to Table 9.1).One problem concerned the regulars there. Every evening during the hot summer, about a hundred and fifty people hung around the park drinking beer, smoking cigarettes and playing music until 7 a.m. the following morning. This was particularly an issue on Friday nights and at weekends. The issue was that the park was, in the words of our commons organiser, 'bombed' with cigarette butts and beer cans. Not only that, but when an old woman resident in the neighbourhood came down one morning with black-circled eyes complaining that she had been unable to sleep for the past week because of the noise, the issue started to become serious. At the time of writing this, I do not know how and if this issue will be solved. But it is interesting to describe the field of forces in which this issue took place. This is revealed in the very moment at which a young woman much dedicated to the park project approached the young people at 2 a.m., asking them to please not toss beer cans on the ground but instead in the bins, and to extinguish cigarette butts in the ashtrays. She recounted that the typical reply was of the 'Do not boss me around' type: 'Who are you, the police?' a youth said to her. Also a polite notice urging people to behave responsibly was torn down because it was thought to be authoritarian. 'The problem is that many of the six hundred people using the park regularly do not participate in the assembly, said another young commons organiser. He continued, 'But it is true that of these six hundred only eighty don't give a fuck. They see it as a hierarchy, a matter of us and them. We asked them to come to the assembly and participate in the decisions, but none of them came. They see it as a question of freedom. 'But it is not a hierarchy,' added the young woman. 'We are not the bosses, we only want to care for the place.'

In spring 2015 I went back to the park and asked whether they did solve the issue of the hanging-about youths and their beer cans and cigarette butts. 'They are gone now,' I was told with a smile by a young man busy fixing a toy, 'replaced by other youth.'

regarding a CPR is usually an uncertain and complex undertaking' (ibid.), often the result of a series of trial and errors. But they also tend to argue that the sources of these uncertainties are not themselves the types of social relations, but are dependent either on the properties of the resource systems, or on lack of knowledge. I briefly review this position, in order later to point out one of the basic shortcoming of this approach.

For Ostrom, the sources of these uncertainties are external or internal to the commons. Among the external sources: 'the quantity and timing of rainfall, the temperature and amount of sunlight, the presence or absence of disease-bearing vectors, and the market prices of various inputs and final products' (Ostrom 1990: 33). Among the internal sources of uncertainty, a major one is

> lack of knowledge. The exact structure of the resource system itself, its boundary and internal characteristics, must be established. Ascertaining the structure of the resource system may come about as a by-product of extended use and careful observation, as in the case of appropriating from a fishing ground or grazing range. Moreover, this folk knowledge must be preserved and passed along from one generation to the next. For a groundwater basin, on the other hand, the discovery of the internal structure may require a major investment in research by geologists and engineers. (ibid.).

There is a clear difference between the way Ostrom and her associates on one side and Marxist and radical traditions on the other tend to view a failure of sustainability and reproduction of commons. While the former see it mainly in light of a failure of the design principles and of the corresponding endogenous forces set in motion, the latter have emphasised power differentials – and violence as one expression taken by this differential – as a key variable in explaining the evolution of the commons and their survival vis-à-vis capital's enclosures (De Angelis 2007a: 133–49). As Caffentzis pointed out, while Ostrom and her associates 'look to endogenous variables ... to determine why one property regime changes into another',[4] Marxists and radicals emphasise that there are no logical reasons why a social centre, a village commune or an indigenous community that has been managing a common-pool resource, sometimes for generations, 'suddenly breaks down even though the logic of the coordination problem had been more or less solved'. While the former 'look to changes in the characteristics of the resource (e.g. whether its value on the Market or the cost of excluding non-commoners has increased) or in the characteristics of the commoners (e.g. the number of commoners has increased) for an explanation of the breakdown', the

> anti-capitalist supporters of the commons ... look to the larger class context to determine the dynamics of 'the drama of the commons.' For it is only by determining the class relations and forces within a particular region and stage in capitalist development that will ultimately determine the existence or annihilation of a common-property regime ... For the particular regime that manages a common-pool resource will be determined, e.g. by the labor needs of the dominant capitalist class in the region and by the commoners' solidarity and political-military power to resist the inevitable force that the desirous capitalists deploy. (Caffentzis 2004: 24)

Thus, there are clear methodological and political differences between the two supporters of commons. Ostrom and her tradition

> see the problem of the commons as an issue of management requiring good institutional designs 'to help human groups avoid tragedies of the commons.' They see the property regimes regulating common-pool resources as offering different combinations of outcomes that can be measured by efficiency, sustainability and equity criteria. The solution to the problems posed by the potential for a 'tragedy of the commons' can be achieved by greater research on common-property regimes throughout the world and greater theoretical comprehension of the variables involved. It programatically rejects doctrinaire neoliberalism that assumes the superiority of private-property regimes throughout the society including the management of common-pool resources. (Caffentzis 2004: 25)

On the other hand

> the anti-capitalist supporters of the commons see the struggle for a commons as an important part of a larger rejection of neoliberal globalising capitalism since it is the commons in the indigenous areas, in the global sense, and in the area of collective intellectual production that is now threatened with enclosure by a capitalism bent on commodifying the planet, its elements, its past and future. Their key issues are how to bring together various aspects of the struggle against commodification and create 'another world' satisfying the needs of global justice. (Ibid.)

The methodological and political differences pinpointed by Caffentzis suggests that we have a tension, between an interpretation of commons as *endogenous* social systems, and commons as systems influenced by *external* social forces, capitalist social forces. In the first case, whether a commons fails or succeeds to reproduce itself depends on its management principles. In the second case, it depends on the power relations vis-à-vis the enclosing (which simply destroys commons) or co-opting (which sucks surplus value by using commons as a way to keep social wages down) force of capital.

However, once we understand commons as social systems, this tension between these two camps is a tension that necessitates productive articulation rather than categorical differentiation. The survival and expansion of commons in larger and larger spheres of lives necessitates the participation of commoners many of whom belong to a working class that has been fragmented and individualised through decades and centuries of capital inscribing itself into social loops. For example, the problem of government of the commons is a problem of envisioning the possibility that commons are and will be viable and desirable, and this implies at least some cracks in old consumeristic habits and aspirations. It is also a problem of organisational and communicational skills among commoners. It is also a problem of breaking habits of delegation and learning participatory methods, as it is a question of resources needed to liberate time from capitalist work and the dependence on capitalist markets and their channelling into practices that trigger, sustain and help the development of commons social forms. In this context, the practical and theoretical difficulty of a political project based on the expansion of commons is to regard commons as social systems whose endogenous dynamics and challenges vis-à-vis exogenous social forces such as capital are *both* necessary for their development and reproduction.

Here suffice to say that the case made by Ostrom is a rough way to pinpoint the fact that *commoners in the reproduction of their livelihood exercise power*, and *how* it is exercised and what it take for a force field to develop out of it are crucial issues to be considered for the survival of any commons system.

On the other hand, the case emphasised by Caffentzis is another way to pinpoint the fact that however this internal power is exercised, it faces a power field and force field differential, social forces that have differing sensibilities and plans, and that will try to enclose or co-opt this commons power for its own ends. Commons live in hazardous environments dominated by capital and the state, a power that either encloses or co-opts and aims at containing the development of a new social force based on commons. The possibility of recomposition among commons of different types, and, even before that, of micro types, requires that emphasis is put on the *endogenous forces* commons are able to trigger, renovate and set in motion for their expansion. But even then, this always occurs starting in a context in which 'sense' has been colonised by the sense of capital, and its rationalisations. *Homo oeconomicus* is everywhere, and is part of us, especially when we *begin* a journey of recomposition. Hence, capital is also inside the commons, part of the horizons that constitute the sense that will frame its operations. The beginning of history is only the beginning of a process. Maybe, only maybe, Ostrom's principles can be an effective guide for beginning a new journey, and imagining a different horizon (P.M. 2014). Look around you, in your towns devoured by garbage and consumption, by Ferraris and waste, by schools falling apart, by crumbling hospitals and superclinics for the rich; in the countryside wasted by pesticides and monocultures and indifference to the earth. The many variegated commons and social movements that have been developed in recent decades are like saying, let our collective reasons and hearth be our guide, and the design principles a yardstick we modify locally with some confidence as they root the commons in thousands of others, and let *omnia sunt communia* be our horizon of peace, freedom and plenty and begin to roll back the end of history.

Chapter 5

The money nexus and the commons formula

Two circuits

In this chapter I explore the roots of the relation between commons and capital systems, in what ways the economy or the markets actually presupposes the commons. Since the 1990s, a literature on the enclosures of the conmons by capital has established that enclosures of commons – that is, often violent expropriations of resources held in common and the establishment of state institutions and a legal framework to protect such expropriations – were a continuous characteristic of capital development and not a one-of-a-time process at the beginning of capitalist development as argued in traditional Marxist literature (De Angelis 2004, Harvey 2003, Midnight Notes Collective 1992). Capitalist development needs to commodify things and people into labour power to be sold for a wage, it needs to acquire things and needs to turn things into capital. In particular, it needs to create a dependency on the commodity form of social relations so that people become unable to escape the capitalist imposition of work (Cleaver 1979). But if capital finds commons to enclose at different moments of its development, commons themselves need to reproduce and develop. At any moment of capital development, therefore, there are commons and, if capital regards these as a barrier to overcome, then it will set out strategies for their enclosure or co-optation. Whether capital succeeds in doing this or not will depend on the relative power each of the opposing social forces are able to deploy. That means that at any given time, capital and the commons exist at a given level of development and relative power relations.

There is, however, a recurrent line of communication and exchange between these two systems, capital and the commons, and that is what is generally understood as 'the economy'. The economy, as we know it today, is centred on money, on money as means of exchange, means of payment and measure of value. Strangely enough, money is also the gateway for two opposite systems, grounded in different modalities, value practices and goals of system production and reproduction. In De Angelis (2007a: 40–1) I used the category *conatus of self-preservation* to refer to a combination of capital's system aspiration, its instinct to accumulation, with its sense of urgency and strategic problematic in overcoming the barriers it encounters. In Volume 1 of *Capital* Marx referred to this as production for production's sake, or accumulation for accumulation's sake: 'Accumulate, accumulate! This is Moses and the Prophets!' (Marx 1976). The original use of the term *conatus* comes from Spinoza, and has recently been picked up by the neuroscientist Antonio Damasio. According to Damasio, Spinoza's notion 'interpreted with the advantages of current hindsight ... implies that the living organism is constructed so as to maintain the coherence of its structures and functions against numerous life-threatening odds' (Damasio 2003: 36). While in my *Beginning of History* I translate the organic setting into a discussion of the forms through which capital as a system maintains coherence against the numerous 'life-threatening' odds provided by that class struggle through commons, in this book I wish to do the opposite, that is, to discuss how the commons systems can maintain their coherence against the numerous 'life-threatening' odds mostly provided by the daily struggle, inertia and foot-dragging against capital. Thus again, to exit one system and enter into the other we need to knock (or knock down) at the door of money.

I do this by using Marx's analytical device in particular, by combining Marx's two formulas for the circulation of commodities. In Chapter 4 of *Capital*, Marx counterposes what he calls the formula for the simplest form of circulation of commodities to the general formula of capital. The former is C-M-C, while the latter is M-C-M', where C stands for commodities and M stand for money and M' stands for more money than originally invested, including profit. This distinction actually is an ancient one, and was noted for the first time by Aristotle, whom Marx acknowledges. Both formulas represent a process in time. The hyphen '-' symbolises transformation, a change of hands (exchange) between two subjects, C-M (selling) commodities into money and M-C (buying) money into commodities. Thus both formulas represents a temporal sequence in a given place or places. These formulas are also called *circuits*, since each element, whether commodities C or money M, are transformed into the other, M or C. Thus, by introducing circuits I am simply suggesting a general system such as a stock-flow framework (Meadows 2008) to begin to analyse specific commons, to locate leverage points, strengths and weaknesses of particular commons in relation to what element of the circuit is critical, to compare it with money circuits, to analyse the degree to which money is relevant in relation to self-reproduced resources, and to adopt a strategic outlook to further the commons vis-à-vis its environment without loss of its organisational unity.

The two formulas have the same elements and are also made of the same actions. The elements they have in common are commodities C and money M. The actions that they both embed are buying and selling. We have here all the basic ingredients to constitute the contemporary neoliberal imagery of a capitalist economy: buying and selling, the market.

In each of the phases of these circuits, 'the same material elements – a commodity, and money, and the same economic *dramatis personae*, a buyer and a seller – confront one another' (Marx 1976: 249). Finally, 'Each circular path is the unity of the same two antithetical phases, and in each case this unity is mediated through the emergence of three participants in a contract, of whom one only sells, another only buys, while the third both buys and sells' (Marx 1976: 249).[1]

These two circuits are different in at least three aspects.

First, what distinguishes the circuit C-M-C from the circuit M-C-M' is the inverted order of succession of the two phases. While the simple circulation C-M-C begins with a sale and ends with a purchase, the circulation of money as capital M-C-M' begins with a purchase and ends with a sale. In C-M-C both the starting point and the goal are commodities, in the other they are money. In the first form money is taken out of market circulation in the act of selling a commodity, in order to be thrown back again to purchase a commodity. In the second, money is advanced in order to get it back. Thus, the first difference between the simple circulation of commodities and that of capital is the goal of the circuit. The first has at its goals the satisfaction of needs, and money here is a mere *means* for the satisfaction of these needs. The second has as its goal the realisation of money: the means becomes here the end.

Second, while in the simple circulation of commodities the two extremes of the circuit are both commodities, and commodities of equal value, 'they are also use-values differing in their qualities' as, for example, potatoes and computers. However

It is otherwise in the cycle M-C-M. At first sight this appears to lack any content, because it is tautological. Both extremes have the same economic form. They are both money, and therefore are not qualitatively different use-values, for money is precisely the converted form of commodities, in which their particular use-values have been extinguished ... One sum of money is distinguishable from another only by its amount. The process M-C-M does not therefore owe its content to any qualitative difference between its extremes, for they are both money, but solely to their quantitative difference. More money is finally withdrawn from circulation than was thrown into it at the beginning. (Marx 1976: 250–1)

This increment in money Marx calls surplus value: 'The value originally advanced, therefore, not only remains intact while in circulation, but adds to itself a surplus-value or expands itself. It is this movement that converts it into capital.' It is this realisation that makes Marx discuss the origin of surplus values in production with its correspondent laws of capitalist development. In the simple form of commodity circulation, instead, no surplus value can appear. M-C-M' and C-M-C appear thus as two chemical formulas, with the same elements but with a different composition and structure and, especially, different goals. It is the realisation of these different goals in certain degrees that allows or not the reproduction of the corresponding system, which can only happen through the reiteration of the transformations.

Third, we have thus the key difference. In the simple formula, the 'repetition or renewal of the act of selling in order to buy, find its measure and its goal (as does the process itself) in a final purpose which is outside it, namely consumption, the satisfaction of definite needs. But in buying in order to sell, on the contrary, the end and the beginning are the same, money or exchange-value; and this very fact makes the movement an endless one' (Marx 1976: 252).

Here we have the difference already made by Aristotle between *economy* and *chrematistic*, the first being the art of house governance within a balanced system of needs, and the second being the dehumanising activity of accumulation of money through the market, aka getting richer.

In the *Politics*, Aristotle argues that chrematistic is only licit if the sale of goods is made directly between the producer and the buyer at the right price; it does not generate a value-added product. In other words, petty trade, systemically linked to the household, is licit. By contrast, it is illicit if the producer purchases for resale to consumers at a higher price, generating added value. Money thus must be only a medium of exchange and measure of value. Aristotle is drawing on a fundamental distinction between two institutions and their goals, or, as I discussed in Chapter 2, the force field where all forces point toward the same region. In Aristotle the polis points towards the pursuit of well-being for the good life, and it acquires the wealth of the household for this purpose. It is the 'good life' that is the goal and limit of the polis's acquisition of wealth from the household economy. In chrematistic's pursuit of money for money's sake, the goal, the force field where all forces point toward one direction, is not external to wealth, but wealth itself. In this conception, instead of the good life we have mere living, becoming instrumental to the pursuit of wealth.

Chrematistic can be illustrated by the endless spiral in Figure 5.1. At every round of greater accumulation of money, more resources have been extracted from earth, more workers have been exploited to create surplus value, more 'externalities' have been dumped into the biosphere and rivers and in landfill, more people have been impoverished by enclosures, more divisions have been created among workers around the globe. This is of course true only with a caveat, and that is that in real processes, people struggle all the time, and are not simply at the mercy of capitalist processes.

I used the word 'people' as in common language. But 'people' is a term that not only reduces the differences to a unity – even if

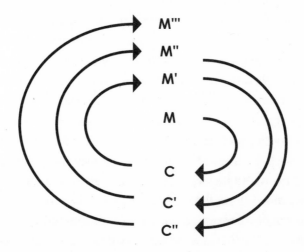

Figure 5.1 Capital's boundless expansion conatus

populations have all kinds of differences (Hardt and Negri 2004: xiv) – but also is oblivious to their internal relations among one another and to their relations to their environment. The same is true of the term 'the masses', the essence of which is 'indifference: all differences are submerged and drowned in the masses. All the colours of the population fade to grey. These masses are able to move in unison only because they form an indistinct, uniform conglomerate' (ibid.). Hardt and Negri contrast this to the notion of *multitude*, 'composed of innumerable internal differences that can never be reduced to a unity or a single identity – different cultures, races, ethnicities, genders, and sexual orientations; different forms of labour; different ways of living; different views of the world; and different desires. The multitude is a multiplicity of all these singular desires' (ibid.). Hence the multitude is many-coloured, rather than grey.

Yet two things are left out of this notion of the multitude. One is that in relation to capital, the multitude is a fuzzy concept: it includes subjectivities that are inside or outside capital, although for Hardt and Negri who do not hold a systemic understanding of society, there is no outside to capital and its empire. Also, because their concept of multitude is 'composed potentially by all the diverse figures of social production' (ibid.) their relative powers vis-à-vis one another should be taken into consideration, something which is part of their 'diversity' constituting the multiplicity. The risk therefore is that the project of democracy of the multitude, when left unqualified in terms of relative power, is not necessarily consistent with social justice, or massive redistribution of wealth, or ecological transformation of social production. There is also another key difference, that of *multitude* and the *working class*, which Hardt and Negri posit with reference only to a use of 'working class' referring only to the industrial working class, that is, subjectivities that are homogenised within the factory work discipline. I believe these terms of comparison are spurious, since for a large body of literature, from Italian Marxist feminists to US autonomism, the working class has always been divided into strata with different powers, the most important division being that between the waged and the unwaged. I will come back to this notion of the multitude and the working class in the following paragraphs, when introducing the dramatis personae, the different actors, inside the different circuits.

Actors' positions: capitalists and commoners

Marx tells us the name for the 'conscious representative' of the M-C-M' movement when he calls this possessor of money the 'capitalist'.

> His person, or rather his pocket, is the point from which the money starts and to which it returns. The objective content of the circulation we have been discussing – the valorisation of values – is his subjective purpose, and it is only in so far as the appropriation of ever more wealth in the abstract is the sole driving force behind his operations that he functions as a capitalist, i.e. as capital personified and endowed with consciousness and will. Use-values must therefore never be treated as the immediate aim of the capitalist; nor must the profit on any single transaction. His aim is rather the unceasing movement of profit-making. This boundless drive for enrichment, this passionate chase after value, is common to the capitalist and the miser; but while the miser is merely a capitalist gone mad, the capitalist is a rational miser. The

ceaseless augmentation of value, which the miser seeks to attain
by saving his money from circulation, is achieved by the more
acute capitalist by means of throwing his money again and again
into circulation. (Marx 1976: 254–5)

Marx does not give a name for those engaged in C-M-C
circuits, but several Marxist traditions have referred to them
as 'petty traders'. But just as capitalists are capitalists 'only in so
far as the appropriation of ever more and more wealth in the
abstract becomes the sole motive of [their] operations', petty
traders are petty traders only in so far as they bring commodities to the market to satisfy their needs. Hence, while capitalists
are capitalists by virtue of their goals measured in relation to
the need of reproduction of the capital circuit, petty traders
are petty traders by virtue of the means they employ to reproduce their system/circuit of needs and desires. In terms of
their goals they are not petty traders, but belong to a larger and
socially segmented category of actors that we may loosely call
commoners. Clearly, here I am not attributing to them a name
necessarily corresponding to their self-proclaimed identity.
In my local market I can probe endlessly with questionnaires
or spend months in ethnographic studies, and most likely the
word *commoner* would never appear. People tend to define
themselves by their trade, by their work, by their status, by their
roles in families, by their nationalities, by their gender groups,
by their religions, by their ethnic group, by their political affil-
iations, by their militancy, by their class, and by their being
human. The self-definition of 'commoner' – once pretty much
in use in England in the Middle Ages – is an intersection among
all these, and one that requires today a reflexivity on the playful

energies, convivial manners, and toil invested in interactions among the diverse social actors and different – if not opposing – social conditions, such as the capitalist.

At this level of generalisation, both capitalists and commoners are intelligible with respect to the circuit they are bringing forth and at the level of market exchange. But for all practical matters, the identification of actual actors is far more complex. Operationally speaking, for example, the function of the capitalists is taken over by managers, and the latter by a management system that increasingly includes different strata of waged and unwaged workers to perform the monitoring necessary to implement the efficiency required for the maximisation of profit.

On the other hand, the definition of 'commoners' is far from being exhausted by that of petty traders, although petty traders are commoners. This will become clearer in the section below where I discuss the commons formula. Here it suffices to note that *commoner* is a more general term than *worker* or 'proletarian'. The term *worker* is generally understood in relation to a *wage*, an identification that, although highly disputed because not capturing the massive unwaged labour necessary to reproduce and sustain capital (Cleaver 1979), has nevertheless consolidated into usage. In this sense, the term *commoner* also captures the waged worker qua seller of labour power, as well as unwaged workers, such as woman mostly, working to reproduce labour power. That is, workers also are petty traders, the commodity they sell in order to satisfy their needs being their labour power. That is also the case if this labour power is qualified and the more the cost of reproducing professional elements of this labour power is regarded as an investment to facilitate employment (i.e. the sale of the commodity labour power).

The term *proletarian* is more general than the term *worker*, and is usually associated with not only the milieu of social subjects who work for a wage, but also those left out of production, the unemployed, and their unwaged families. The term, however, is difficult to reconcile with the modern segmentation of the working class which includes subjects with different typologies of access to means of production held in commons. Its Latin roots defines proletarian as a member of the lowest class of Roman citizens, who contributes to the state only through having children. In the radical tradition, it specifies a social subject in a particular relation to capital, that of the exploited or contestant. Just as the term *proletariat* include that of waged worker, without exhausting it, the term *commoner* includes that of proletarian, without exhausting it. Commoners are defined in relation to capital, whether through the wage or not, or through petty trade or destitution, but they are also defined in terms of their constituent powers. Commoners are social subjects that, as I argue below, are engaged in the reproduction of commons and for which the relation to capital is often necessary, but does not exhaust their social being and activity. It is precisely this characteristic that makes the category of commons interesting for a discourse on social change and on commoners, the name I give to the actors operating within the commons. Hence, whenever we are looking at the relation between these commoner subjects and capital, the term 'working class' or 'proletariat' can suffice. However, whenever we aim also at including the self-activity of this class in so far as the many-faceted (re)production of livelihoods outside capital is concerned, the term *commoners* is a better specification because it captures both an underpinning relation to capital and a quest for the production of alternatives.

The money circuit of capital

Marx expanded the capital circuits formula to reveal the social activity that goes on outside the sphere of commodity circulation and inside the realm of capitalist production. The same can be done with respect to the simple formula, although this is not something that Marx has done.

In the circuit in Figure 5.2. as usual I indicate money capital with M, while the sum value of commodity capital – that is quantum of money and commodities understood as moments of the self-expansion of capital – with C. In processes of capitalist production, this commodity C takes two forms in turn. The first, LP, indicates labour power – a given articulation of human powers, of powers to, whether material or immaterial, and whatever the level of skills, ability and complexity of work required – sold on the labour market by wage workers. The second, MP, stands for means of production, that is, all the other 'fragments of nature' used in the process of production, whether as raw materials or the result of a more elaborate process of transformation by means of social production: tools, machines, computers, buildings, and so on. Means of production and labour power come together in the process of production ...P... which, from the perspective of the human subjects involved, is nothing else but a sensuous process of life practices, in which labour power is turned into abstract labour, a social force appropriated by capital and its measure, an expenditure of human energy consumed (brain, muscles and nerves) in order to produce a new commodity and a profit for the capitalist, while the emotional states and life experience of workers are subordinated to the value practices of capital. Clearly, workers can resist, drag their feets or struggle openly. This is when their value practices clash with that of capital. This conflict is embedded in every moment and transition in Figure 5.2 (Bell and Cleaver 2002).

The production process ends with new commodities C' being produced which their owner will take to the market in the hope of selling them and pocketing money M' and profit ΔM as before.

This circuit of capital illustrated in Figure 5.2 should not be taken as an illustration of what occurs at a given time, but simply as the sequence of conditions which are necessary for capital – as a particular form of human production – to reproduce itself at a greater scale. In order to do this, each moment must turn into another. Capital reproduces itself only if the previous phase is accomplished. Failing this, there is a crisis (Bell and Cleaver 2002). Thus, the valorisation process – the actual phase of production (...P...) in which life energies are expended in the form of living labour through what we will see are conflicting value practices – presupposes that capital is able to find workers who are willing and in a position to sell their labour power and supply a given set of skills. The phase of realisation, C'-M', presupposes that actual living labour has been extracted out of the workers and objectified in the form of monetary value. The phase of purchase, M-C, presupposes that money is concentrated as accumulated wealth, whether through credit from the banking system or company financial resources, that it is available and that it is thrown into the process as investment. Each of the phases in this general formula is located in one particular

$$M - C\{LP; MP\} \ldots\ldots P \ldots\ldots C' - M'$$

Figure 5.2 Expanded capital circuit

moment in time and represents a qualitative transformation, and therefore it is opened to the possibility of a rupture, of a crisis or of a bottleneck.

The overall circuit of capital thus represented in its sequential process tells us what must happen if capital is to be reproduced on a larger and larger scale, if growth must proceed. However, as Bell and Cleaver (2002) have pointed out, because each moment of the circuit of capital is a moment of struggle, this may affect each of these moments and/or circulate to the subsequent moments, thus making it difficult for capital to sustain accumulation. Struggles for wages affect profitability, so the struggles for working time and rhythms in ...P... Investment M-C depend on profit expectations, which in turn depend on a combination of past profits, on the 'cost-effectiveness' of the expected ability to extract work from workers during the moment ...P... relative to other workers elsewhere, on making them accept new restructuring and job cuts, on the ability to make the extraction of raw materials cost-effective, on the ability to increase social productivity by the building of infrastructures that might be contested by environmental groups or local communities, and so on. In turn, the moment of realisation C-M' depends on the ability to sell, which depends on purchasing power, but also on the struggles among competitive capitals. The latter struggles in turn are a reflection of the differential ability of individual capitals to turn their employed or precarious workers into objects of production (objects of restructuring which increases productivity, or objects of wage cuts), their differential ability to exert command over their living labour. The formula in Figure 5.2 thus implies that capitalist accumulation, in order to occur, requires strategic intervention to overcome the inherent crisis of each of its moments. The emergent patterns of the sum total of these strategic interventions and purposeful actions predicated on corresponding value practices is what Marx calls 'laws' of capitalist development, and as such they have nothing deterministic. Indeed, precisely because these laws include counter-tendencies, they are the result of strategies; each moment in the capital's circuit, at any given moment in time, is a situation in which different social subjects in different positionalities give rise to different and often clashing social forces running in different directions, thus affecting the overall pattern of the circuits.

The coupling of circuits

The money circuit of capital is linked to the simple circuit by a myriad different connections. In general, and in principle, every purchase or sale of the circuit of capital can be done with agents of a simple circuit. Marx was of course preoccupied with one particular actor of the simple circuit, the seller of a particular commodity, what he called labour power. But Marx stopped at the analysis of the role of the owner of labour power as seller of this commodity, and as labourer within the money circuit of capital. He did not study the process of production of this commodity, even in its general characteristics. In Marx's formulation therefore, the money circuit of capital abstracts from what is a central, yet invisible, component of capitalist production, namely the work of reproduction of labour power, which is mostly unwaged. Building on the insight of radical feminists in the wages for housework campaign (such as Dalla Costa and James 1975; Cox and Federici 1976), we can represent the work of reproduction as a subcircuit of the money circuit of capital. In this way, it is possible to visualise the relation between the work

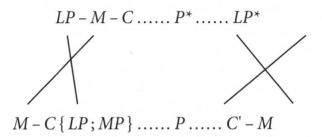

$$LP - M - C \ldots \ldots P^* \ldots \ldots LP^*$$

$$M - C\{LP\,;MP\} \ldots \ldots P \ldots \ldots C' - M$$

Figure 5.3 Coupling between production and reproduction circuits

of reproduction and the capital valorisation process and the strategic importance that struggles over reproduction have in relation to the overall circuit. This relation is depicted in Figure 5.3 where a circuit of reproduction is written above the money circuit of capital.

In the circuit of reproduction, the money (M) obtained in exchange for labour power (LP) is used to buy commodities (C). Commodities however need to be processed in the household through an expenditure of labour P*. This expenditure of reproduction labour allows the physical and psychological reproduction of labour power (LP* = regenerated labour power), which can then be sold again to capitalists. The circuit of reproduction does not tell us who is performing this work of reproduction, although to the extent that patriarchal relations are dominant, women do the great bulk of this work. In any case, the interlinked circuits of capital described only give us a broad framework in which to conceptualise the link between reproduction labour and capital's accumulation. The top circuit could in principle be used to illustrate other forms of unwaged labour, such as student work. Here, the flow of money from the bottom to the top circuit can take the form of transfers (student grants) or be simply erased with the abolition of student grants, while the process of reproduction P* represents the process of producing what economists call 'human capital'.[2]

The circuit in Figure 5.3 could be seen as outdated since the reproduction of labour power occurs at numerous sites: schools, hospitals, day care centres, unemployment offices, training centres, prisons, and so on. I thus understand the circuit in Figure 5.3 in its generality and not necessarily as located in the household, although the latter constitutes a large chunk of reproduction labour. If it were to be assigned a monetary value – as calculated by the Office of the United Nations High Commissioner for Human Rights – it would account for between 10 and 39 per cent of GDP (UNHR 2013). What is important here is to highlight the interconnection between the money circuit of capital and the circuit of labour power reproduction. For example, a fall in the work of reproduction in P* in the upper circuit means for example a deterioration of the labour power in production, and thus a negative effect on P. All the same, capital may try to find ways to increase reproduction work P* by shifting on to unwaged labour the cost of, say, cuts in health expenditure so as to reduce the social wage it pays, while the household internalises more care work. While this modification of Marx's analysis allows us to put at the centre what mainstream economics makes invisible (work of labour power reproduction), this modification also throws light on the other bulk of human activity made invisible by mainstream economics (and mainstream Marxism): unwaged labour. In the neoliberal era the disciplinary mechanisms that regulate social cooperation through the markets also increasingly pervade the realm of unwaged labour, especially through the disciplinary role of international finance capital movements and Third World debt management, which together enforce global austerity on public spending. Cuts in public spending on elderly care or childcare for example, imply, all things being equal, that for the household there is an increase either of direct unwaged work of care within the household, or the labourer must do more work to acquire the salary to pay for care work.

The circuit in Figure 5.3 highlights the fact that both waged work and unwaged work are moments of capital's sequence of transformation and therefore they become complementary targets of capitals strategies, realms for capital's value practices and value struggles. It also suggests that capital's working day is 24/7 long before the emergence of post-Fordism and 'communication work'.

Thus, capital's strategies on the side of reproduction such as the shape of educational system or the level of population growth, or the shape and size of expenditures on public services – strategies that pass through the discipline and control of real bodies, or, to put it in Foucault's term, that define the realm of biopolitics – are complementary to strategies on the side of production to define which sectors to promote or how to regulate the social wage. On the other hand, cuts in the social wage and in transfers to families accompanied by an increase in transfers and subsidies to companies have the double effect of restructuring production and reproduction work. All the same, struggles in one circuit can and often will circulate in the other, or define a point of resistance to a strategy initiated in the other, as for example women's struggles in the 1960s and

1970s which, by disrupting and subverting the micro-state of the patriarchal family, have also shaken the overall social fabric which facilitated capitalist accumulation in the Keynesian post-1945 period. These women's struggles did this by threatening the reproduction of male workers in particular forms and routines, which then contributed to shake the 'social peace' predicated on collectively bargained growth in wages and productivity for the unionised workers of the Fordist deal.

The commons circuit

The analysis can be further generalised, if we zoom out of the specific reproduction of labour power, and regard the top circuit in Figure 5.3 as applicable to any commodity, that is, if we return to C-M-C in the form of C-M...P...M-C. In this general form, C-M-C describes not only the general metabolism of the reproduction of labour power, but also the circuit of production of commodities involving self-employed, petty producers, craft people, small organic farmers, reclaimed factories, water associations and so on, as they bring their commodities to the market and couple their system circuits based on needs to the economy. But since human needs and desires both can be fulfilled in many social forms and modes of coordination, if we zoom out even further we see that C-M-C is itself but a moment of social reproduction. How important this moment is in intensity and scale is entirely a historical and contingent question. The point is that unlike the capital circuit, the simple commodity circuit is just a means, hence scalable, depending on the external context, to the structure of needs and desires and the resources that can be mobilised in non-commoditised forms (through for example pooling, gift circuits or administrative transfers).

In this sense, the commodities in C-M-C circuits are a moment of a social process of production that runs parallel to and is socially integrated with, in specific forms and modes of coordination, a non-commodity production. This allows us to locate the C-M-C as a sequence within a broader circuit, which we may call the *commons circuit*; this is illustrated in Figure 5.4, the formula for the commons.[3]

In Figure 5.4, the constituent elements of the commons (Cs) are common resources or commonwealth (CW) and an associated community (A), in brief, an association. It does not interest us for the moment how this association came about, whether it is through kinship (like an *ayllu* in the Andes), a political affinity (like a social centre in Europe), proximity (like a neighbourhood association in the USA), a cyber encounter in a software development project (as in P2P), a local custom (as in an Indian village), or an affective choice (a household or a network of friends in Europe). The types of commons vary, among other things, in relation to the type of structure formed by their elements, which in turn comprise material and immaterial characteristics. Material elements are biophysical: the people's bodies comprising A, or the characteristics of the land they share as CW, or any tools, technology, building they share. Immaterial elements are more intangible but no less real, and with no less tangible effects: the cultural horizon of the community, the knowledge base, the dispositions and so forth as I have discussed in Chapter 3. Also,

$$ {}^{NC}_{C} \Big\}\, {}^{A}_{CW} \Big\}\, Cs \ldots cm \ldots Cs \, \Big\{ {}^{A}_{CW} \Big\{ {}^{NC}_{C} $$

Figure 5.4 The circuit of the commons

the constituent elements of the commons form and are formed in turn by particular relations among themselves. The association is a whole comprised of relations (customs, roles, conflict, rules, norms, institutions) and elements (people). The great bulk of CW comprises a set of non-human forms of life within particular ecological processes (what we call 'land', 'water', 'air', 'ecosystems', etc.) and their material substratum (stones, minerals, etc.). The element Cs (commons) at the beginning and end of the process thus indicate the commons as the unity between an associated community A and commonwealth (CW).

In turn, CWs are here divided into two main types: ones that are pooled together within the sphere of the commons, that is, those that take on a non-commodity form (NC), and the ones that must be acquired from within the market economy as commodities (C). To access the monetary means through which these commodities may be acquired, the commons must either enter the market economy as buyer – on the left hand of the formula – and sellers (at the right hand of the formula), or receive money as a transfer from an outside source (the state or another organisation, such as an NGO).

Finally, the middle term cm in Figure 5.4 indicates the commoning activity that is required to reproduce the commons in this basic unit anew, as I discussed in Chapter 3.

Further reflections

The commons circuit in Figure 5.4 is a derivation from two major circuits of money that are rooted in diverse philosophical and economic thinking. While neither Aristotle, who made the first distinction between *oeconomia* and chrematistics, nor Marx, who developed the circuit of capital to identify the source of exploitation, nor Keynes, who understood the distinction between the two circuits[4] – none of these figures ventured to question what is behind the C-M-C and M-C-M' circuits. As I mentioned, this was the merit of Marxist feminist scholars and activists in the 1970s, interested to show that the invisible labour of reproduction of labour power was done in the domestic sphere by women and monitored by men who thus reproduced patriarchal relations where men inside the family acted like foremen and monitored women's housework. Women's domestic labour thus contributed to the value of labour power. This was the basic argument grounding the international campaign for wages for housework. To the extent that the proletarian family of the post-World War Two era was made functional for the process of capital accumulation and the Keynesian deal between mainly male factory workers and trade unions, the power relations of the factory were replicated into the domestic scene, and the family – notwithstanding the form of the formula given in Figure 5.4 – was turned into a distorted or corrupted commons (Hardt and Negri 2009) where the man acts as the foreman of the woman. Today, many families are certainly turned into another type of corrupted commons, that is neoliberal families (Garrett, Jensen, Voela 2016; Barbagallo 2016): two-income rampant enterprises in competition with others for everything: careers, best schools, best carers, best neighbourhoods to move into. These neoliberal families are engaged in a competitive war that sees the richest succeed, while the poorest succumb to a life of poor schools, poor services, and poor housing. Yet the formula shown in Figure 5.4 indicates that there is more to the family micro-commons than patriarchy or neoliberal subjectification. To the extent that the commons circuit is (re)produced through values and practices that are alternatives to these, rooted in mutual support, love and conviviality, the circuit of the commons (re)produces the commons, not its corrupted form.

This also applies for larger commons than families. One can imagine a large variety of commons organised in the way captured by the commons circuit formula, from households to farms, from community associations to self-organised *centri sociali* and sites of cultural production.[5] Let us make a simple stock-flow illustration of a night in Forte Prenestino, a self-organised social centre in Rome that occupied an old fortress more than thirty years ago, and that often, among several other activities, organises concerts and cultural and political events. The non-commodity circuit represents the relational, cultural, and knowledge practices that have been (re)generated in previous circuits and enter now as reproduced (and developed) resources. The 'outputs' or the regenerated resources occur before the 'inputs' of the next round, since also cultural resources are reproduced or regenerated resources. This is also because the process of production of culture and knowledge of the community implies development at each round, and so it is not a static repetition of routines but a dynamic process. Each input is not necessarily the same as the previous one, since the output that each input has as a precondition may be different from the previous one. This is even more likely if the community we are considering – largely also a political community – faces a hostile environment (fascist groups, a degree of indifference or even hostility from surrounding communities, and an enclosing state). A hostile environment requires adaptive strategies and therefore it urges the commons into courses of development. Also anything material that is gifted or found in a 'common pot', plus some basic material resources, belongs to these circuits, regenerated communally from a previous event via maintenance, cleaning and reordering (chairs, toilets, benches, tables, musical instruments, lights, as well as drinks, food, pamphlets and other political materials that needed to be produced). The commodity circuits are also present in these events, but they are of the nature C-M-C, which limits markets to the metabolic function of social reproduction. The community beer makers sell beers at the event but can also be part of the group governing the space or connected to it by affinities that go beyond market exchanges. Thus market circuits are entangled with the commoning (cm) within the larger commons systems of the fort that contains it. Some of the monetary resources obtained through the selling of beer may in turn be pooled together with that of other producers to purchase material that is used in the commons, while the remaining money resources enter the circuits of domestic commons of the producers. Through the analysis of systemic circuits, and the interactions of all possible stocks and flows, the different processes become intelligible, the boundaries between one system and another become clear, and the choices to make these boundaries what they are, including the constraints faced by subjects and their tensions in overcoming them, become discussed among commoners.

Part three

Commoning: the source of grassroots power

Chapter 6

Mobilising social labour for commoning

In this and the next chapter I will deal with the third element of commons systems, the most crucial because it is generating the system. Commoning is the life activity through which common wealth is reproduced, extended and comes to serve as the basis for a new cycle of commons (re)production, and through which social relations among commoners – including the rules of a governance system – are constituted and reproduced.

Commoning as a mode of exercising powers

Commoning, doing in common, relating, governing, making, creating, producing, reproducing in common: obviously commoning is a social activity, but wage labouring or slaving also are social activities, and thus to say that commoning is a social activity is not enough. The first very general key characteristic of commoning is that it is social labour bounded in space/time, by a given amount of accessible resources and within a commons circuit as shown in Figure 5.4, hence within goals and *modes* of organising labour set by the commoners. I will discuss this element of autonomy in the next chapter.

I hesitated to use the word 'labour', so loaded in political meaning, so charged with both positive and negative aspects which makes reading it and interpreting is a very ambiguous affair. Perhaps I was following the contemporary hesitation in the commons literature to use the word 'labour' in reference to commons. The best and most vivid example is Michel Bauwens (2015), who refers to commoning as 'collaborating', not labouring. Of course, Marx taught us that collaboration can only be a form of social cooperation, which in turn implies the expenditure of social labour (Marx 1976: ch. 13). Sophistry is not necessary to assuage our fear that commons may also become exploitative places. Labour is not always exploitation, while exploitation always is a particular amount of surplus labour.

I want thus to stick with an Early Marx definition of labour as activity that includes both immaterial and material aspects, and that, depending on how it is carried out and through what relations it is actualised, positions our species in its unique place of either destructive or reproducing itself as *nature*. Marx wrote, 'Man [sic] lives from nature, i.e., nature is his body, and he must maintain a continuing dialogue with it if he [sic] is not to die. To say that man's [sic] physical and mental life is linked to nature simply means that nature is linked to itself, for man [sic] is a part of nature' (Marx 1977: 328).

In other words, this mental and physical life linked to nature is social labour, social doing. Commoning in this general sense is a form of social doing. But social doing comes in a million different forms. Even autonomous social doing does: people can take things into their own hands and kill one another into family or community feuds. Obviously, this is not the commoning, or the autonomous social doing that we are talking about. Instead, I want to connect to that doing that has been theorised by John Holloway (2002) as the true force of production, as the human force that breaks the chains of the deed, chains that under the dominium of capital over people's lives take the grey tone of fetishism. The doing is in this sense the exercise of many human powers, understood as *powers to*. To talk about commoning is to talk about a constituent force of new social relations, but within a setting, a context, in which these *powers to* encounter the limit of capital's *power over*. However capital's *power over* is ultimately nothing less than the expression of a clash between opposing *powers to*, that is, its ability to turn many social powers towards capital's own systemic ends: accumulation. *Power over* is nothing else than a net result, a particular balance of powers within a power field, one type of *powers to* (the commons' one) being organisationally outflanked and outgrown (Mann 1986) by another type of *power to* (that of capital/the state). We must therefore approach our analysis of commoning as social activity, as *powers to*, without forgetting that *power over* is still a relation to *powers to* that runs in the opposite direction, part of a force field as discussed in Chapter 2.

Here it suffices to note that commoning brings to life the essential social elements of the commons. The life sequence of commoning, its rhythms, pauses, cycles, draw on and craft anew networks of relationships turned into community by repetition of iterations, building expectations of reciprocal obligation of care and aid – *munus* (Esposito 2006) – and shared understanding that are things that belong to all of us. On the other hand, commoning reproduces the community as well as resources, thus giving shape to the *conditions* of production of the next round of commoning. As I will argue in the next chapter, commoning also develops the conditions of autonomy and auto-production (autopoiesis) and the features of the boundaries separating one commons from another, defining lines of inclusion and exclusion. Commoning therefore, in terms of both its internal relations and its external relations, is a highly *political* activity, even when the commoners themselves are unaware of this.

Commoning thus is flow-like in its praxis: like a bike chain it continues to rotate, to iterate, to start anew a new cycle, literally converting the reciprocating, valuing and cooperating motion of the commoners' labour into rotational motion of the commons, (re)producing resources and commoners, and in turn (re)producing the commons at new levels and in new forms (see Figure 5.4). There are, of course, people at the heart of this system, not civil society, not citizens, but commoners who come together to co-create and co-produce their life in common. They do not need to wait for others to solve their problems, they do not ask politicians for representation in order to act, although they would not necessarily refuse a helping hand from them in the right conditions.

Commoning thus is an alternative way to make decisions and act upon those decisions to shape the future of communities without being locked into market competition and its anxieties, the blackmail of profit-driven companies, and state agencies. Commoning is the way the struggle for freedom is actualised: by being free. This is not the same as being free in the bourgeois sense, as an individualistic passion for the most idiosyncratic behaviour, in the sense of free will. Your freedom is not in any danger in the commons. You can always fight in the commons, you can always leave it, or you can overcome deep pride to agree with others when that is sensible. The freedom that the commons gives you is a freedom you will find nowhere else: that is, the freedom to shape, together with others, the condition of your doing, of your caring, of your commoning. Freedom as auto-determination, to determine autonomously. And, since to determine is to select from the complex realm of the possible, to determine is to set limits, thus to set limits autonomously. Clearly, this freedom is as relevant as the powers of the commons, their relative development, the resources they mobilise, the number of connections they make with other commons, and the counter-forces acting upon them. For these reasons, commons have a particular way of sustaining themselves through adaptation and development, which in turn often implies an intensification of network links through what I call *boundary commoning* (see Chapter 8). The development of commons is thus the expression of two interrelated things: the way a particular form of commoning in given contexts operationalises commons reproductive circuits (including expansionary circuits through boundary commoning); and the counter-forces present in the field of forces in which any specific commons is located.

Commoning goes down deep in human history in all civilisations. As a practice, it has adapted and transformed itself to stay alive through empires, genocides and waves of enclosures taking away lands, dwellings, rivers and coastlines to put them in the hands of some profitable or military enterprise. It developed across generations, it moved from rural places to cities and vice versa, always bringing memories and resources of all types which were pulled into new contexts: on shop floors among co-workers, in lavatories among women, along rural roads being mended by entire communities. It gave birth to children, it nurtured them, it healed them, it cared for them, it played with them, it fed them, it educated them.

Commoning is a social labour flow pushed by needs, attracted by desires and oriented by sense horizon and aspirations; it is a life flow in which money, if necessary, is only a means to a human end – unlike capital flows whose only rationale for moving is a gap, a delta, a plus sign, a quantitative increase in money. The loss of the commons in successive waves of capitalist development has also robbed people of their autonomy to meet basic needs for sustenance and economic security, of their social fabric and network of solidarity in those contexts. But if it is true that the expropriation of the old commoners is 'written in the annals of mankind in letters of blood and fire' (Marx 1976: 875), it is also true that the fire, however tremendous, has not been sufficiently big, and the blood spilled was not sufficient to stop common-ing from adapting, redeveloping and recreating new social connections wherever the commoners were displaced to. Simi-larly, twenty-first-century enclosures in the form of the current land grab in Asia and Africa (Daniel and Mittal 2009) occur at the same time as new forms of resistance and commoning are developing as a social force of regeneration (Pushback 2011). Five hundred years of genocide have not stopped the indige-nous cultures in Latin America – and other parts of the world – from developing their own commons to meet the challenges of the day. In the Zapatistas' area in Chiapas, the Caracoles repre-sent the administrative areas where 'We are learning ... how to govern ourselves, to walk alone without help from the federal government' (Ross 2005: 41). Throughout the Andes, villages, neighbourhoods and associations managing water and schools, building community houses or organising protests are governing themselves. The same developments are occurring in different forms in Africa, Asia, Oceania, Europe and the Americas.

In our daily life commoning is also evident as a self-directed form of cooperation through the most simple relations of our lives or in the most energising social movements of our time. Moreover, we can look back at the diversity of people's history and in spite of all distinctions, diversity, peculiarities of culture, we can distinguish the shape and form of that social force articulating subjects through solidarity, mutual aid, conviviality and different forms of sharing. This is a social force in which subjects themselves create in often unanticipated ways, and that mobilises social powers, power that 'arises from co-operation itself' (Marx 1976: 447). It is a form of social cooperation that resists the dominant paradigm of modern life, that operates outside the code and protocol of capitalist-dominated social cooperation; it is a form of social cooperation in which profit for profit's sake, expropriation and competitiveness are not the dominant drivers of the forms and goals of cooperation, and that thus provides fundamentally different meanings and sustenance for life in common.

And through commoning we imagine, because imagining is playing, and playing, as children of history, is part of commoning. We imagine and also we remember through commoning. Memory, as imagination, is a quality of commoning. We remember massacres and we remember moments of conviviality and events in those moments, things that have happened to us, discovery of ourselves in relation to people we love or we respect. We remember events we participated in and organised. We remember heart-breaking moments, we remember in anguish, and we remember with joy times of just having received a gift in life and being touched by others, or having felt that feeling of exuberant 'excess' in struggle with others (Free Association 2004). They are all memories *through* commoning, and of moments *of* commoning, or of the commoning necessary to defend the commons from a threat, as if when life seems to stop after a massacre in a village, and then the survivors emerge from their hiding places and pick up the pieces, comfort one other, organise a soup kitchen and burials, take care of orphans, rebuild houses, churches and clinics. Commoning does not have just one emotional dimension: a whole range of human emotions is circulated through commoning in different contexts, from joy to sorrow, from anguish to exuberance. Entire networks of affects are reproduced through the iterations of commoning. The same goes for knowledge, technology, cultures, and values. Commoning is also a way to tap into the hidden chamber within our imaginations that harbours vivid images of different ways to live, to relate, to define goals.

To be resilient, commoning must depend on an open attitude that embraces traditions and projection into the future, history and contemporaneity, memory and immanence. We are not just discovering the commons – we are (re)inventing them as well. As we rediscover how to interact and take responsibility in ways that are both old and new, and as we discover more elemental ways of interacting and organising social and economic life, even with high-tech communication tools, when we common we engage in the oldest ways of doing things and relating, the most convivial and democratic: as The Singer remarks in Brecht's Prologue to *The Caucasian Chalk Circle* (1944), 'Mixing one's wines may be a mistake, but old and new wisdom mix admirably.' Not all cooperative or collaborative enterprises are commoning. Negotiating deals with bosses cannot be commoning and nor can working in a team with your line management when it is understood that she will discipline you or grass you out with an even higher line management. Likewise the rhetoric of 'we are all in this together', used by politicians to assuage fear of cuts in social entitlement while at the same time they prepare for massive cuts, is not indicative of commoning, but only of the neurotic spectacle of control. So, for example, if a lady worth £340 million sits on a gold throne, and, wearing a crown encrusted with over 2,800 diamonds, unveils a government's 'one nation' policies announcing measures that include freezing benefits, clamping down on strike action, seizing migrants' wages and removing automatic housing support for young people, it does not feel as if there is any real commoning here, in spite of the 'we are all in it together' rhetoric.[1] Rather, again with Brecht, it's like the case of the man that asked the worm to go fish with him.

Setting commoning in motion: lessons from the Andes

How do a group of people decide to come together in a particular area or a particular network and common together? How are these people and their labour mobilised? Capital 'commands' or mobilises its social labour through direct coercion or through the shaping of the social and economic context in such a way that people have little choice other than to be put to work under capital's measure. I use here the term 'command' to relate this concept to classical political economy's notion of labour commanded, which is the labour set in motion by a given quantity of money. Under capitalist relations, labour commanded depends on the wage rate, so the lower the wage rate (maybe as a result of high unemployment or poverty intensifying competition between workers and outflanking their struggles), the greater is capital's power of money to command labour, to mobilise it into social labour for its own profit. So, for example, if the wage rate is on average $10 an hour, with $1 million you can mobilise 100,000 hours of labour, or 12,500 days of work at 8 hours of work a day, or, which is the same thing expressed in a different way, 100 workers working 125 8-hour days.[2] The commons mobilises labour in radically different ways.

There are two general ways to set in motion social labour in the form of commoning. I call these communal labour and reciprocal labour. Both cases are embedded in particular social and cultural norms that regulate individual and households' participation, the planning and conception of work and so on. As I argue in the next chapter, however great the similarity with capitalist work and despite the most general point that both commoning and capitalist work are forms of social labour, the key difference between the two is that the commons establishes its own autonomous measures of what, how, when and how much labour, while for capital all these measures are prevalently defined from the outside condition of markets, competitiveness and the particular needs of capitalist profitability.

Communal labour is the social labour that a community of commoners pulls together for particular common objectives following convocation. *Reciprocal labour* is the form of social labour that is intertwined with perceptions of reciprocity, gift, or mutual aid; it is the labour that subject A performs for subject B, B for C and C for A (circular reciprocity) or simply A for B (where karmic feelgood is the reward). Blood donation is a contemporary type of gift that is connected to the time spend in donating it, hence a form of reciprocal labour, since in donating blood we expect that others will have donated it if and when we need it (Godbout 2000).

Communal and reciprocal labour are distinct but complementary. While communal labour represents the labour that a community of commoners pulls together for particular objectives following their convocation, reciprocal labour is the weaving of the social fabric of a community through circuits of reciprocity. All the forms of what is generally referred to as mutualism that are not based principally on sharing labour but on sharing goods or money, are ultimately derived from these or are its preconditions (as in the case of resource pooling). However technologically interconnected or 'cognitive' is the type of post-capitalist commons, my hypothesis here is that communal labour and reciprocal labour represent the spectrum within which any form of commoning could be mobilised, even as a hybrid form between the two and in a different time–space context.

A different concept from communal or reciprocal labour is that of *organisation* of labour. By organisation of labour I mean the overall coordination of *different processes necessary* to carry out the production of a good or a service. So, in principle there may be division of labour and *organisation* among different communal labour nodes in order to produce a canoe (Malinowski 1922) or an open-source tractor (http://opensourceecology.org/wiki/LifeTrac). When carried out in the commons, a division of labour does not need to be the instrument of alienation and exploitation and hierarchy of conditions of labour; it can instead be an instrument to work less. The division of labour could also be simple: a rotation over the same tasks (with some variation). P.M. (2014: 37; see also the rotation in the tasks of administration of a water system described in Box 6) did the calculations for a neighbourhood commons kitchen (or club) in which people take turn to cook for everybody: '44 members divide into 11 cooking teams of four. Every team cooks, washes up and does all the work four times a year and pays for all the food. This means that you can eat 40 times for free and have time to communicate without having to help (it is essential that help is forbidden!). P.M. describes two of such food circles in Zurich which have operated respectively for twelve and twenty years.

The following brief discussion of communal and reciprocal labour is premised on the fact that imagination (and mathematics) is the only limit for ingenious forms of organisation to maximise conviviality, resilience and ecology, and to minimise work as work.

Communal labour

As noted above, communal labour is the labour that a community of commoners pulls together for particular objectives following their convocation, while reciprocal labour is the weaving of the social fabric of a community through circuits of reciprocity. This is work that is not paid with a wage, although different traditions tend to end the period of work with parties or banquets.

The works generally benefit the whole of a community. A dam for irrigation, containment walls, a road, a place of worship, a community centre, an aqueduct, a storage house, a park or a school can be built or renovated by a community, as it is the restructuring of an occupied social centre. Here the 'joint effort results in a shared product. The members of the collective gather once or several times to work together, for the production of a good from which they all hope to benefit when it is ready' (Van der Linden 2008: 83).

This form of social labour was deeply rooted and widespread thorough Europe when the continent was a mainly agricultural society. My own grandfather, up until the late 1940s in the Emilian Apennines in Italy, participated in communal labour together with other farmers to lay roads and build walls to keep the river from flooding the country in what they called 'fare un cantiere'. In Europe at least, the tradition has survived through a plethora of large or small, formal or informal associative moments, although its survival is generally culturally subordinated to the limited presence of waged work as a 'proper' mode of commanding labour that serves as the standard of reference. Throughout the Andes, this form of labour is known as *minga* or *minka* (see Box 5) and its use is quite widespread and culturally rooted. This cultural and economic practice allows indigenous communities such as the Aymara peoples of Bolivia, the Quichua of Ecuador or the Mapuche of Chile and Argentina a large degree of autonomy from the capitalist economy. This cultural economic base is perhaps one of the reasons why an indigenous resurgence has happened in South America. In Bolivia, indigenous struggles have translated into the demand for 'plurinationality' first adopted by the Bolivian constitution of February 2009 after a wave of struggles against neoliberal privatisation policies expropriating common resources of the indigenous population, the so-called water wars (Olivera and Lewis 2004). The new Bolivian constitution is important since for the first time the state acknowledges the plurality of socio-economic organisations, which include private, state, cooperative and communal organisations.

Unlike the voluntary character that communal labour may take in Western society – say, following a public call to clear a beach of rubbish or to participate in a demonstration – a character greatly due to the much looser community ties developed within the context of highly pervasive market societies, *mingas* are not generally voluntary, but, once you enter a given association, community or neighbourhood, they are obligatory. Apart from the generally accepted moral obligation to participate in a communal project, the community also tends to establish systems of enforcement and punishment to assure wider participation in *mingas*, obviously taking into consideration mitigating circumstances that justify absences, such as illness, infirmity and the like. This is of course contemplated by Ostrom's fourth and fifth commons design principles described in Chapter 4, regarding monitoring and sanctioning freeriding, a mechanism which the community must somehow implement if it is to sustain itself. Clearly, this is not the same as an autocratic reaction by a line manager firing or fining workers for taking a toilet break, and my impression in visiting some of the water associations in Cochabamba and *mingas* in Ecuador and Peru was that there was a very relaxed implementation of such rules. For example, some community water associations around the area of Cochabamba require obligatory attendance at decision meetings and at meetings to decide the rota of work for maintenance of the infrastructure. The penalty for not participating repeatedly could be fines, a double work shift or even a cut in the water supply. The system is apparently generally little used since, in the word of an informant, 'we generally always find ways to solve conflicts amicably'. The same claim was made to me by others. Clearly, the opposite could be true in different contexts. In other instances, community members are required to participate in demonstrations, as when entire neighbourhoods descend in protest from El Alto areas into downtown La Paz.

The great anthropologist Bronislaw Malinowski provides powerful descriptions and beautiful photographs in his classic work on the coastal population of the South Sea islands in the Western Pacific (Malinowski 1922). Here he gives accounts of communal work building canoes, in fishing and in growing gardens (the latter has a magisterial accent in Malinowski (1935)).

Other work has accounted for the role of communal labour in colonial times. Okia (2012), for example, has written an account of how the British colonial power in the early twentieth century was able to co-opt existing community labour practices or even invented them anew in order to use community labour to build and maintain infrastructure needed by the colonial power and to save large sums of money. In these conditions 'communal labour' was hardly communal. Heavy punishment for violations of the colonial 'community labour' rules were imposed and defended with the fiction that such practices were at the basis of African culture.

In pre-Hispanic Inca times, when the ties of dependence within a particular community (*ayllu*) were strict, repeated noncompliance with *minga* obligations could give rise to the maximum penalty: expulsion from the group. This would have turned the individual or the nuclear family into a wandering pariah with no rights, no access to land and to the network of support and gift exchange, and no hope of joining another *ayllu*. Thus 'there remained only three possibilities: to become beggars, to become bandits', or to serve the Inca nobility (Soriano 1997). I am not sure whether this is the case today, although if mobility is acquired in modern societies, it is always possible to reconstruct affective and obligation networks and non-kin commons pretty much everywhere.[3]

Reciprocal labour

If communal labour is mostly based on the principle of community sharing, both in terms of labour and the products of labour, as for example the sharing of a meal and music, reciprocal labour is based on principles of equality matching (EM) (Fiske 1990; Fiske and Haslam 2005). As I will discuss below and in the next chapter, these are two of the four ways people cognise others while coordinating action with others. According to this model, to analyse how people coordinate is to analyse how 'they create relationships that are intrinsically motivating, that evoke emotions, and that they constantly evaluate with respect to shared modes of how people should coordinate with each other' (Fiske, Haslam 2005: 267). There are of course endless numbers of culturally specific ways to model social relations, as social and cultural anthropologists can tell us. However, from the perspective of social theory, the interesting and most useful aspect of the Relational Model Theory (RMT) developed by John Fiske (1991, 2004) is that these endless specific forms can be reduced to four basic generative models in various combinations. The four relational models are community sharing (CS), authority ranking (AR), equality matching (EM) and market pricing (MP). 'These four models are the structures out of which people construct, understand, evaluate, sanction, and motivate most joint activities' (Fiske and Haslam 2005: 268). Communal labour and reciprocal labour are closest to what Fiske identifies as CS and EM. In CS, the only meaningful social distinction 'is to consider whether a person is the same or different with respect to the relevant aspect of whether people are coordinating'. EM 'is a relationship in which people keep track of additive differences, with even balance as the reference point. It is evident when people organise 'turn taking, lotteries, the framework of games and sports, co-ops, and eye-for-an-eye vengeance' (Fiske and Haslam 2005: 271).

In the literature, reciprocal labour is also called exchange labour, cooperative labour or rotating labour. It consists of an interchange of labour among individuals or groups (such as households, villages, neighbourhoods, networks, churches), a very antique form especially rooted in agricultural societies, but also evident in networks of friends in modern urban centres. Here one person or a nucleus first 'consumes' the labour of the rest of the group. After this, it is the turn of another person/ nucleus and so on. In agricultural societies, it is a form of labour that follows the agrarian cycle, in which different domestic units (that is, commons at a lower social scale) borrow the labour of some other domestic units with the implicit obligation to return the favour. For example, harvesting time requires the pooling of more labour than a family unit can mobilise, hence the need to borrow labour from other families. Who, in turn, requires more labour than they can afford for the harvesting in their own land. Travelling through the Andes and witnessing practices of *ayni* – the Quechua name given to this type of reciprocal labour – really brought home the point to me, because these practices are the same practices of my ancestors from the Italian regions of Emilia-Romagna and Marche. The difference is that our economic development has erased even the name for it (in the Emilian Appenines it was called *ovra* or *cambio*), while their political development in the Andes in the course of five hundred years of struggle against colonisation has saved the names, renewed the practices, and built a social force upon them.

Nicolaas van Meeteren describes one such arrangement on Curaçao, which was popular there until the first decades of the twentieth century:

Whenever one needed to weed, plant or harvest, the custom was implemented that was known as 'saam.' All neighbors then agreed to work for each other once or twice in the week in the evening by moonlight. The beneficiary of the work provided rum and refreshments. As the workers encouraged each other by singing in turns in 'guenee' or 'Macamba,' the work went smoothly and everyone benefitted by it.' (Van Der Linden 2008: 5)

A saam had the advantage that the work was done much faster, because workers encouraged each other, which is very important, especially for strenuous labour in the fields. (Van Der Linden 2008: 6)

Reciprocal labour does not only involve strictly agricultural work. The 'barn raisings' common in the USA in the nineteenth century are another example: every first Sunday of the month, a group of farmers would built a new barn for one of their members, until every member of the group had had his turn (Van der Linden 2008: 83). In the Andes, it is a custom for the house of a newlywed couple to be built by shared community labour.

Mobilising social labour for the commons in modern societies

In urban capitalist societies, these reciprocal and communal forms of labour are reinvented anew, since agricultural cycles are far distant from urban realities, and modern agribusiness models do not need such forms because of heavy mechanisation and oil dependence.

Yet forms of communal or reciprocal labour still pervade the social field. In centres where there exist factories that concentrate workers and tie them into industrial rhythms of work, networks of labour reciprocity among workers' families - often maintained and reproduced along ethnic or national lines - are often the basis of broader labour union constitution and organisation. All the same, there are neighbourhoods in modern Western cities that for a variety of reasons have managed to keep up networks of reciprocity and communal labour, allowing them to maintain a social cohesion which is very useful when the neighbourhood is threatened by neoliberal urban 'regeneration' processes.

In some anti-foreclosure movements in the USA and especially in Spain, a hybrid of communal and reciprocal labour occurs, as when groups of activists help residents to resist a bank's bailiffs and in turn the residents are required (or invited) to join the struggle and help someone else in the same conditions (reciprocal labour); these types of network represent a significant break from the otherwise individualising tendency of the metropolis. In the USA, however, eviction 'communal labour' blockades have often been bypassed at gunpoint (Gottesdiener 2013). It has been a different story in Spain, where the Platform Afectados for la Hipoteca (PAH) began in 2011as a way to help both materially and emotionally those foreclosed by the bursting of the housing bubble in 2008. Born from the street, the movement has also developed an *Obra Social*, with the aim of relocating families in houses owned by banks. PAH do not consider these as 'illegal occupations' since citizens bailed out these banks with public funds and didn't receive any social goods in return. So, rather, these amount to 'legitimate recuperation' of social wealth. The public reclaiming of these occupations, and the procedures advised by PAH to create maximum impact in the negotiation against banks, imply different forms of communal labour are activated, whether with neighbourhoods or with other activists (PAH 2013).

Both ways to mobilise labour for commoning, that is, both reciprocal and communal labour, are generally inversely related to the centrality of money. For example, the LETS systems (Local Exchange Trading Systems) or time banks (Ruzzene 2015; Collom et al. 2012; Lee et al. 2004) are generally instituted as ways to organise and rationalise reciprocal labour in conditions of social fragmentation and in an attempt to overcome them. These forms of mobilisation of labour generally grow in periods of economic stagnation and decline in periods of economic boom. Classic examples of this trend are the experience of Argentina in the 2000s and of the UK in the 1980s. Crisis thus opens the way for alternative modes of social interaction, which in any case follow the general model of reciprocal labour or communal labour. The political problem becomes how to sustain these forms, making them resilient against capital's power and even able to overcome it.

It goes without saying that communal labour that depends on customary norms within a community, or reciprocal labour that follows regular agrarian cycles, do not set standards for all possible and conceivable forms of commoning. *These two general forms of labour only set the two axes defining the plane in which the labour necessary for commoning is activated as a social force: either as communal labour, which is an aggregation and a concentration of forces in one point, or as relational labour, which is a circuit; or a flow of forces circulating spatially and temporally, or alternating rhythms of both.*

To mobilise the social labour necessary for commoning requires some aspects of coordination and cooperation. Sometime individuals are employed by the community with a salary to do a job that requires a certain regularity, such as coordination and administration. This subtracts nothing from the commons character of communal labour if it is inserted and subordinated to the commons circuit as in Figure 5.4.

In any case, there are key questions that only commoners in given contexts can answer. For example: how will coordination occur? This depends on the norms established by the commoners themselves, as well as the characteristics of the pooled resources, the objects of labour, the relational dance among the commoners and their values, the broader cultural and political-economic context in which commoning operates, the struggles within the community, the historical stratification of norms, cultures and codes. Does this mean that we can say nothing about commoning in general? No, there is indeed one feature about commoning as a form of human cooperation that distinguishes it from capital. And this is the fact that, unlike capitalist work, the social labour in commoning *is not subjected to one dominant measure*, one way to understand value, *but by a plurality of measures*, often posited by different members of the community in different positionalities, and must be articulated through communicational and labouring processes. In other words, social cooperation occurs notwithstanding the fact that diverse social activities are subjected not to the one measure of profit, but rather to the plural measure of a community that reproduces itself, its relations and its resources. I will discuss this in the next chapter.

Chapter 7

The production of autonomy, boundaries and sense

Commoning as creation of autonomy and self-reliance

In Chapter 6 I discussed the forms through which common-ing is mobilised. In this chapter, I discuss some key aspects of commoning itself, what commoning produces besides the particular immaterial and material goods that are part of its focus. Thus, the commoning necessary to (re)produce water resources, a theatre, a occupied social centre, a church, a social movement, (re)produces not *only* these 'common goods' and the community, but a range of other features of the system.

The first such feature is autonomy. To discuss this I begin with the relation between commoning and the state. In his book *The Magna Carta Manifesto*, the historian Peter Linebaugh (2008) traces the origin and development of this crucial constitutional text as emerging from the commoners' struggle to have their rights to the commons recognised and acknowledged by the state. In this context, commoning is the activity of the commoners in organic relation to the 'commons' (as pooled resources that need to be sustained and reproduced) and to one another. This implies that commoning is an activity that develops relations preoccupied by their (re)production and therefore – to use a modern term – crucially founded on their own 'sustainability' and resilience.

Commoning is also constituent of rights, the 'commons rights', which should not be confuse with 'legal rights'. The latter are granted within the context of the state, by the powerful. Commons rights instead originate in their being exercised, and therefore the state can only, at most, acknowledge them, and confirm them (or else deny, restrict them, etc.). This recognition is precisely what happened in the history of the freedom charters discussed by Linebaugh – the 1215 Magna Carta and the 1225 Charter of the Forests. These rights were taken by the people, which forced the king to acknowledge them. For the state (the king) to reach the point of confirming commoners' rights, itself implied, in fact, that the commoners were already commoning; people were taking their lives into their own hands before commons rights were granted. Equally today, therefore, the state does not only (and does not, in fact, tend to) grant common rights, but (rather) confirms rights (if it does) already exercised by the commoners, as in the case of the customary rights confirmed in thirteenth-century England.

If the origin of commons rights is in commoning, an element of commons, we are in the presence of a social system generated by its own operations, codes and values, what we will discuss below as autonomous and autopoietic systems. Inevitably, these are framed by the context of their circumstances. Thus, from the perspective of the medieval English commoners, the right to common does not come from the high palaces where the powerful are located, but is embedded in a particular ecology and a correspondent local husbandry (Wolcher 2009). The issues that preoccupy the commoners are thus moments of a commons reflective stance grounded in the needs of resource and social relational sustainability. Commoners don't think first in terms of who owns the property, who is in possession of a title deed, rather they think in terms of human needs. What can we grow on this land? Shall we till it or use it for pasture? Are there any water sources? Research and exploration are central to the practices of commoners, even early ones (Wolcher 2009).

Communication and research are therefore all embedded in the same activity of commoning. But commoning is not only arranging selections through communication, as it also involves communicating through actions, through labour: going 'deep into human history' – in fact, as far into that history as that history goes – 'commoning is embedded in a labor process; it inheres in a particular praxis of field, upland, forest, marsh, coast'. Therefore, 'Common rights are entered into by labor,' and 'commoning is collective', and 'being independent of the state, is independent also of the temporality of the law and state' (Linebough 2008: 44-5).

One key feature of commoning thus is autonomy: this is a striving of communities to take things into their own hands in respect of certain material or cultural aspects of their (re)-production. Autonomy has different meanings, depending on the domain in which it is applied. It can refer to a state or institution's right of self-government, or to community self-government. It may indicate a Kantian notion of the freedom of the will giving itself its own laws or class autonomy vis-à-vis capital. But commons are not individuals, and nor are they states or classes, though they can relate to them all.

In order to understand commons autonomy, I am inspired by the biological definition of autonomy at the cellular level, from which I derive – with all due precautions in translating the biological into social realms – an understanding of autonomy in the commons. I argued in Chapter 1 that just as for Marx the commodity is the cell form of capitalist wealth, so the common goods is the cell form of postcapitalist society, but just as the commodity presupposes the capitalist system, so the common goods presuppose commons systems. In the biological cell, autonomy refers to a condition, the condition of autonomy, of some organic unity controlled only by its own laws and not subject to any other. With respect to a commons social system, the question of autonomy thus can be derived in two senses. The first is from the point of view of a social system vis-à-vis others, where autonomy defines a commons dynamic vis-à-vis (other) systems in their environment, namely, the state and capital. At this level, autonomy is pretty much understood as a political struggle, a clash of values, and does not require much elaboration. It means first of all the establishment of an autonomy in relation to heteronymous pressures coming from outside, in terms of measures, in terms of cultures, in terms of what and how production processes and ways of life should be.

Politically, today, this means establishing an autonomy from (against, in response to, thus defined by) the values and rationales of capital. Institutionalised capital wants us to eat GMO food? Commoners develop commons that promote permaculture, agro-ecological methods and networks of community support to agriculture that reproduce ecologies while producing food. European capital enforces austerity in terms of basic as well as consumer needs? Commoners develop solidarity economies linking different commons in order to meet needs and reframe desire, as in Greece since 2009 (see below), or organise to relocate in houses held by banks, as in Spain. This autonomy has clearly a quantitative and qualitative dimension. The former concerns the amount of commons resources and numbers of commoners mobilised within a given space, and the fact that the

latter are still in a minority in relation to the capacity of mobilisation of capital is simply a strategic condition and problem of
commons development. The latter, qualitative dimension refers
to the quality of the relations generated in the commons.

Besides an understanding of autonomy as a relational aspect
in terms external to the commons, we must ask how are 'its own
laws' and social relations generated? For a commons to establish
autonomy vis-à-vis capital, organisation of other production
processes vis-à-vis capital in the manner of resistance is a social,
economic, and political matter as well as a question of setting
new forms of governance and non-state 'rules'. At this point, the
question of autonomy posed by the biologist Francisco Varela for
biological unities is equally relevant for socio-economic systems
such as capital and the commons, only obtained through different practices. Thus, for Varela, autonomous systems are

> defined as a composite unity by a network of interactions of
> components that (i) through their interactions recursively regen-
> erate the network of interactions that produced them, and (ii)
> realise the network as a unity in the space in which the compo-
> nents exist by constituting and specifying the unity's boundaries
> as a cleavage from the background … (Varela 1981: 15)

From the perspective of a social system, autonomy is thus the
property generated by the recursive interaction of components
across a social network in such a way that the network that
produced those interactions is regenerated and a boundary is
defined. The network, therefore, is reproduced through a recursive
loop. Recursion here generally means that an object – a network
of interaction among components – is produced (regenerated) by

the network itself. Thus, the network of interaction can define a boundary vis-à-vis the outside and thereby constitutes a unity. It is this unity identity – continuously reshaped and redefined by the recursive interaction – that gives the commons system its autonomy. For the commons, I translate these recursive interactions as commoning in its various determinations.

The components of commons internal networks – the subjects and the resources, the latter comprising immaterial wealth and the elements of commons material wealth available to the pool – lie dormant in their respective locations – locked in the human memories and in the physical and virtual places of origin – unless and until they are metabolised, transformed from material and immaterial elements of commonwealth through commoning, into utilisable commonwealth. In a forest common (for this and many other traditional commons examples, see Princen 2005; Deb 2009), in order to share the wood of a forest for construction or to burn it to create heat in the houses of a town, it is necessary to share not only the trees but also the logs, which obviously involves a collective process to produce them. A collective production process is at the same time a process both of social labour – the mental and physical exertion of energies towards a goal – and of social relations among the commoners. In this light, commoning is thus the recursive social force and life activity that regenerate and develop the social relations constituting the commons; it is the socially defined life activity that reproduces the social relations among subjects and their metabolism with the common resources.

Networks were regenerated and developed, for example, in solidarity movements in Greece during the height of the recent crisis, as when unemployed communities blocked access to the tribunal where dispossessed houses were auctioned, and where they reinstated electricity to poor households when this was disconnected. Networks at the basis of commons are also regenerated and developed when workers threatened by redundancy occupy their factory, convert it, connect it to newly created solidarity networks to sell their produce, and open up the space for children and other community activities. To each of these, and many other events, corresponsd a social activity, in which a network is regenerated and developed and a boundary is drawn.

But what, then, are the interacting components of commons as social systems? Commonwealth and commoners, that is, resources and people that bear the mark of commons components, that are recognised as such, that are socially 'initiated' as belonging to the system of meanings and values constituted and reproducing the commons. Thus, *commoners can reproduce themselves only via the medium of commonwealth, and commonwealth can reproduce itself only through the medium of commoners' activity.* Commoners are not objectively but relationally defined – so the commoner who abandons the sphere of commons and enters the sphere of capital or the state just disappears, magically turned into worker, commodity labour-power, employee, civil servant, administrator, consumer at whatever level of significance we are looking for, even if they have the same body and knowledge. The commoning recursive loop is broken, at least momentarily.

It is the same for the commonwealth. The ostensibly same (im)material things and knowledge and experience (know-how) of individuals transforms from common wealth into capital (or public goods), in so far as some agents aim to 'invest' it into (or subsume it under) a capitalist (or statist) production process, defined by another recursively generated autonomy and another system unity. It follows from this as a fact of everyday life that people, we, as (self-conscious) subjects daily bouncing in and out of commons and capitalist and statist circuits, bear witness to this: it is we, the self-same subjects who go to work in a company factory or government office by day, for example, but who go commoning in a social centre or a local bar – and at home – by night. Thus our subjectivities change, our identities become multiple, and we shift between them as we move between qualitatively different systems circuits (the circuit types of capital/ state and commons), which may require certain different types of skill and lead to forms of psychic fracturing.

Just as production in capitalist/statist circuits secretes capitalist/statist values, so does production in commons systems secrete commons values. The recursive character of social interrelations along the network is possible only through value practices, a sense of what is good or what is bad, that governs social labour and interactions within a particular social system. Thus the value practices of capital tells its managers to select only those practices that maximise profits and minimise costs (including our wages). In the case of the state, the value practices embedded in this system reproduce hierarchies, and obedience to rules, principles and procedures, even if we think that they are pointless, even if they clash with the values practices generated in our commons, even if they are unjust and biased. Commons production through commoning, on the other hand, is based on value practices among which selection is made contingently by the collectivity (either during the process of production and distribution through feedback mechanisms, or in moments of collective decisions). Commoning thus relies on a *dance of values on the floor of community sharing.* Internal autonomy thus reproduces relationships through a variety of values, but produces the commons as a whole unit, with a character that in terms of value production distinguishes it clearly from capitalist/statist unities.

To the extent that commoners pool a commonwealth (i.e. components of an internal network), and to the extent that commoners interact with one another qua commoners – establishing, thereby, broad horizontal relations adjusted, of course, to the shifting authority of some in given contexts due to their contingent know-how – each of these components recursively interact, they regenerate the commons networks and define its boundaries. System autonomy implies that subjects of the community constitute the systems of interactions as a unity, recognisable in the domain in which the process exists, and this implies the constitution of a boundary between the systems of interactions and the environment. Of course, the existence of a boundary does not mean that nothing passes through; rather, it operates as a filtering membrane, in this case connecting this commons to its environments. It also means that often this boundary becomes the front line that defines the clash of the commons with state and capital.

Communities giving shape to commons around the world have taken things into their own hands in the double sense of autonomy: one, mentioned above, of regenerating and developing their own value practices, and the other of generating communities of struggle and resistance. In particular, since the late 1990s we have witnessed the emergence of activist commoning, a form of grassroots movement that makes horizontality and direct action two key principles of their political praxis. It is a politics grounded in the particular circumstances of the current phase of the neoliberal capital–state dynamic. Ceaseless organising across networks has defined clear boundaries between them – as communities of resistance – and the privatising and enclosing 'enemy', multinational companies, for example, taking away community land to build a dam or to establish new mining operations, or patenting the information systems – genes – of life itself.

Networks of activists are first generated through the concentration of forces on a new goal, acquiring and securing the place, whose repainted walls physically institute the commons, functioning as a protective and insulating boundary – which then further expands and regenerates further networks through the socio-cultural events. Both senses of autonomy – that in relation to the capital/state forces opposing it and the recursive autonomy established through the activity of commoning – constitute and (re)produce their commons boundaries. In the first case of autonomy especially, the boundary might be an immediately antagonistic front line, as in the case of squatting, but establishing filtering mechanisms such as anti-racism and anti-fascism. And with the generation of solidarity activities with migrants, the state migration laws and organised xenophobia confront established commons. In the recursive sense of autonomy, the boundary may instead take a more symbolic or cultural form, and the new commons has the chance to generate a cultural opening-up of new horizons for generations permeated with mainstream values, or a site where it is possible to express new artistic forms and new social and economic experimentations.

Further observations on autonomy

The autonomous force based on commoning often encounters – in different contexts – the issue of legality. For example, many self-organised social centres in Italy began their journey of commoning outside the law, by squatting. Where they gained a sufficient degree of legitimacy in the community, they also acquired a certain power to negotiate with the state their permanence on the site, perhaps turning their illegal situation into a legal tenant's contract, usually at a low cost. Legitimacy is thus the first resource that must be generated and accumulated by many illegal commoning practices, and the key question faced by many movements is how not to be criminalised. This involves the participation of widening circles of communities within the extending boundaries of the commons, the communal use of premises, the organisation of networks of social reproduction and so on. In many instances, wider community legitimacy of a commons is thus an acquired commonwealth that can, in sufficient degree, be used politically against state criminalisation of commons activities. Like any other elements of commonwealth, also, legitimacy is (re)produced through commoning.

We should not, however, see the issue of autonomy and self-reliance as something necessarily sited outside a given legal framework. This would be forcing the argument onto an ideological ground. To be for creating alternatives to the capital/state implies first of all mobilising commoners and commonwealth into commoning, and in many situations, this is possible only within existing laws as the power field at our disposal is still too limited. In other situations, we can safely reclaim a resource abandoned by capital/state – detritus of their failing loops – working to get the support of the surrounding community to gain strength and legitimacy. In other words, contexts and local conditions and commoners' shrewdness – and not a fixed idea of how to organise things – are the elements of a commons development.

In the case of disused buildings, for example, the alternative to squatting of pooling money collected through donations and fundraising so as to rent represents a strategic choice, a developmental trade-off between what many perceive as an ultimately impractical (unsustainable) radical ideological correctness and what others see as a 'selling out' for some degree of bourgeois stability with the aim of organising a free space whose inhabitants can have a relative peace of mind. In Italy, many old squats have become rented social centres. In Greece, a classic case is *nosotros* in the centre of Athens, whose legal status has allowed its members to open up the site for language courses for migrants and other support practices. In other words, the choice about how to take and hold the means to take things into one's hands, to do direct action on one's own life, involves contextualised options specified by the relation of forces on the ground, by tactical shrewdness and, especially, by strategic ambition. What is certain, however, is that regardless of the manner in which one gains and maintains access to the means for collective direct action, commoning autonomy requires the imagination of independence.

Indeed, commoning expresses a strive for autonomy and self-reliance that often contrasts with the depressed (oppressed) condition of alienation and *detritus* which communities live when coupled to capital's loops. The condition of *detritus* is constituted by the layers of waste inscribed in the body and in the environment and that emerge out of capital's loops. The waste inscribed in the body can be understood, for example, in terms of the energy – exhausting participation in disciplinary mechanisms of the markets, what in *Capital* Marx calls the expenditure of labour power, or the anxieties and insecurity lived while in unemployment and precarity. The waste inscribed in the natural environment is growing more evident in our polluted cites, in climate change, in the loss of biodiversity, in ocean acidification, all products of capitalist loops and capital's obsession with accumulation. In this sense, *detritus* is the common material condition (in different contexts and at different points within the wage hierarchy) in which the problematic of social reproduction is uniquely in the hands of waged and unwaged 'dispossessed' and their capacity to common. In other words, social reproduction dramatically depends on the effectiveness, organisational reach and communal constitution of struggles and the ability to reclaim and constitute commons in a condition of *detritus*, whether this is simply to reproduce labour power to be siphoned back into the circuits of capitals, or to *live* through autonomous practices of constitution beyond capital's value, that is, practices of commoning. This autonomy and self-reliance are actualised by a process that creates and revitalises communities, through some form of access to the means of production – whether through squatting, renting, pooling or redistribution – and the creation of material and social and psychic rewards, which feed back into the system in multivarious ways, including the human motivation to continue, to enter further into commoning relations, which in turn energises the recursive. The rewards are not just individualised payoffs in so far as they are important precisely in reducing people's dependence on both capitalist markets and increasingly blackmailing state benefits; commons also reward through their staying together and learning from one another, through the forming of affective links to replace the tenuous, formal or alienated connections that exist in the neo-liberal city always on the run.

There is in this autonomy also a first element with which to understand the relationship between commoning and the quality or state of being worthy of esteem and respect, or *dignity*. If esteem in the capitalist market is established with the outer symbols of conspicuous consumption as Veblen argued in 1899 (Veblen 1973) and under state tutelage through a formalised position in its apparatus, then in commoning it is established by the daily struggle to overcome *detritus* and to develop new sensitivities and mutual support. In the same way that biomass decomposition by millions of diverse biological and chemical iterations in ecosystems reproduces conditions of earth fertility and allows the production of new plants, so does commoning turn *detritus* into a social humus in which new ideas can flourish into new practices and bloom with new wealth.

Commoning as generative force of autopoiesis

Another aspect of autonomy is auto-production, or autopoiesis. Autonomy and autopoiesis are related but not the same, since autopoiesis is a particular aspect of autonomy, one that coincides with a higher degree of resilience (see Table 9.1), in which *not only the interactions among components of a system and its own rules are regenerated but also the components themselves*, namely, here, the commoners and the commonwealth. In autopoietic commons, therefore, not only are the *relations* among subjects and the metabolism between commoners and commonwealth (re)produced, but also *these components themselves*: the knowledge, the mind and the bodies of the commoner subjects, the material and the immaterial resources. In Varela's (1979: 13) words:

An autopoietic system is organized (defined as a unity) as a network of processes of production (transformation and destruction) of components that produces the components that:

1. through their interactions and transformations continuously regenerate and realise the network of processes (relations) that produced them; and

2. constitute it [the system] as a concrete unity in the space in which [the components] exist by specifying the topological domain of its realisation as such a network.

With the components of commons being commoner communities (relationships of subjects qua commoners) and commonwealth, commoning (re)produces the bodies and subjectivities as commoners and the wealth as common wealth. It does not matter whether some material aspects of the wealth come from outside the commons or if the subjects have a predominantly non-commoner subjectivity, so long as (and to the extent that) the recursion established by commoning recreates subjectivities and resources as components of the commons.

Here, an analogy with capitalist circuits is helpful. In a capitalist circuit, the sum of the exchange values of, on the one hand, the physical components of capital (raw materials, tools, and machines understood and valorised as capital) and, on the other, labour power (the capacity to work, sold for a wage), provides the whole capital invested (at the beginning of a capitalist circuit). Both of these elements have a price tag that makes it possible to measure their cost, in spite of the fact that they constitute quite different (categorically distinct) things. The final result is a new commodity, which, if sold on the market, would autopoietically reproduce the components of the capitalist system for the next round of capitalist production, that is capital (through amortisation and profit) and labour power (through wages).

In this example of the autopoiesis of capital, the system's components are not machines and labour power, but constant and variable capital, the value expression of those commodities. Also, they are capital only in so far as it is expected that their use will bring more value at the end of the labour process, a profit. Therefore, the process of accumulation reproduces these components as capital. Analogously, but through radically different measures, the autopoiesis of commons is obtained through commons circuits that reproduce the commons as a social system. After the pooling of commonwealth and the gathering of commoners who will at one point engage in commoning as determined by their collective engagement and internally generated values, autopoiesis of the commons involves the reproduction of the resources and subjects involved in the commoning as new commonwealth and commoners, agents of these commoning circuits.

The fact that some resources pooled as commonwealth do not have (are not measured as) a common monetary exchange value, simply because at no point have they been commodities, does not affect their useful character in the commoning process. For those resources that the commons have to buy on the market, it will be necessary to find a source of monetary income. However, the budget of the financial ins and outs only describes one part of the operations of the commons. For a household commons the selling of labour power and the buying of consumer goods are only one moment of the reproduction of the household – the other being the multifaceted labour of reproduction; likewise the larger-scale commons may still depend on some form of market exchange, but its set of practices are far from being exhausted by it. The commons have other goals than profit (even if some revenue may be one of their goals) and other measures than those impelled by capital's relative and absolute surplus value strategies. If the commons must trade commodities, this is generally done in order to buy other commodities that are necessary for the reproduction of the commons, or to give revenues to communities with which the commons holds solidarity links, not to accumulate. Exchange value is a measure that appears only in those commons that have to relate to the market, and even then it is routinely subordinated to other features that contribute to the measures of commons (the value expression), such as equity and sharing, solidarity and conviviality. Indeed, the fact that the financial resources utilised are pooled makes them also (reproduces them as) components within that commons. The health of a commons depends on an appropriate density and balance of all relational circuits, including mutual aid, solidarity and affective circuits.

This implies that autonomous systems – and the autopoietic as a part of them – change their state in response to external events and are realised and propagated only within the networks of processes that produce them and, therefore, through the value practices that these networks set in operation.

Going back to the commons circuit and the capital circuit

Both commons and capital in the formulas of Chapter 5 describe and schematise the basic moments of the process of systems' auto-reproduction, that of the commons system and that of capital's systems – that is, that of their *organisation*. In biology, the term 'organisation' is unambiguous; it 'signifies those relations that must be present in order for something to exist' as a member of a specific class (Maturana and Varela 1998: 42). For me to recognise something as a bicycle I have to recognise certain relations between the parts I call saddle, wheels, frame, pedals, handler, etc., in such a way that mobility is made possible with my leg's movement (i.e. the function of the bicycle actualised). It does not matter whether the tyres are tubeless or not, or whether the frame is made of heavy or light metal, or whether it has a shift gear, or whether it is white or black. All these latter features constitute the *structure* of a particular bike. The structure of any unity 'denotes the components and relations that actually constitute a particular unity and make its organisation real' (Maturana and Varela 1998: 42).

Thus, when I speak of commons and capital as social systems, I in the first place point to their unity, that is, their common character in relation to non-social systems, what distinguishes them from non-social systems (for example a psychic, a biological or a mechanical system). In this sense, both commons and capital involve processes of self-generation, which in turn involve people and expenditure of their life energies, and also involve communicative processes, the establishment of goals, and particular social relations. *Autopoietic organisation* is a term we use to indicate processes of systems regeneration. An autopoietic system reproduces the elements it consists of through these elements themselves and their operations. Social systems are *autopoietically closed* in the sense that while they use and rely on resources from their environment, those resources are only the substrata of the systems' *functional* operations. Although these resources are necessary, it is not these resources that generate the autopoietic operations of the social system, but every type of social system develops its own system-generated autopoietic operations. In the process of operating, they (re)produce the social relations and the social meanings of components through which they operate.[1] This fundamental view applies to the commons as to any other social system, although in different *modes*. We can thus recast the Marxian concept of *mode of production* in terms of the specific ways in which autopoiesis occurs and is structured.

Let me make an illustration. If I sell my labour power to a capitalist factory, office or educational establishment working on a laptop on some project, the computer becomes constant capital while I become, in Marx's term, variable capital, that part of capital that, together with constant capital such as machineries and raw material, contributes to the creation of exchange value, but that unlike other forms of capital has the ability to create a surplus value pocketed by the capitalist through labour. I am a temporary capitalised subject here, part of the autopoietic process of the capital system. If, however, on the way out I take that laptop (the company trusted me on that) and go into some self-organised community centre to write a leaflet denouncing work or contract conditions or environmental conditions in my neighbourhood, or even give it to my kids to play some videogames on, I turn that laptop in a material element of the commons as much as I am a commoner with a particular vector of values.

The key questions therefore are: what is the organisation that defines commons as a class of social system? And what is the organisation that defines capital as a class of social system?

Commons are social systems in which not only resources are shared and communities set rules for this sharing, but the goal of autopoiesis is the reproduction of these shared resources and communities. The commons (Cs) and its elements, an associated community (A) and common wealth (CW) occur both at the beginning and at the end of the formula given in Figure 5.4. All the same, in the money circuit of capital, money M occurs both at the beginning and at the end of the formula in Figure 5.2. This illustrates the fact that the commons and money are, respectively, an end in themselves in the two different systems, or, to put it in another way, they are autopoietically closed self-reproducing systems, systems that reproduce themselves through the renovation of their elements and the recasting of their relations. While in one case, commons are for commons' sake, in the other, the capital system's money is for money's sake.

An immediate conclusion about the specific autopoietic requirement of each system is that what we conventionally call 'economic growth' is only an indispensible requirement for the sustainability of capital systems, not of commons systems. Commons systems could reproduce themselves in a condition of what some environmentalist thinking has called 'de-growth' (Latouche 2009), that is where M' is less than (<) M in the capital's circuit, without at all undermining their expanded reproduction and improvement in the perceived quality of their processes. Thus, overall reduction of gross domestic product (GDP) could be compatible with (a) extension of C-M-C circuits, for example coinciding with relocalisation of commodity chains and a decline in the scale of productive activities (small workshops, local farmers' markets, etc.) and/or (b) extension of the realms of non-commodity exchanges, such as administrative or gift exchanges in Polanyi's tradition, or commons circuits. Indeed, both (a) and (b) can be and have been conceived as part of a virtuous hybrid. Take for example Community Supported Agriculture schemes, the schemes in which a group of consumers supports the income of farmers in exchange for products, bypassing multinational distributors. They involve both commodity exchanges (i.e. farmers selling their produce to consumers) and at the same time commoning between consumers and small farmers to negotiate the quality, quantity and price of farm produce, guaranteeing an income to farmers.

Boundaries

One important implication of this understanding of organisational closure of autopoietic systems is that systems change their state in response to external events and are realised and propagated only within the networks of processes that produce them and, therefore, through the value practices that these networks set in operation. In Chapter 2 we encountered the notion of a system as a unity between the system S and its own environment E, as S/E. To define commons and capital as autopoietic systems is in the first place to draw a distinction between them and their correspondent environments. In system theory, the distinction system/environment is crucial. From an observation point situated within the operating of each system, whatever is outside the system's autopoietic operations constitutes its environment. Each social system (integrative function systems such as the economy or politics, or organisations such as a household, a company, an association, etc.) has other social and ecological systems as its environment. This implies that what constitutes an 'environment' is always relative to the system, hence there is no single environment. Incidentally, this also means that sense and meaning are constituted within the relation between a 'system–environment unit': 'Thus my environment is the world as it exists and takes on meaning in relation to me, and in that sense it came into existence and undergoes development with me and around me.' (Ingold 2000: 20). It also implies that the boundary is constituted by this system–environment distinction.

System/environment

The distinction between an autopoietic system and its environment leads us inevitably to pose the question of a boundary. The system/environment (S/E) split is made the autopoietic system S and the environment E. The boundary '/' is part of S in the sense that it is constituted by its autopoietic operations as illustrated in Figure 7.1.

In Figure 7.1. boundaries are the result of social system internal operations, which, following Niklas Luhmann, divide it from a complex and chaotic exterior (for a more exhaustive discussion of complexity see Chapter 8). Boundaries thus allow for operations to take place within a workable scale by establishing some order which makes operations possible, by virtue of reducing the

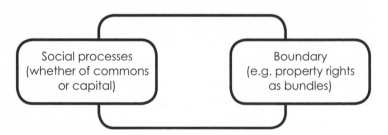

Figure 7.1 System's reproduction of its own boundaries

complexity of the domain within which operations take place. By complexity I thus mean, with Luhmann (1995: 24), 'a problem-oriented concept', that is, a strategic concept for the singular system that has to deal with it. Thus:

> when the number of elements that must be held together in a system or for a system as its environment increases, one very quickly encounters a threshold where it is no longer possible to relate every element to every other one. A definition of complexity follows from this: we will call an interconnected collection of elements 'complex' when, because of immanent constraints in the elements' connective capacity, it is no longer possible at any moment to connect every element with every other element.

Take for example water associations in Cochabamba, Bolivia. Here we have community associations established to deliver water services (including infrastructures) in conditions in which the state cannot deliver them and the market can deliver them at very expensive cost to households, and conditions of sanitation are very poor . Each water association is generally organised at neighbourhood level, its members doing the administrative, strategic and manual work necessary to build and maintain the infrastructure, as well as pooling funds to pay for equipment and material. Thus, water associations in Cochabamba have reached a threshold where, given their common wealth CW and the number of households a water association is comprised of (or association A), the association cannot deliver more water to more members. This is a threshold that is encountered regularly given the limited amount of material and financial resources and the increase in urban population. The associations thus have to select who is part of their membership (in terms of neighbour-hoods, and other criteria). Alternatively, they have to select ways to integrate the operation of different water associations to increase the scale of operation, by sharing equipment and expertise among the different associations and thus overcoming differentials in power fields. A water association can also put pressure on politicians in order to access resources present in its environment (resources, for example, that could be mobilised by the state). In all these cases, the associations give rise to second-order associations; that is, they create nested commons systems. Also, in all these cases, selection is the way to reduce complexity and make operations possible. The system–environment distinction is thus marked by three interrelated elements: first, the zone of reduced complexity as the interior of a system in which communication operates by selecting only a limited amount of all the information available outside; second, an outside of the system zone of greater complexity and out of the system's control; third, a boundary through which the system filters and selects.

At the most general level, both capital and commons have a twofold environment. Capital's first environment is the commons, that is, social systems that reproduce the various facets of life in non-commodified ways. In the commons, access to money is, at most, only a means through which needs are satisfied and not an end in itself, as it is for capital. When the purchased commodities exit the market sphere and enter the spheres of social cooperation (households, associations, networks, etc.), they often enter the complex, culturally and politically diverse and variegated sphere of the commons. It is here that the cultural and physical reproduction of labour power, the value-creating commodity so critically important for capital, occurs – outside the control of capital but, of course, strictly coupled to it. On the other hand, the commons' first environment is capital, that is, social systems that reproduce the various facets of life through capital's loops seeking accumulation.

The other system that both capital and commons depends on as their environment is the ecological system upon which all life and social organisation depends. The ecological crisis of natural ecosystems caused by capital in its endless quest for greater resource extraction and cost-shifting externalities (such as the free use of the atmosphere, land, and water as a waste dump) is a crisis that also threatens commons (re)production.

The reality that, first, as social systems commons and capital share an environment (ecosystem) and that, second, they are an environment to one another has important implications. The unit 'system plus environment' should 'denote not a comparison of two things, but one indivisible totality. That totality is, in effect, a development system ... and an ecology of life ... is one that would deal with the dynamics of such systems' (Ingold 2000: 19).

One final observation. Boundaries also exist in between commons, and for many reasons: because they are simply in different, not yet connected domains, or because they are alienated from one another, because they are indifferent to one another, because they are competing with one another, and because some of them attempt to free-ride the benefits of other commons, without joining in their governance (see Box 8).

Boundaries, commoning and abstract labour
Boundaries filter the relation between a system and its environment, but they do so through the internal operations of the

continued on page 250

Box 8 No free water if you free-ride

In 2006 I visited Orange Farm, a township near Johannesburg, South Africa, of an estimated 360,000 families (in the late 1980s there were 3,000 residents). I arrived in the midst of a movement against water (and electricity) privatisation (see Naidoo 2010 for a great account of the dynamic of the struggle against privatisation in Orange Farm). Privatisation was actually happening and the private company was trying to introducing pay meters for water distribution. I remember feeling the great strength of the movement, even though I never had a chance to witness any of the movement actions to prevent meters from being installed in people's houses, or to defend the neighbourhoods where people had taken out the meters. I only heard stories, and visited some houses – accompanied by activists of the APF, the Anti Privatisation Forum – to try understand the day-to-day reality of the water and electricity commons.

Those households who wanted their water meter removed could do so with the help of the movement's plumbers, who reconnected house after house to the mains pipes running under the middle of the street. This involve some digging and plumbing work. I visited the house of a woman who told me why she chose to join the movement of water reclamation. She said that the water bills had escalated, and that she certainly could not manage with the 'trickle', a washer the diameter of a water tap, with a very small hole in the middle. This was one of the things suggested by the water company to 'help' people to reduce their water consumption and 'manage' water. Inserted in the water tap, this device would substantially reduce the flow of water to a trickle. Imagine a household of twelve people depending on one tap in the yard fitted with a trickle. Anyway, the incredible thing that hit me was that in the middle of the conversation the woman went to her liberated-from-the-meter tap, put a chain around the tap and locked it. I asked her, 'What are you doing?' She replied that the evening was approaching and she needed to close the tap. 'But why do you need to do that? You do not need to pay for water.' She candidly replied to me that this was true, but there were neighbours who did not join the movement, and at night they would come to her yard to collect water. If they needed water because they could not pay, they should come to her and ask her and she would give it to them. Clearly she wanted them to face up the fact that they had not joined the movement. A boundary, a filtering mechanism, was here drawn vis-à-vis other household commons as part of the dynamic of movement building. Being in the movement has risks, and she faces those risks. A free-rider would not even have acknowledged that, and therefore would have avoided being accountable for her own choice of not participating in the movement.

Incidentally, there were several reasons why not all Orange Farm people joined the movement, which anyway was a massive movement. The one that struck a chord with me was the boundary, the division, running inside households between the older and the new generation. The former were loyal to the African National Congress (ANC), the party in government, which had led the struggle against apartheid and delivered the post-apartheid deal. The younger generation did not have such a loyalty, and reacted to the skyrocketing bills resulting from privatisation in the same way that their parents did when the apartheid regime tried to increase prices for utilities: with a riot. This was truly the sad contraposition inside families, and in many cases it was the head of the household who decided whether to accept the ANC meter or to join the water movement opposing meters.

system. Two things therefore follow. One, the typology of this boundary is not a given, but depends on the operational and relational processes that are constituted within the system. Second, the gatekeepers, that is, those in a position to enforce or monitor given boundaries, are part of the system and its internal operations. Putting into question given systems boundaries is therefore always putting into question both the internal operations of a system and the structure of given positionalities.

In commons the internal operations take the shape of commoning, while in capital they take the form of abstract labour. Both are forms of social labour, and involve forms of social communication and cooperation, but they differ in terms of the system's attitude towards the social form of expenditure of human energy. In capital, where profit dominates the horizon of systems' reproduction, social labour tends to become abstract, in the Marxian sense of 'human labour power expended without regard to the form of its expenditure' (Marx 1976: 128; for a discussion see De Angelis 1995). Here the subjects appear as components of systemic loops that lock them in with respect to the standard of measure of their life activity, what Marx calls socially necessary labour time (SNLT). SNLT is the measure of value emerging from an ongoing process of capitalist social production, pitting producers against one another, and turning them into the object of heteronymous market measures of doing things that they have to meet or beat. If this does not occur, they will pay the heavy penalty of losing means of livelihoods. This is another way of saying that the boundaries of a capitalist autopoietic system, defined by who is in and who is out (employment), who gets and does what (internal structural hierarchies), are continuously reproduced through abstract labour, through an endless rat race aimed at attracting resources from market circuits. Capital reproduces itself (i.e. accumulates) through abstract labour, and the people whose life activity is 'abstracted out' to produce profit and allow M-C-M' system reproduction, while also growing the *detritus* in our bodies and the natural environments we all have to face. Commoning is another matter. As an 'activity', commoning is in the first place a form of social labour, that is, a social activity that requires the exercise of mental or physical human effort and that requires some form of coordination, communication and cooperation. This of course was also the case for abstract labour. But the general character of this activity is different from abstract labour in the sense that (a) it establishes a degree of autonomy from capital and its measures and (b) it connects organically with the 'commonwealth', that is, with the pooled resources that need to be sustained and reproduced, and with the 'community'. It is ultimately human labour power expended *with* regard to the form of its expenditure, and *with* regard to goals and orientations defined by the community itself.

Autonomy from the capitalist market does not mean that the commons do not access the market, rather that the market, and the market in a particular form or on a particular scale, is contingent on a particular situation, ecology of commons, place, culture, social rules. Through commoning, the commons not only can develop new forms of social cooperation with other commons to meet new needs, or increase the non-commodity (NC) diversity of its resources (human and not), it can also establish new markets with rules that are alternative to capital's markets (such as participatory guarantees or some aspects of fair trade), and bring to the markets goods that fill an old need in new ways, with attention to environmental issues, producer pay, quality or minimisation of distance travelled of goods. Commoning also produces local supply chains to reduce the dependence of an area on capitalist commodities and revitalise a local economy. Commoning thus can organically articulate existing skills and resources over a territory, helping a depressed region to realise the wealth that resides hidden within it.

The organic aspect of commoning highlights a related aspect concerning the purpose of autonomy. In general, if there is one thing that characterises the 'organic' and distinguishes it from what it is not is the fact that it lives, that is, that cells, organs and organisms all strive to reproduce themselves, and they do so through ingenious and evolving forms of cooperation, feedback processes and relations among their elements. (Re)production – and (re)production through structural change of its elements – is therefore the basic aspect of what define the organic. An organic relation is a relation that allows the (re)production, sustainability and development of an organic form. In a commons system, commoning is the social activity that (re)produces, sustains and develop the commons social system. But it does not (re)produce it in a vacuum, rather within fields of power relations that influence its structure both from within and from the outside of a commons system.

Boundaries and property rights

Many commoners begin their commons journey by pooling resources through a variety of means, including accessing some land or a building. Inevitably, implicitly or explicitly, they are confronted with the issue of who legally owns that property, indeed it is the first main boundary they face in their common adventure.

According to the classic definition of old institutional-ism, property rights are enforceable authorities to undertake particular actions in a specific domain (Commons 1968). For our purpose here, it is not relevant how these authorities are enforceable, whether through the state or through a system of sanctions embedded within social customs. In either case, property rights define some actions that individuals or insti-tutions can take in relation to other individuals or institutions regarding some 'thing' and within a definitive scale of social action. If one individual or institution has a right to an action, some other individuals or institutions have a duty to observe that right, to let it happen (Ostrom 2000). But if property rights define authorities for a range of possible actions, then it is not very useful to understand the right of alienation as the only relevant action defining them. Indeed, Schlager and Ostrom (1992) identify a bundle of five property rights, which comprise: access, withdrawal, management, exclusion, and alienation. Property rights as a bundle of rights to pursue certain actions, that is, a bundle of socially protected powers to, have a broad application. Table 7.1 summarises the bundle of five rights in relation to 'things' as reported by Schlager and Ostrom in rela-tion to particular social positions.

Once decomposed into different elements, the property rights shown in the first column of Table 7.1 can be assigned in different packages to give rise to specific positions. For example, they can be assigned to different individuals so as to construct different social positions in relation to particular resources; or they can be attributed to individuals or collectives. In the last case, is there a particular combination of rights that is necessary to define a commons?

Table 7.1 Property rights as a bundle of rights

		Owner	Proprietor	Claimant	Authorised user	Authorised entrant
Access	The right to enter a defined physical area and enjoy nonsubtractive benefits	X	X	X	X	X
Withdrawal	The right to obtain resource units or products of a resource system	X	X	X	X	
Management	The right to regulate internal use patterns and transform the resource by making improvements	X	X	X		
Exclusion	The right to determine who will have access rights and withdrawal rights, and how those rights may be transferred.	X	X			
Alienation	The right to sell or lease management and exclusion rights	X				

Note: My elaboration from Schlager and Ostrom (1992), Ostrom (2000).

The two interrelated elements in Figure 7.1, that is, the relation between the dynamism of the system and its boundary, point at an answer. If boundaries of a system (i.e. practices that filter access and withdrawal rights) are constituted through the peculiar dynamism of the system (i.e. the regulation of internal use patterns and transformation of resources) then a commons is obtained when its members (community) have the rights to exclude (and not exclude) and the rights to manage. These two rights are the rights that commons systems in particular must have at a minimum in order to exist. Thus, for example, Ostrom argues that:

> Groups of individuals are considered to share communal property rights when they have formed an organisation that exercises at least the collective-choice rights of management and exclusion in relationship to some defined resource system and the resource units produced by that system. In other words, all communal groups have established some means of governing themselves in relationship to a resource. (Ostrom 1990, 2000: 342)

A collective-choice right is the right to set collective-choice rules. These in turn 'affect operational activities and results through their effects in determining who is eligible to be a participant and the specific rules to be used in changing operational rules. These change at a much slower pace' than, say, everyday operational rules (Ostrom 2005: 58).

For this reason, for example, a capitalist factory or a university as a whole is not a commons, to the extent that 'management' asserts for itself the 'right to manage' to the exclusion of workers (and even outer layers of user communities such as customers, students, etc). On the other hand, the same factory is a social space in which commons systems reproduce along a vertical hierarchy and often clash: management commons, workers' commons, blue-collar commons, white-collar commons, students' commons, and so on. To challenge managers' right to manage, in these terms, would be at the same time to challenge the rights of exclusion from management decisions, that is, to reformulate the domain of management commons. Only when the plurality of users of a university (or a subplurality in limited spaces) obtain and exercise the right to manage and redefine boundaries, can we say it is actually a commons. When this is not the case, to claim a resource (or an institution) as a commons helps to define the journey that is necessary to undertake to actually turn it into one.

Along a parallel example, workers' co-ops that give themselves the right to manage through representatives that can be recalled at any time are commons, since the collective choice right is in the hands of all the workers. However, if these co-ops are engaged in cut-throat competition with other companies (whether co-ops or not) in a market system, their survival increasingly depends on adapting to productive norms and practices outside their control, and therefore the source of their dynamism becomes closer to self-exploited abstract labour than to commoning.

In most complex situations where common wealth is not formally and legally owned by the commoners, commons thus develop qua commons with the development of (a) the democratisation of collective choice rights and (b) the autonomy of communities to set their own 'measures' as the basis of their dynamism, i.e. commoning. Commoning in turn redefines boundaries.

The relation between property and boundaries is all-pervasive in human relations, and for this reason we should not conflate property with 'private property', which is dominant in capitalist relations. Property boundaries are in the first place the social membrane that surrounds a social system. In biology, one of a cell membrane's main functions is to be selectively permeable, to operate, in other words, as a filtering mechanism for flows entering and exiting the organism. In this way, the membrane allows in specific substances and keeps out others. In social systems the same occurs. Instead of using a lipid structure as in biological cells, social systems' membranes are composed of aggregates of individuals making decisions in forms and organisations that are historically and culturally determined – what are generally called institutions. For example, contemporary socio-economic membranes of a company are composed by job interview panels, protocols and procedures for hiring and firing, sales and purchase departments following particular policies, security guards, and civil and criminal laws backed by the state apparatus. Within these aggregates, there is of course the possibility that the selectivity criteria are also constituted by phenomena such as corruption, racism, prejudices, sexism and so on. Households have different criteria of entry and exits, but in general they rely on a mixture of political-economic, legal, symbolic and emotional-affective circuits (marriage/divorce, kinship, friendships and so on). Some cooperatives and associations depend on different criteria for membership. Entries in other forms of human associations simply depend on 'getting involved' without any other criteria (volunteering in a community association, for example). In others, filtering mechanisms of the property boundary require you to share an interest (club), a skill (profession), a political affinity (political organisation), a religious faith (churches) and so on.

The property boundary is not necessarily a fixed thing, although at a given moment it is a given. Yet this 'given' character always has some degree of fuzziness, due to the fact that any social system participates in metabolic flows with others and the singularities carrying the social metabolic messages around may well participate in the lives of several social organisms. Fuzziness seems also to be the property of the boundaries in the exchange among all biological organisms. An analogy is the boundary between a human being and its environment – which is experienced through the skin. Is the air we breathe through our lungs and through our pores still part of the outside world, or is it already our own? If we eat food and digest it, where is the boundary between the human being and its environment? Where is the source of my thought? Is it my brain, is it my nervous system or is it the stimuli that I receive while conversing with you? The fuzziness of property boundaries in an interconnected world allows commoners to make and remake sense, and observe the world with new eyes, by even melting into the air what seems fixed and realistic, and reconfiguring it as part of a commons system.

Production of boundaries through meaning and sense: measure

As I have argued following Luhmann, a system is defined by a boundary between itself and its environment, dividing it from an infinitely complex and chaotic exterior. It follows that the interior of the system is a zone of reduced complexity. In other words:

> [s]ystems lack the 'requisite variety' [Ashby's term (cf. chapter 10)] that would enable them to react to every state of the environment, that is to say, to establish an environment exactly suited to the system. There is ... no point-for-point correspondence between system and environment (such a condition would abolish the difference between system and environment). This is why establishing and maintaining this difference despite a difference in degree of their relative complexities becomes the problem. The system's inferiority in complexity must be counter-balanced by strategies of selection. (Luhmann 1995: 25)

Thus in social systems, this lower complexity of the system in relation to the complexity of the environment encourages the system to process meaning and sense that enable the selection of information and social organisational order relevant to the autopoiesis of the system within the environment.

Social autopoietic systems like commons and capital are founded on specific communication patterns. The operations of communication in turn depend on situated observers. When communication is orderly, it manifests itself in sequences or patterns of communicational events, which emerge from what Luhmann calls 'double contingency'. Double contingency means that the selection in communication is contingent upon two sides. In this way, communication can be established as the unity of announcement, information and understanding. Communication that is not mutually understood will not go on. For example, within a simple educational relation, such as teaching a class, it is understood by the class that by entering the room and switching on its PowerPoint machine, the teacher announces that she is ready to teach. Also, what is on the screen visibly informs the students of the theme of the lecture. In the operation of this communicational event, the class begins to set its boundary which distinguishes it from its environment and to set its internal order.

But this is an order that depends on a shared sense among teachers and students within that communication event, however that shared sense is brought about. Imagine, however, that one day students enter into the class with a different sense than the one allowing educational routines, say when they intend to occupy it and establish a teach-in instead. In this case, a subversion of roles is established: now it is the students who announce their intention with banners and by walking in, and inform the teacher of the new situation. A different boundary corresponding with a different order is then set in place, as when the class registers are in all practice declared void and open participation in the teach-in is encouraged. It goes without saying that both these opposite forms of communication also imply different forms of social labour.

An economic transaction is also a distinct communication event that creates its boundary. Selling is only possible when the seller can expect the buyer to pay her money, and when the buyer in turn can expect that the seller understands she has to deliver the goods. It also requires that the buyer understands the price announcement by the seller and informs her of her intention to pay. The communication event established by the economic transactions creates its boundary, its distinction from non-economic communication. Imagine for example that a group of precarious workers now enter the supermarket with banners and megaphones and announce their intention to practise price self-reduction, to inform the seller of their intention to pay less than she requires, so that she will understand that she has lost control over the right of alienability of her commodity at her own decided price (Arie 2014). Obviously, we are no longer in the realm of economic communications here, although indeed, commodities pass hands, and a price is announced. It goes without saying, also, that if she calls the police, their arrival may announce that the demonstration is no longer tolerated, and inform the demonstrators of the deadline by which they have to leave the premises or else (and the police will make sure the demonstrators understand the consequence of the 'else'). Also in these cases it is clear that all these different forms of communication imply different forms of social labour.

Boundaries and sense are therefore two sides of the same coin. Communication events, oriented by shared sense, create boundaries. Repeated communication events develop into patterns and create systems we call institutions. When the sense is not shared, other communication events, other boundaries and other social systems have the opportunity to be set in place in the interplay of different or conflicting senses. Sense is the medium shared by both psychic and social systems. It 'is the "sand" into which each concrete thought or communication imprints a specific footprint' (Moeller 2006: 225–6). And 'Since the making of sense is always a construction by a system, it can also be defined as a selection within the horizon of what is possible' (ibid.). Sense provides an orientation plane, a measure between the actual and the possible. Luhmann uses the example of a ship, which through its movements uses the horizon for orientation.

The direction chosen by the ship (the actual), is just one selection within a range of the possible provided by the horizons. I refer to this sense thorough the book as *sense horizon*. I must underline that the direction chosen by the ship (the actual), is just one selection within a range of possible selections. Here we find the source of potential epistemic decoupling among social systems. If two systems do not share the same horizons, and capital and commons do not, any selection of what is possible by both systems may, or may not, coincide at any given time, but a bifurcation will occur at some point.

Part four

Social change

Chapter 8

Boundary commoning

Political recomposition and social revolution

The commons initiated and (re)produced by commoning are a necessary but insufficient condition for overcoming capital's hegemony as a mode of production and the existing socio-economic divisions generated by capitalist processes and statist orderings and selections. They are necessary, in that the production of new systems of life and production requires the development of social systems such as commons that exercise their autonomy and autopoiesis vis-à-vis capital and the state, that is, by positing their different measures, values and senses of things in praxis, by engaging in the construction of another common sense and another material life, by experimenting and establishing new sustainable, socially just practices in a convivial and participatory atmosphere. This parallels Marx's idea that social rather than political revolution is a primary condition for overcoming the capitalist mode of production and its state apparatus and opens the way to identify three 'fallacies' in the construction of radical discourse for another world, the fallacy of the political, the fallacy of the model, and finally the fallacy of the subject (De Angelis 2014a).

The fallacy of the political is the idea that a political recomposition could generate and sustain, through any sort of political representation, a radical change in social relations and systems

continued on page 268

Box 9 School trespassing and temporary boundary commoning

Just imagine any school in Europe during breaktime (any schools, that is, that still have some breaks): the kids pouring into the yard and playing with that typical noise of a crowd of children running loose. Just imagine some strange kids wanting to enter from outside, together with a couple of adults … what is the chance that these outside kids – and the adults – are let in to play? I guess the chance is higher that school 'security' calls the police, and the police arrive accompanied by social services to check on the parents' behaviour.

One day in March 2010, my 2-year-old son was banging his head against the closed gates of the school complex in Misahualli, in the Napo region of the Amazon forest during breaktime. He loved playing ball and he saw quite a few balls on the other side of the gate, as well as kids from 5 to about 14 screaming, running and having fun. His 6-year-old brother was a bit more cautious, but clearly would also have loved to share some fun time with the kids on the other side. My partner and I instead were boringly hushing him away from the gate, telling him the 'right thing' : no, come away, love, they are at school, we cannot enter, and all the sweet bla bla to transmit to him the no trespassing' rules that we are accustomed to. One day only a couple of months before, our 6-year-old could not play with his own schoolmates because he had missed school in the morning, and this was sufficient to make him an outcast during playtime in the afternoon! So, while we were talking and our 2-year-old kept banging his head, a young woman approached the other side of the gate, undid the chain, and opened the gate. Unlike us, our 2-year-old did not hesitate and ran in. We looked at the woman and asked with some wonder, 'Can we get in?' 'Claro que si,' she said.

On what authority could the woman open the gate for us? She was nothing less than one of the two woman traders who get into the school for half an hour each day during recreation (breaktime), selling candies and ice creams.

But her action was tacitly endorsed by a caretaker who greeted us as though nothing had happened, and by a couple of teachers walking about the yard who nodded with a smile to acknowledge our presence. We wandered around the large yard during the remainder of the breaktime, the kids playing basketball and handball, and running up and down the slides.

Our 2-year-old was a bit puzzled when the couple of hundred kids around him started to disappear after the bell rang, and he kept running after the last kids until the end. When all had disappeared, he turned the corner to find that an older boy was still hiding away playing basketball ... we all joined in for a while, until he felt he really had to go and run towards his class.

Boundary rules are rules that filter access to commons, that define the porosity of boundaries and therefore the type of relation with the outside world. Without some type of boundary rules, there would be no commons, because commons are not open access but involve some community working out, governing and defining the rules of access (see Chapter 7). In the nature of these rules as it is revealed when they are implemented, the community shows what type of commons it has built, or, which is pretty much the same thing, what types of human beings they are in relation to 'the other'. This little episode illustrates how a gateless school where anybody from outside could get in and out is not necessarily the answer to a closed school where nobody from the outside could get in and out. The answer is the power to open the gate exercised by people of the community, the power of individual judgement (the woman who opened the gate) and the power of collective control (the caretaker and the teachers observing and, in this case, agreeing with the action). This shared power is really what ultimately enhances our sense of security without at the same time undermining our common sense.

of social reproduction. My stand is that political recomposi-
tions – that is, social movements across a diversity of actors – are
certainly necessary to create momentum for change by initiating
chain reactions of sociality and channelling social energies into
particular objectives and directions with efficient thrust. In this
sense, phases of political recomposition and the corresponding forms of political representation are important for opening
up opportunities for the radical development of new social
relations and systems. In themselves, however, they do not radically change social systems such as capital into something else:
they can only perturb them. Capital reacts and adapts to these
perturbations by developing new forms, absorbing, enclosing,
channelling, redividing within the wage hierarchy, co-opting
and repressing, and the mix of these will depend on the cost
and benefit calculus in given situations. Keynesianism and the
welfare state as developed in the period after World War Two
(De Angelis 2000) is a case in point.

The fallacy of the political involves, therefore, a conception of radical change, of 'revolution', that is aligned to Marx's
conception of social revolution (rather than to Lenin's of political revolution). In the first place, a social revolution is not the
'seizure of power' engineered and led by a political elite (whether
through reformist or political revolutionary means) (Holloway
2002), but the actual production of another form of power, which
therefore corresponds to the 'dissolution' of the old society and
of the old 'condition of existence' (Marx and Engels 2005: 19) or
a change in the 'economic structure of society' that is constituted
by 'the totality of the [social] relations of production' (Marx
1977). Secondly, precisely for its characteristics of being constituent of new social relations reproducing life (and dissolving old

relations), social revolution cannot be reduced to a momentary event, a 'victory', but instead it is epochal and configured by a series of 'victories' and 'defeats'. Marx thus speaks of the 'beginning' of the 'epoch of social revolution' (Marx 1977). How long this epoch is, none can say (although climate change and the massive crisis of social reproduction are putting some constraints and urgencies on the horizons). This distinction between social and political revolution does not imply that social revolution is not itself 'political'. Social revolution is political in the sense that it acts as a crucial perturbation of established dominant systems and poses the socio-economic basis for a new polity, for new forms of governments of networks of social cooperation.

This priority of social (rather than political) revolution also implies that to bring about radical transformation we do not need to have a worked system to replace the old one before dreaming of or wishing its demise. Quite the contrary, and indeed, we have here the second fallacy that I think underpins discourses on radical social change.

The fallacy of the model is the widespread idea that in order to replace the current system (model), another system (model) needs to be ready to take its place. Unfortunately, this is not the way history works, or systems, any systems. Alternative systems can certainly be imagined and problematised, but it is not through their 'implementation' that the development history of the modes of production occurs. Systems are not implemented, their dominance emerges; and their emergence occurs through the related processes of social revolution and political revolutions, with the former creating the source from which the latter get their power to perturb capital while at the same time developing their autonomy. This is the way, for example, in which the dominance of capital has developed from the phase of commercial capital to industrial capital, and today to the hegemony of finance capital, an evolution that was unimaginable at the time of the mercantilists or Adam Smith's writings.

The process of social revolution is ultimately a process of finding solutions to the problems that capital systems cannot solve, because it has created them, and the rest of us have an urgent need to address them: social justice, a dignified life for all, climate change, environmental disaster. This implies the establishment of multi-scalar systems of social action that reproduce life in modes, systemic processes, social relations and value practices that seek an alternative path from the dominant ones and that are able to reproduce at greater scale through networking and coordination. What has become increasingly clear from the various movements in the recent decades, from the Zapatistas in the mid 1990s to the Occupy movement in 2011, is that whatever the alternative put forward by an idiosyncratic section of the movement – whether micro or macro, whether participatory budgets, reconfiguration of social spending by the central state, transition towns, renewable energy cooperatives, self-managed factories, non-criminalised cyber-activism, defence of traditional communities along a riverbed threatened by enclosures, general assemblies, self-managed public squares and so on – they all depended on some form of commons, that is social systems at different scales of action within which resources are shared, and in which a community defines the terms of the sharing, often through forms of horizontal social relations founded on participatory and inclusive democracy. These two elements of commons emerge through concrete life practices developed on the ground, their systems of values utterly distinct from the value practices of capital – concrete life practices that develop and reproduce the social power necessary to sustain and give forms to the commons system. This social labour and corresponding forms of cooperation located within commons that (re)produce them is what we call 'commoning'.

The relation between social and political revolution is thus the relation between the social systems that underpin them, that is, commons and movements, and I suggest we should take Marx's warning about radical transformation beyond capitalism seriously, when he says in the *Grundrisse* that if we do not find concealed in society as it is the material conditions of production and the corresponding relations prerequisite for a classless society, then all attempts to explode it would be quixotic (Marx 1973: 158).

Commons are those concealed, latent material conditions in which a classless society can be given form. But to modern cosmopolitan urban subjectivities, many contemporary urban or rural commons often seem messy, disempowering, claustrophobic, patriarchic, xenophobic and racist. These are obviously not the commons we want for an emancipatory perspective, and the strategic intelligence we need to develop should really learn to deal with the resistances and struggles against all these which are located in any commons.

It would be dishonest and dangerous, however, to select these out of our theoretical radar just because these are not desirable characteristics of the commons we want. The more our 'postmodern' condition facilitates subjective nomadism (to escape relationships, jobs, places to live, group identities) and communication, the greater are the opportunities to escape the entrapment of these reactionary commons. People do this all the time. However, although nomadism, like communications allow subjectivities to change their situations, it does not necessarily change the social systems through which subjectivities are articulated and it does not prevent the re-emergence of these reactionary traits in new social systems. So, for example, in many parts of Africa, women are escaping the commons while demanding land reforms to change communal practices embedded in customary laws that have often discriminated against them, with respect to land inheritance and even land use. In these commons only men have control over land, and land rights are required for empowerment and for providing livelihoods for their children. The risk however is that 'this movement can be used to justify the kind of land reform that the World Bank is promoting, which replaces land redistribution with land titling and legalization' – unless, of course, the demise and/failure of a patriarchal form of commons is met with 'the construction of fully egalitarian commons, learning from the example of the organisations that have taken this path, like Via Campesina, the Landless Movement in Brazil, the Zapatistas' (Federici 2011: 49). Reactionary traits, however, can easily resurface even in 'politically correct' commons as soon as commoners seek shortcuts to decide questions of system boundaries (who is part of the commons?), of the division of labour or of distribution of payments, or have to deal with the perceived free-riding of one group of commoners, and so on.

The solutions that commons can offer to tackle problems depend obviously on particular situations, on the specific cultural mix of existing communities, for example, and on the particular resources available for pooling. However, in a situation in which capital and commons are both pervasive systems that organise the social, it is clear that often a solution will imply a particular deal between these two, that is, a particular form of their structural coupling. If together with others I set up workers' cooperatives to sell commodities on the market in order to provide a form of income to a community, and I ground this on horizontal participation and self-management, I still have to meet particular standards, use money, enter particular institutions that are given to me. Also, I have to engage with the problematic of profitability (of competitiveness, of efficiency, of cost minimisation and so on), a problematic that frames my competing commons (co-op) also as an individual capital system articulated to others via the market, and this in spite of the social objectives and value practices of the co-op. Any contemporary institution located within broader fields of social relations, therefore, is the realm in which structural coupling between very different social systems (commons and capital) present themselves in particular forms. Is the recognition of 'deals' with capital a step towards selling out? One could argue that, in fact, from the perspective of true radical transformation beyond capitalism, the problem is the deal, because the function of every deal for capital is to allow its reproduction as a social system. While formally true (deals do allow the reproduction of capital), this position fails to recognise that social reproduction (in households, communities, or in 'services' such as care, health and education) is to a large extent at given times also coupled to the reproduction of the capitalist social system. This means that deals with capital also make it possible to reproduce life in given circumstances. Therefore, for the commons understood as a social force of transformation, whatever deal we are able to cut in particular phases of movements is never enough because it excludes something or someone from benefiting from it, thus it contributes to the reproduction of hierarchies and hence it is the basis for the need for new phases of perturbation (struggle) and it is the basis upon which capital will develop new forms. The strategic horizon therefore is not to avoid making deals, but how to make a given deal the basis upon which commons can develop new forms and try to outflank capital by including the issues and the people who have been excluded by it.

However, this advancement of commons implies sooner or later a collision with other social systems governing them. And it is also clear that the force that alternative systems can sustain in this collision course with other social systems (their system's resilience) is proportional to the degree of the multiple social powers they are able to mobilise. By a social system's resilience I mean the ability of a social system to retain function and a sufficient degree of prosperity, reproducibility and social cohesion in the face of the perturbation caused by the shocks and crises of outside systems such as the ecological, state and capital systems. These shocks and crises (such as the loss of income caused, for example, by unemployment and economic crisis, or state victimisation criminalising particular struggles) have put to test commons' resilience, forcing commons to adapt and evolve. The path of this adaptation however is open, and it can lead to a greater domestication of the commons within capital's loops (like for example the patriarchal nuclear family in the period after the Second World War) or, on the contrary, the development of the autonomy and resilience of the commons in spite of capital's circuits (for example the experience of occupied social centres or the universe of grassroots voluntary associations socialising different aspects of reproduction).

My approach here seems at odds with the narrative of classic post-Marx Marxism. According to this a class, the proletariat, is the social force that brings capitalism to its knees and, through a revolution, will abolish the capitalist system and replace it with a new one, socialism, in which the state will direct economic activities and regulate the market. This situation will then progress to full-blown communism, in which Marx's dictum will prevail: to each according to their needs and from each according to their abilities. In this classical narrative, the proletariat revolts against the rhythm of life and work, the threat of pauperism and the exploitation of the bosses. Aside from the fact that the proletariat is actually a far larger class than just the employed industrial workers, the core of the matter for us here is that what was imagined in this old narrative is that a revolutionary class will bring about a postcapitalist scenario: as if a political revolution is sufficient for bringing about a new mode of production, a new ecology of social systems. This was actually acknowledged by the post-Marx Marxist narrative. As revolution was directed against old elites, they assumed that if it was successful, new elites could take their place and socialism could be proclaimed. From all this the revolutionary workers would thus have some advantage in some aspects of social reproduction, but ultimately the elite would define the road through 'socialism' into 'communism', and the old rebels would go back to work under the old discipline with 'socialist spirit'.

My conception is different and intersects with many traditions such as council communism, autonomism, eco-feminism and others who emphasise bottom-up dynamics. It is only when a class of social subjects emerges out of a new mode of production that they helped to shape, sustain and develop that there emerges a new social force to contrast with capital and the state, to deeply transform them, even to commonise them and abolish their worst aspects. Thus the *class for itself* that Marx contrasts with the class *in itself* defined by capitalist exploitation, is the class of struggling *commoners*, the new subjectivity empowered by the new ecology of social systems they have set in place and intertwined: the commons. This conception obviously implies that for a historically defined period, both commons and capital/state cohabit the social space, their struggles and relative powers giving shape to it, with the result that unevenness and contradictions are many, as well as strategic games to colonise the other's space with one's own values and decolonise one's own space from the other's values. The struggle is therefore continuous.

My underpinning hypothesis thus is that a social force like the commons only emerges, expands and create effective transformative powers vis-à-vis other social forces such as capital and the state as a manifestation of its own powers, and this only to the extent necessary for its preservation and reproduction (and the preservation and physical/cultural/emotional reproduction of the commoners comprising it). In order to problematise social change, therefore, we need to problematise social forces, and to do so implies that we understand social systems, in particular commons.

The development of capitalist commons

The transformative journey that commons have in front of them as a social force shares some features with the journey capital undertook in the centuries of its expansion. The development of capital occurred through a twofold terrain of the positing of new methods to organise social cooperation under its own value practices, and the struggle against other modes of production and their measures and value practices. In the first case, for example, the imposition of capitalist measures in the factories (as local rules) offered temporary 'solutions' to the masses of the poor and the dispossessed created by previous iterations of enclosures. It also developed on the terrain of struggles against alternative value practices, alternative ways to coordinate social reproduction, whether these alternative ways were the methods of the old (feudal) ruling class, or whether they were the self-organised methods of the communities they enclosed and destroyed, or whether they were the emergent patterns of mutual aid and solidarity inside the factories and working-class communities fighting for a shorter working week, increased wages and labour rights. The key here is that *capital developed through struggle*, accommodation, alliances, strategic timing pursued by a variety of elements, movements and organisations of the bourgeoisie.

In the various phases of world capitalist development in the last five hundred years, power blocs have modified their government of stratified power relations and class conflict in order to reabsorb this conflict and turn it into the mechanism of accumulation and therefore of development of its form. The struggle against other modes of production and of organising senses did use intellectual tools to help rationalise and prefigure the workings of the desired system, but these tools never ended up predicting the forms actually developed. So, for example, the world capitalism we live in today would have been unintelligible to Adam Smith. (Yet Smith's metaphor of the 'invisible hand' of the market – the idea that competing capitals with no interference from the state will in the end provide for the common good

– is still today, in spite of the oligopolistic powers of modern transnational corporations, an evocative image, one that can still inspire and give confidence to the planners of market expansion and privatisation in spite of all experience.)

Likewise, analysis of the continuous character of enclosures opens the door to its mirror image: the continuous character of the commons, their construction in a variety of ways, depended on different subjectivities and situated realities. Indeed, new forms of capital enclosures often correspond to capital's attempt to close down previously achieved forms of commons (however inadequate, bureaucratic and instrumental to capital accumulation we may have regarded them, such as the 'welfare state').

The fallacy of the model thus leaves us with the problematic of the development of alternatives as latency, as a period between the presence of alternatives and their explosion as dominant forms or modes of production. But this explosion of alternatives up to the point of constituting a hegemonic social fabric of production is not possible if these latent alternatives fail to overcome existing divisions within the social body, within the working class, corresponding to the middle-class hegemonic sense of what constitutes 'betterment' and therefore constituting 'social order' along a wage hierarchy (De Angelis 2010). It is not only capital's systemic forces that create divisions of power: the deals we cut with capital reproduce or reorganise divisions. A world in which these divisions are overcome is part of the puzzling equation that needs to be solved in order to address our question, 'how do we change the world?'

These divisions cannot be overcome through an ideological appeal to unity – as often these divisions are based on material conditions, and ideologies do not constitute grounds for hegemonic unity. To the extent that the crisis intensifies and proletarises conditions and prospects, it creates the conditions for the flourishing of reproduction commons, domains of social action in which communities of all types, religious creeds, national or ethnical groupings and political persuasions pool or seize resources together and develop ways to increasingly meet their needs articulating and waiving their differences in common projects.

According to systems theory, diversity within systems is what allows them to increase their resilience and adaptability to new conditions. Diversity of strands of wheat seeded in the same place allows greater long-term adaptation to the environment, and thus greater resilience. It goes without saying that this is not automatic, as the crisis also pushes for divisions. The avoidance of this depends on organisational resources put on the ground. In many countries of the Global North, it depends on the ability of radicals, cosmopolitan commoners, to mesh with the 'mainstream' and sustain productive interactions that give rise to reproduction commons and advance value practices that push open the boundaries of commons.

To develop such an attitude for strategic problematising requires, however, that we come to terms with the fallacy of the subject: the idea that somehow the 'working class' can be thought of as a unified body vis-à-vis capital, or, if divided, could be recomposed through some sort of ideological terrain or some other cultural or income homogeneity or representational affinity. Instead, I want to pose its existing division – both objective and subjective – as a founding condition of the real, and problematise it in terms of the radical transformation of the present. In another place (De Angelis 2010) I have problematised power hierarchies within the social body in terms of the 'middle class', which I define not as a homogeneous social group, with a given level of income, but as a stratified field of subjectivity disciplined to a large degree to the norms of behaviour of a modern society in which capital has a fundamental role in organising social production through disciplinary markets, enclosures, governance and its profit-seeking enterprises. In other words, 'middle-classness' is constituted through an idea of betterment and order achieved within the boundaries of capitalist system. I claim that from the point of view of radical transformation, one basic conundrum is that alternatives cannot be achieved either with, or without the middle class. It is for this reason that I proposed the thesis of the 'explosion of the middle class' as a necessary element of this process of radical transformation. I understand this explosion as a sudden increase in the volume of social cooperation and a corresponding release of playful energies, in such a way as to create a socio-cultural shock wave corresponding to the emergence of commoning across systems boundaries, national borders and through the wage hierarchy. This is a commoning through which boundaries, borders and the wage hierarchy are problematised and dissipated as result of social cooperation and a common platform of struggles. In so far as the latter is concerned, much inspiration comes from the working-class struggles that demand equal wage increases for all strata of the working class, so that the lower strata get a greater percentage increase in their income than the higher strata. This was the case in the struggles of the late 1960s and early 1970s in Italy, which united blue- and white-collar demands. Today, the battle for a basic income would serve this purpose, but could only be successful if accompanied by a large movement of commons that begins to communalise some of the social services functions of the state and explores and develops new forms of reproduction commons.

The stuff of explosion: multiplication, interweaving and tipping point

How could be such a fundamentally self-referential system as the commons be at the basis of social revolution?

When I talk about social revolution I am talking about an explosion and multiplication of new creative energies, energies that design and implement new commons systems, systems that are based on and further encourage alternative values and that orient towards corresponding values of social justice, environmental sustainability and a new economic paradigm, and provide the basis for waging new and more powerful struggles vis-à-vis capital and the state. But several things are missing between individual commons autopoiesis and this big revolutionary scenario. The first of these is a principle of multiplication of existing commons, what in biology is called reproduction. Second is a principle of coming together and interlacing of the different commons so as to leverage social powers and constitute ecology and scale. Third is a principle of dynamic evolution, which includes the notion of adaptation and least-resistance path for a large number of commons, a *class of commons*.

Let us examine these in turn.

Multiplication

The word *reproduction* has many different meanings depending on the areas in which its meanings are constructed. A first meaning has a macro dimension and is referred to as *social reproduction*, the capacity for the entire social system to recreate the conditions of its existence and production.

Another meaning of *reproduction* was emphasised by Marxist feminists in the 1970s and it is applied specifically to the reproduction of labour power (Dalla Costa and James 1975; Federici 2012). Reproduction thus is a kind of work, reproduction labour, that regenerates the physical and emotional capacities to work (i.e. labour power) so that the waged workers can be physically and emotionally fit to go to work the following day. The same can be applied to the relations between reproduction labour and schools (where students are reproduced at home) or care of the sick (Cleaver 1979). Ultimately it is biopower, 'an explosion of numerous and diverse techniques for achieving the subjugation of bodies and the control of populations' (Foucault 1976: 140).

As a result of feminist struggles and the entry of many women onto the labour market, this reproduction labour has undergone a big transformation in many parts of the world, especially in the Global North. Given also the intensification of work and relative declines in wages, the wages of two working parents is becoming necessary to ensure the reproduction of labour power, and many of the classical functions of reproduction – nursing care, shopping, cleaning and so on – have now been commodified (Barbagallo and Federici 2012). There is more to reproducing labour power, however, because, as Federici argues, reproduction is 'simultaneously a production of valorisation of desired human qualities and capacities, and an accommodation to the externally imposed standards of the labour markets' (Federici 2012: 99). As I have argued in Chapter 4, many of the activities that go on in families, in neighbourhoods, in churches, social centres or associations are valorising labour power in order to enable people to enter the capitalist labour market, but they are *also producing* other values, other ideas and other things. They are qualities that belong to other modes of production.

There are, therefore, other meanings of the word *reproduction* that I want to underline besides the reproduction of labour power and desired human qualities. I think that if we scale up from the reproduction of individual commoners to commons systems, there are two other meanings we need to give to reproduction.

First, *reproduction* in a context of commons systems denotes the commoning activities that maintain or increase the autonomy of commons circuits vis-à-vis the capital/state circuits. This *commons reproduction (as opposed to* reproduction of labour power) includes all the activities that provide material autonomy to the commons: reproduction loops such as care, food, energy and housing. These are *reproduction commons (and corresponding commoning)*, because a hypothesis of social revolution requires a growing autonomy in general conditions of living. Take for example the key issue of food sovereignty, advanced since the mid 1990s by Via Campesina – a global movement with about 200 million participants in 164 local and national organisations in 73 countries (described in Box 10).[1] In this context, in short, food sovereignty means autonomy and self-management of territory, biodiversity, and commons governance of seeds and water. In other words, the development prefigured by the food sovereignty movement would be a huge step towards not only feeding us all in justice and health, but also making a major reduction in greenhouse gases (Against the Grain 2011) and avoiding potential food blackmail from the state and capital (Cleaver 1977).

continued on page 286

Box 10 Food sovereignty

The concept of food sovereignty is in direct opposition to that of food security embedded in the the final report of the 1996 World Food Summit organised by the Food and Agriculture Organization (FAO) of the United Nations, which states that food security 'exists when all people, at all times, have physical and economic access to sufficient, safe and nutritious food to meet their dietary needs and food preferences for an active and healthy life' (FAO 1996). In the context of neoliberal agro-export, based on the neoliberal logic of free trade, privatisation and the commodification of land, water, forests, fisheries, seeds, knowledge and life itself, the notion of food security would bring ruin and devastation to farmers, as well as health hazards to consumers around the world (Patel 2007). This is because the neoliberal agro-export model is guided by a drive for corporate profits and the boosting of production for export; it is responsible for the increasing concentration of landholdings, resources, and chains of production and distribution of food and other agricultural products in the hands of a few corporations; it is also responsible for massive land grabs as a result of use of land for biofuel or carbon-offsetting plantations, for food dumping by the European Union or the USA into local markets, pricing local farmers out, and for low wages for farmers and workers. It is also responsible for a chemicals-intensive model of agriculture that causes incalculable damage to the environment and to the health of producers, workers and consumers alike; a high percentage of meat consumption and a high dependence on food transported over long distances, implying that the agro-industrial model is responsible for 35 per cent of global greenhouse gas emissions.

For Via Campesina, the unqualified availability of food is not sufficient. What is necessary is also the right, claimed by rural social movements worldwide of all peoples, countries or state unions, to be able to define their own agricultural and food policies, without policy imposition by multilateral agencies or any dumping in their local markets by third countries (Patel 2009). The concept of food sovereignty was developed by La Via Campesina, and brought into public debate during the World Food Summit of 1996; it has since been endorsed by a broad range of civil society organisations around the world, and it has become a major topic in the international agricultural debate, including that within UN bodies. The notion of food sovereignty has also evolved, and moved from a notion of state sovereignty (the demand that the state exercises its sovereignty with respect to food policies against the demands of the multinationals) to a notion of local and regional self-determination of farmers and consumers (Agarwal 2014). The latter formulation of food sovereignty underlies the Declaration of Nyeleni:

Food sovereignty is the right of peoples to healthy and culturally appropriate food produced through ecologically sound and sustainable methods, and their right to define their own food and agriculture systems. It puts those who produce, distribute and consume food at the heart of food systems and policies rather than the demands of markets and corporations. It defends the interests and inclusion of the next generation. It offers a strategy to resist and dismantle the current corporate trade and food regime, and directions for food, farming, pastoral and fisheries systems determined by local producers. Food sovereignty prioritises local and national economies and markets and empowers peasant and family farmer-driven agriculture, artisanal fishing, pastoralist-led grazing, and food production, distribution and consumption based on environmental, social and economic sustainability. Food sovereignty promotes transparent trade that guarantees just incomes to all peoples as well as the rights of consumers to control their food and nutrition. It ensures that the rights to use and manage our lands, territories, waters, seeds, livestock and biodiversity are in the hands of those of us who produce food. Food sovereignty implies new social relations free of oppression and inequality between men and women, peoples, racial groups, social classes and generations. (CADTM 2007: 2)

This formulation sees food production as independent of the grip of agro-business, and evokes the commons in that no individual alone could manage territories, waters, seeds, livestock and biodiversity. Evidence shows that this model is potentially more productive per unit area (Altieri and Nichols 2012; Holt-Giménez et al. 2012), far more environmentally sound, and far more capable of providing rural families with a decent, dignified life while providing rural and urban consumers with healthy, affordable and locally produced food. A further development in the food sovereignty revolution would be a huge step towards not only feeding us all in justice and health, but also achieving a major reduction in greenhouse gases (Against the Grain 2011). Importantly, it would also be a great step towards the autonomy of commons from capital, which could no longer use food – a key condition for subsistence and culture – as a weapon of blackmail to impose its own dictates for geopolitical purposes (Cleaver 1977).

Reproduction has also a second, broader sense. In cellular biology, reproduction designates the capability of a cellular system to give rise to two cells and, as a result of a number of such occurrences, to give rise to organs and living organisms made of different specialised parts. Reproduction here is not like replication, which instead occurs 'whenever we have an operating mechanism that can repeatedly generate unities of the same class' (for example, a factory which, applying the same process, produces cars, computers etc.) In replication, 'production mechanism and the product are operationally different systems, and the productive mechanism generates elements independent of it' (Maturana and Varela 1998: 59).

One the other hand, reproduction is not copying. 'Copying is whenever we have a model unity and a projective procedure for generating an identical unity …' (Maturana and Varela 1998: 61). It is impossible to copy commons in all their features, since different physical and cultural contexts make for different commons, even if the organisational rationales are the same. With reproduction something of one or more commons (one or more subjects, some key resources, know-how, etc.) goes towards the formation of a new commons which, as a result of this transfer, can now establish commons loops but present different features of the original commons. I am thinking here of a wide range of activities that encourage the reproduction of commons in this sense, as the creation of new commons: from educational and training activities to resource pooling and militant activism; from crowdsourcing to commons foundation by nomadic subjects.

Intertwining into commons ecologies

The multiplication of commons implies the multiplication of spaces in which commons systems operate. Commons ecologies are the interrelations among different commons and their environments brought about by a particular type of commoning that put them into communication and sustained cooperation, that is *boundary commoning*. I will discuss boundary commoning in more detail later in this chapter; here it suffices to say that boundary commoning is that type of commoning that crosses boundaries, activates and sustains relations among commons thus giving shape to commons at larger scales, pervading social spaces and intensifying the presence of commons within them. Commons ecologies consist of webs of interrelated commons, cooperating at different scales and intensity. One finds commons ecologies in social spaces such as commons supply chains – where for example cooperative producers of low-gluten antique strains of wheat are turned into flour by a stone mill, whose milling process preserves all the nutrients of wheat, unlike industrial milling. The flour is then sold at prices high enough to cover costs and guarantee a revenue and low enough to allow greater access to the products by a local family bakery with a conscience. Such networks are being formed in many parts of Europe, where each cooperative producer seeks other ethical producers and consumers in order to weave sustained relations.

Commons ecologies are also formed by interactions among reclaimed factories and community associations and social movements, proving a market outlet for the factory products and an avenue for the community to meet for a variety of initiatives. In my youth, in the contexts of the pervasive social movements in Italy in the 1970s, commons ecologies were also pervasive. They brought together women's clinics to allow women access to safe abortion procedures while abortion was still illegal, and created 'Red rescue' networks of activists and lawyers to defend workers in occupied factories, incarcerated activists, and common criminals who participated in prison struggles to guarantee their autonomy from prison mafia circles. Occupied social centres were beginning to grow, allowing a myriad collectives to find spaces for photo or music labs, collective cooking and childcare, banner painting and rehearsal of anti-repression practices. High schools, universities, social centres, factory canteens, neighborhoods and the streets were turned into commons ecologies. Commons ecologies are visible today too in indigenous markets, many farmers' markets and militant fair-trade networks. The effect of a significant number of commons ecologies in a single area is intense: it produces a new culture, norms, networks of support and mutual aid, virtuous neighbourhoods and villages. For sustained social change to occur, commons ecologies need to develop and intensify their presence in social space up to a point where they present a viable alternative for most people. This point is the point of *critical mass*.

Critical mass and tipping points

Critical mass is a term that has been used in several fields including film, gaming and music, nuclear physics, sociology and social movements.

The term originated in nuclear physics where it indicates the amount of *fission material capable of sustaining a continuous or chain nuclear reaction*. A reaction in which the number of neutrons decreases in succeeding generations, thus not continuing, is called a *subcritical chain reaction*. A reaction in which the number of neutrons remains constant in succeeding generations is called a *critical chain reaction*, and is the type that powers nuclear power stations, while a reaction in which the number of neutrons increases in succeeding generations is a *supercritical chain reaction*. A supercritical mass of uranium or plutonium is necessary to produce a nuclear explosion (Nato 1996).

In sociology, an associated notion is that of threshold or tipping point, where a critical mass of participants decides to abandon a social form or a particular behaviour and adopt another (Granovetter 2009). How could we apply it to very large transformations, as in for example the passage from the dominance of one form to another mode of production? Ruef (2014) applied a retrospective view of the threshold model with respect to the passage from the slave-based plantation system to share-cropping in the USA.

The term *critical mass* also came to prominence amongst cyclists in the early 1990s in San Francisco and London. By 2003, critical mass rides had occurred in more than three hundred cities around the world. Although their participants see these events as celebratory and spontaneous, rather than as protests, so as not to be obliged to reveal advance notification to the police, in effect critical mass is a social movement that reaches a sufficient number of bicycles concentrated in the street to be able to slow traffic and prevent cars from crashing with bicycles and hurting cyclists. In practice, these initiatives are temporary commons that affect changes in the space they are allocated. Since major bike accidents occur because car and truck drivers seem not to 'see' bikes, critical mass movements make bicycles visible, not just to car drivers, incidentally, but also to urban designer and planners. Critical mass rides were born out of a variety of self-help movements within bicycle culture in which

> the bicycle has become a cultural signifier that begins to unite people across economic and racial strata. It signals a sensibility that stands against oil wars and the environmental devastation wrought by the oil and chemical industries, the urban decay imposed by cars and highways, the endless monocultural sprawl spreading outward across exurban zones. This new bicycling subculture stands for localism, a more human pace, more face-to-face interaction, hands-on technological self-sufficiency, reuse and recycling, and a healthy urban environment that is friendly to self-propulsion, pleasant smells and sights, and human conviviality. (Carlsson 2008: 115)

In light of these different uses, I can propose the following hypothesis: to be able to contribute to a social revolution, it is necessary for the *commons* in general and reproduction commons in particular and associated frontline struggles to reach a critical mass above which the multiplication and diffusion of commons can develop freely as if there is insufficient friction or counterforce, since the methods, rules, values and cultures of reproduction commons are viewed as offering the best chances for life in different conditions. This tipping point would be when the commons come to be helped by large sections of society to develop further, to multiply, to integrate, and the entire society begins to mutate into something else, because commons are desired by the vast majority as the social form to reproduce life and produce commonwealth.

It is difficult if not impossible to predict what is this critical mass of commons that can allow us to reach tipping point, especially as it is a matter of opposing forces. However, the very fact that a tipping point corresponding to a critical mass to take us there is conceivable, can make the idea of social revolution more real, and open up the debate on how we can move in the direction of reaching it starting from current conditions.

Recomposition, scale, and network: the magic of boundary commoning

As already discussed, the social force that creates and sustain commons ecologies is boundary commoning, which *produces structural coupling between and among different commons.*

This structural coupling among different commons systems constituting a commons-systems environment does not simply involve the sharing of goods or information or acts of solidarity among commons. Rather, through the continuous interactions brought about by boundary commoning, structural coupling allows 'the boundaries of one system [to] be included in the operational domain of the other' (Luhmann 1995: 217). This means that the first system makes its own complexity 'available for constructing another system'; furthermore, to make this complexity available for the other system is to make its own 'sense' available to other systems, 'and with it indeterminacy, contingency, and the pressure to select' (Luhmann 1995: 213). Through boundary commoning, new senses are developed that modify the horizon in relation to which strategic decisions are made. In other words, the structural coupling that boundary commoning implies corresponds to the construction of a commoning sense and the constitution of 'a state in which two systems shape the environment of the other in such a way that both depend on the other for continuing their autopoiesis' (Moeller 2006: 19).

Through coupled repetition of relations, structural coupling among commons may drift into different social forms, giving rise to a commons phenomenon never seen before. If we were to follow the indication of biology, we would identify two general directions for the drift: that of (towards) symbiosis and that of meta-commonality (meta-cellularity in biology) (Maturana and Varela 1998: 88). Symbiosis occurs with the inclusion of the boundaries of two (or more) commons into one unit (Figure 8.1). An example might be the self-managed Forte Prenestino social centre in Rome (see page 196), which since 1986 has been collectively managed by an assembly of diverse groups and projects that share a basic ethical code and are involved in a variety of activities, including an infoshop, music and dance labs, and a wine cellar, bakery and farm market. Each group retains its own identity, autonomy and autopoietic processes while operating within the boundaries of the self-organised social centre that hosts it and from which it derives greatest visibility. On the other hand, the fort as a whole has an impact on surrounding communities and general archipelagos of radical-alternative subjectivities as not only an alternative point of aggregation and socialisation, but also a place of a plurality of activities, knowledge, and services that anybody can access, thus benefiting the fort's reputation as a whole. Inside the fort, therefore, there is an ecology of commons.

Meta-commonality occurs instead when the recurring structural coupling among the commons units maintains each common's identity and internal commoning, while at the same time establishing a new systemic coherence among two or more commons. An example could be when reclaimed occupied factories in Argentina or Italy not only change their structural components by changing their production methods and outputs,

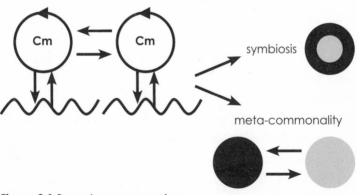

Figure 8.1 Boundary commoning

but also establish ongoing links with the community and its organisations (for childcare, training, festivities, meetings, etc.), thus developing commons outside the reclaimed factories related to the latter for mutual resilience. Another example could be solidarity networks across regions and continents as in the case of Via Campesina or the Zapatistas' coffee cooperatives, in which, Wikipedia says (giving no source), 2,500 producers produce hundreds of tons of coffee that go to solidarity markets around the world paying a higher price to producers (around 10 to 15 per cent more) than commercial markets do.

To show how boundary commoning operates in the production of meta-commonality I conclude this chapter with a discussion of the Genuino Clandestino network of farmers and consumers in Italy.

The case of Genuino Clandestino

Caruso and Mara (only their names are made up) have three children and work on a few hectares of land in the hills surrounding Bologna, producing vegetables in the summer and beer in the winter. They sell their products mostly in markets in Bologna – but these are not normal markets. The small agro-firm they operate is neither a price maker nor a price taker. It is a price co-maker. The price at which they sell beer and vegetables is a price that is decided at regular assemblies among consumers and the 84 local producers of the Campi Aperti association. Caruso and Mara and their three children constitute a household commons. The Campi Aperti association is also a commons, but on a larger scale. Camp Aperti is also part of the Genuino Clandestino (Genuine Clandestine) network, a social movement aiming at promoting participatory food sovereignty practices, joining and designing campaigns for the advancement and protection of grassroots agriculture. Each commons is nested into a larger one.

Before helping to set up Campi Aperti – the largest and perhaps most innovative node of the Genuino Clandestino network – in the early 1980s Caruso and Mara produced vegetables for the wholesale market. Economists usually distinguish between two different types of sellers. Price takers are those that are so small in relation to their competition that they have to take the price that the market offers them. In contrast, large oligopolists or monopolists are price makers, in that they have the power to *make* the price. In their early years as a family farm, Caruso and Mara were price takers, and low price takers, selling their vegetables to a few large powerful distributors, as thousands of farmers still do today. It was only at the end of the 1990s, with the rise of the alternative globalisation movement, that Caruso and Mara met 'consumers' in a self-organised social centre in Bologna and began a regular market there. At the beginning, they told me, it was quite difficult to convince farmers to join them. Now, they have long waiting lists before they can process the accreditation for farmers to enter the network. 'Although slowly, Campi Aperti is growing and growing,' they said.

The Campi Aperti network of farmers and consumers has developed a space outside of state-regulated organic certification. Usually, in order to obtain the label 'organic' and thereby enter the organic trading circuit, farmers have to pay a private agency to come and check their land and take soil samples for laboratory testing. This certification process has become an expensive procedure for small farmers (costing hundreds if not thousands of euros), one wide open to corruption.

In response to this, a commons approach has emerged with the establishment of Campi Aperti, an association that promotes and operates through relations of trust. This trust is founded on proximity and repeated interaction between consumers and producers, as in the village community, where reputation is mainly built on or damaged by the quality of foods supplied, and local people can easily check on the farming conditions (the type of fodder used, the living conditions of animals, the revenue and working practices of farmers and their co-workers, and so on). In other words, proximity creates reliability of product through trust in the process at the level of human relations and so without the need for state intermediation; this trust is secreted by commoning processes in a variety of forms

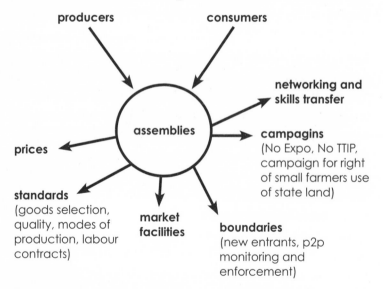

Figure 8.2 The market assembly, the core institution of the Campi Aperti

in the locality and distributed through networks of friends or acquaintances. In the conditions of the modern city, however, the conditions of a village cannot be replicated: some form of social innovation is therefore required. Camp Aperti extends the sense of community from the physically located (bound to the land) to the socio-economically defined (thus unbound), generating trust throughout trading networks that extend into urban spaces.

Trust among consumers and producers is maintained in several ways. In the first place, this occurs through established procedures monitoring association bonding and filtering membership. New producers have to apply to join by filling in a form describing their products and their methods of production and this is evaluated by a committee of one of the market assemblies. Each of the five weekly markets has an assembly of producers and consumers, one role of which is to scrutinise applications for membership. The new applicant is brought in front of the assembly to explain their case and the assembly can probe. Finally, a team of existing producers and consumers (at least two producers, one of whom belongs to the same trade) visits the working premises of the new applicant. Even when a new applicant has been accepted, and especially for the initial few months, producers and consumers in a given market vigilantly check that the new entrant truly and only brings to the market the foodstuffs that they were certificated for and not, say, the produce of friends who have not been through the market community's certification process. It is a key principle of the markets of Campi Aperti that each producer must *only* bring to the market their products. This reduces the complexity of monitoring quality. Clearly, sellers reduce the variety of their supply of produce, and the market as a whole increases the overall variety by expanding the numbers of producers. The need for this monitoring also highlights the appeal that this network has for small farmers, who face the alternative of selling their produce at a very low prices in the large distribution system. The network is open to farmers, but farmers have to accept rules and must participate in the creation of new ones.

In the second place, trust is also reproduced through regular meetings in the market assembly, through informal conversations at the markets (Figure 8.2), and through public initiatives and parties.

Consumers are welcome to visit the farms, and, in some cases they work on one of the farms at harvest or other busy times, especially on the farms that they administrate together with farmers. Figure 8.3 presents an overall view of the network among producers, markets and food types in Campi Aperti, all developed in a few years through boundary commoning and institutionalisation of collective rules.

Each of the five assemblies of the five markets meets monthly; at each, producers and consumers deal with questions of boundaries, quality and prices. Each market posts agreed prices, so that price competition is not an option (another issue that is monitored). The level of trust is so significant that one cooperative linked to Campi Aperti – Arvaia – decided to dispense with boxes and scales. The members of the cooperative just take the fruit and vegetables they need from a warehouse, having paid at the beginning of the year an amount proportional to the number of the people composing the household so as to guarantee the farmer's income. The rest of the farmer's produce is sold in the Campi Aperti weekly markets.

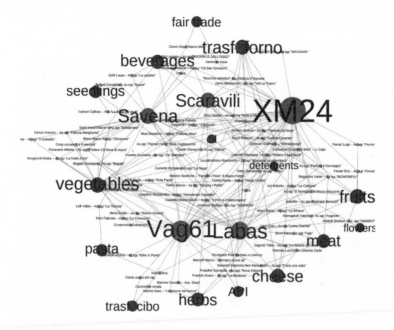

Figure 8.3 Producers-consumers-markets-goods network, Campi Aperti, Bologna. (Thanks to Juhana Venäläinen for this web "scraping" and data visualisation.)

Bimonthly assemblies are held involving all five markets together, where strategic and political decisions are made. Annual assemblies and meetings are organised at the national level – to discuss strategic issues of expansion, analysis of the political situation, and strategic intervention – by the national network Genuino Clandestino, which politicises the practice of participatory guarantees and promote campaigns such as the movement to prevent the sale of state land in favour of a policy to incentivise social cooperatives with missions analogous to that maintained by the network. Genuino Clandestino is thus a movement working to multiply the type of participatory guarantee markets across Italy, from Sicily in the south, to Milan, Turin and Val di Susa in the north. What is significant in the experience of Campi Aperti, and Genuino Clandestino in general, is that the process of commoning involves the pooling of occupied, rented, owned and public conceded land, owned or shared tools, know-how and market spaces, shared with self-organised social centres or public concessions. Clearly, autonomy of production is decentralised to farmers, as is autonomy of consumption to consumers. However, both producers and consumers meet together to institute rules, and constitute spaces in such a way as to create benefits to all. The coordinated construction of the organisation, the network, the prices, the quality standards, the boundaries and also the scale of operations – all are agreed in the various assemblies (Figure 8.3).

Scale here is determined by the number of nodes (or markets made up of producers and consumers) that enter into a participatory relationship to one another; these relationships can be even at the national or international level. In the area of Bologna alone I have estimated a total of 168 to 252 hectares used by Campi Aperti farmers (between 2 and 3 hectares per farmer times 84 farmers), a size that, taken in the aggregate, is far above the average European farm size of 15 hectares and is comparable to the average US farm of 180 hectares which generally makes heavy use of chemical fertilisers and pesticides. To put it in different terms, it is as if in the area of Bologna there were between 204 and 307 large Premier League football pitches dedicated to organic and *genuine* agriculture,[2] with both producers and consumers having power to decide on the what, how, and how much of that production. That begins, just begins I know, to be considered scale. The following text, which I found on a poster at the entrance to one of their markets, is very much in tune with their practice:

> A revolution is happening: always more citizens look for a healthy, local non-alienated food, respecting people and the environment. Always new peasants look for a way out of the global markets and organise themselves to sell their products directly in the city. An encounter that can produce social cooperation, democracy and the invention of more socially just modes of production, distribution and consumption of food. A wonderful revolution. Food and land as common goods.

Across Italy, we have a situation in which distinct farmer–consumer commons engage in their autopoietic operations (in terms of creating and reproducing their own products, rules, regulations, market spaces), while at the same time forming structural coupling links with one another that give rise to a network which is not just a network of acquaintances who occasionally meet but a meta-commonality that organises a range of campaigns and events and propagates a method and philosophy of doing agriculture based on food sovereignty and trust building. Thus, through a process of boundary commoning, many agriculture commons have come together to form a network of commons with its own autopoietic process scaled up from the autopoietic processes of the individual commons. Finally, within this commons conglomeration, repetitive relations among commons and subjects/commoners give rise to and reinforce ways of interacting within this environment, (re)produce affective relations across boundaries – for a new commoning sense.

There is another important aspect of the experience of these organised farmers in Bologna. This is the fact that each farmer pays up 5 per cent of their income and most of this money goes to pay market taxes to the local council (only four of the five markets actually pay taxes because one is within a squatted social centre hosting the market). Interestingly, this point was the precise reason for a small group of activists leaving Campi Aperti. Their idea of 'alternative' did not contemplate any deal with the state, not even when these taxes were halved after Campi Aperti went to the council complaining that they were paying a high tax even though their markets offer the best guarantee of quality control of any market in the city and they leave the market premises completely clean (these markets recycle all boxes and beer glasses are reused). The council cut the tax using the 'common goods' law, which allows it to valorise certain activities. What is interesting is that on other occasions as well, Campi Aperti has developed a working relationship with the council, keeping at a certain distance and complying with basic laws regulating markets, but at the same time implicate the council into being accountable for any favouritism. Campi Aperti knows that their self-organised practices provide the best controls on the quality of food sold, with no 'biological'-certified logo and no verification by external agencies. When I asked what the condition is for continuing to negotiate with the city, I was answered: autonomy. 'Our autonomy is never under threat, otherwise we would refuse to comply' (see also Chapter 9).

Chapter 9

Commons and capital/state

The previous chapters were all intended to analyse the commons and their positions in the world, to frame their internal dynamics, to single out the engines of power at the basis of their multiplication and to probe the constitution of commons ecologies as an effective social force. What sparked me to work through this framework is a great belief in the possibility of social cooperation beyond capitalist wage labour and state control, beyond financial regimes and enclosures and exploitation, a belief that is shared among many social movements around the world. I argued that in given circumstances and with some ingenuity, commons can grow in scale through networking (the boundary commoning that gives rise to metacommonality in given contexts) or can become plural poles of attractions for subjectivities who can then build other commons through symbiosis. Commons therefore are capable of interrelated ecologies of existence and development. There is of course a big difficulty: that is, the state of subjectivities which are symbolically and materially dependent on a world shaped by capital, and in which the state can favour capitalist development, expropriations and repression and its own mediations can leave the commons playing a relatively subordinated role, that of reducing the cost of social reproduction to the state and capital (Caffentsis and Federici 2014, De Angelis 2010, Dowling 2012).

Does this mean that the development of commons is a pointless strategy? No, for two reasons. One is that commons developments are often *necessary strategies to face crises,* to pursue particular values practices negated by capital, to simply be able to reproduce bodies, cultures, values, desires. The detritus left by the capitalist processes of accumulation and its externalities, both on the body of nature and on the bodies of commoners, is a vast space that require nurture, healing and another type of development that, through commoning as its basic social force, shapes recursively new subjectivities through the modification of their *sense* of things as I discussed in Chapter 7. The development of commons is not pointless, second, because the question of *how* the development, reproduction and multiplication of commons occurs is not just an issue of necessity, but is linked to the central issue of their interconnection and recomposition vis-à-vis capital, especially when capital – in its 'boundless drive to accumulation' – becomes an enclosing force: to face all this the commons then can become a political force. To illustrate both these points, I will first tell the story of Cochabamba water wars of 2000, and will then make some further observations regarding structural coupling between commons and capital/ state, and the spectrum of opportunities and dangers that this coupling can give rise to.

Commons movement: the Cochabamba water wars of 2000

In the story set of the water wars of 2000 and the material and stories about water commons I collected ten years later when I visited Cochabamba, a series of elements that I have dissected in earlier chapters come alive, especially the principle of commoning and boundary commoning creating scale, and of commons movement.

Cochabamba is the third-largest city in Bolivia, a city of half a million people blessed with a late spring weather all year round. The city has been pretty much cut in half, the northern part being wealthier (middle class and up) and the southern part poorer, populated in recent decades by waves of migrants from the countryside and miners from closed-down mines. Among the problems facing the southern part of the city, the greatest was the lack of access to clean and cheap water. The public water system did not reach the southern part of the city and people had to buy water from private traders; this was trucked in and deposited in outdoor metal canisters, leading to major health problems caused mainly by rusting metal and atmospheric agents.

Frustrated by the lack of state provision and poor private provision (traders offered water in unsafe water tanks and at three or four times the price paid for public water in the wealthier, northern part of the city), communities originally took things into their own hands by digging wells, laying pipes and building systems of urban water storage and distribution (see also Zibechi 2009). Through thirty years of activities involving urban migrants and rural networks, commoners established water associations drawing and distributing water communally. Then they established associations to facilitate coordination among local community associations and effective intra-community sharing of resources (water pumps, cistern tracks, skills, etc.) and to constitute institutions of political representation vis-à-vis the state. These associations created for and from the primary associations thus operated as a secondary tier, as second-order commons, giving rise to the initial stage of meta-commonality structure with community associations nested into the second tier (see Box 4).

Between January and April 2000, a series of protests in Cochabamba captured the imagination of millions of people around the world, especially those who were involved in what emerged as the alter-globalisation movement and had had its media baptism in the Seattle protests against the World Trade Organisation on 30 November 1999.[1] The protests were against the privatisation of the municipal water supply. Under pressure from the World Bank – led by its president James Wolfensohn – which threatened not to renew a $25 million loan to Bolivia to unless it privatised its water services, the Bolivian government under President Hugo Banzer agreed to the terms of the sole bidder Aguas del Tunari, a consortium led by the British company International Water Limited, the Italian utility Edison, the US Bechtel Enterprise Holdings, the Spanish engineering and construction firm Abengoa and two Bolivian companies, ICE Ingenieros and the cement maker SOBOCE. The plan was to provide drinking water to all of the people of Cochabamba which, in the words of the World Bank, was a 'city that was crying out for water privatization', due to the fact that 'most of the poorest neighborhoods were not hooked up in a network, so state subsidies to the water utility went mainly to industries and middle-class neighborhoods; the poor paid far more for water of dubious purity from trucks and handcarts' (Finnegan 2002). The government signed a forty-year concession to the multinational consortium for $2.5 billion, under which the latter would provide water and sanitation services to the city's residents and generate electricity and provide irrigation for agriculture in the nearby areas. The consortium was guaranteed a minimum of

15 per cent annual rate of profit in real terms, as it was to be annually adjusted to the USA consumer price index.

To ensure the legality of the privatisation, the Bolivian government passed Law 2029. Under this law, Aguas del Tunari had the right to instal meters and begin charging at the independently built communal water systems which were never part of the state municipal water agency SEMAPA; it could have also charged residents for the installation of those meters. Some began to fear that the government would require people to buy a licence to collect rainwater from their roofs.

As soon as Aguas del Tunari took control, water rates increased, under the threat of turning off supply, by an average of 35 per cent, to about $20 a month which, in a country where many of the water company's newly acquired customers earned about $100 a month, meant that they were paying more for water than for food.

La Coordinadora for the Defence of Water and Life was soon set up and became the core of the opposition to the policy. It represented the coming together of organisations of peasant farmers who relied on their own irrigation, as well as local professionals, engineers, environmentalists, and a confederation of factory workers' unions and water associations. As the street protests mounted with barricades and occupations of squares, they were joined by retired unionised factory workers, pieceworkers, sweatshop employees, and street vendors, students and the growing population of homeless street children. A four-day general strike paralysed the city, while on 4 February two days of clashes began with police and troops sent from Oruro and La Paz, in which almost 200 demonstrators were arrested, and 70 protesters and 51 policemen were injured.

Throughout March 2000, the Bolivian hierarchy of the Catholic Church tried to mediate between the government and the demonstrators, but the government rebuked that there was nothing to mediate. In April things escalated further, with the arrest of the leaders of the Coordinadora who went to a meeting with the governor. They were released the following day, but other demonstration leaders were arrested in the days that followed, some being transferred to a faraway jungle prison on the border with Brazil. But the demonstrations spread quickly to rural areas of the country and to cities such as Oruro, Potosí and La Paz. The effect of the wave of protests was the expansion of the protestors' demands, which were no longer confined to repeal of the water privatisation policy but also included calls on the government to resolve unemployment and other socio-economic problems. The coca growers of Bolivia led by the then congressman Evo Morales (who would be elected President of Bolivia in December 2005) had also joined the demonstrators while at the same time demanding an end to the US-sponsored programme of eradication of their crops. This gave the government the opportunity to stigmatise the demonstrators as agents or pawns of drug traffickers, alleging that it was 'impossible for so many farmers to spontaneously move on their own'. But the coca growers – with the strength of a popular tradition that uses coca leaves for chewing and tea and makes a strong distinction between coca and its derivative cocaine – had no difficulty in rebutting the government's claims. Felix Santos, a leader of the farmers, said 'We are protesting because of higher gasoline and transportation prices and a law that will charge us for the use of water'. Teachers of state schools in rural areas also joined the protests by going on strike calling for salary increases; students in urban areas such as La Paz fought battles with the police.

In what was now a broad social recomposition wave, protests spread to the point of blocking highways in five of Bolivia's nine provinces, and even inspired police officers in four La Paz units to refuse to obey orders until a wage dispute was settled. The settlement was reached on 9 April, when the government granted police a 50 per cent raise; it came after a group of some eight hundred police protesters fired tear gas at soldiers on 9 April; the soldiers responded by shooting their guns in the air. Following that wage agreement, police went back to work enforcing the state of siege against other protesters in La Paz.

The settlement with the police was necessary to consolidate much-needed military power against the protesters, since on 8 April President Banzer had declared a 'state of siege', the seventh time such a decree had been declared by the Bolivian government since the return to parliamentary democracy in 1982. The state of seige suspended some constitutional guarantees and allowed the police to detain protesters without a warrant, to restrict travel and political activity, to establish a curfew, and to enforce mass arrests in nighttime raids. Freedom of the press was also severely curtailed, some newspaper reporters were arrested and some radio stations were taken over by the military. Internal exile followed the continuous clashes among the police and protesters, rubber bullets and tear gas versus stones and Molotov cocktails with a balance of 40 injured and 5 deaths. On 9 April in Achacachi, close to Lake Titicaca, soldiers opened fire in an attempt to remove a roadblock. They killed two people, including a teenager, and wounded seven others. Angry campesino residents retaliated by taking some of the soldiers' weapons and attacking and wounding local military officers. The protesters later dragged an army captain from his hospital bed, beat him to death and dismembered him.[2]

The clashes intensified up to the dramatic episode, recorded on television, of a Bolivian army captain, Robinson Iriarte de la Fuente, who fired his rifle into a crowd of demonstrators, wounding several people and killing high school student Víctor Hugo Daza with a shot in the face. Widespread and intense anger erupted, with the result that the police could not assure the executives of Aguas del Tunari of their safety. The executives then fled from Cochabamba to Santa Cruz,[3] while La Coordinadora signed a concord with the government – demonstrating the grown political power of the movement. This guaranteed the removal of Aguas del Tunari and the turning over of Cochabamba's water works to La Coordinadora, the release of detained demonstrators and the repeal of Law 2029. The day after Víctor Hugo Daza's funeral, Óscar Olivera – one of the leaders of La Coordinadora – proclaimed victory from the union office's balcony, but the demonstrators declared that they would not give up until Law 2029 was changed. To get a quorum to amend the law the government even rented planes to fly legislators back to the capital.[4] What was left of the now-defunct policy was the squabble between the Banzer government and Aguas del Tunari over compensation. On 19 January 2006 a settlement was reached between the Government of Bolivia (then under the Presidency of Eduardo Rodriguez Veltze) and Aguas del Tunari. The two parties agreed that the concession was terminated because of civil unrest, and hence that both parties would drop any claims for financial compensation.

*

The point of this story is that when the commons are able to establish a commons movement (the highest form of boundary commoning across different sections) and this in turn is able to reach a critical mass (see later) on the streets, then it is like pushing backwards a line, to draw a line in the sand further on, to establish a taboo, to give material force to a 'NO' (Holloway 2002) by means, however, of a *plurality of organised yeses*. The yeses, the exercise of powers, the force fields that are necessary to say this 'no' are not qualitatively the same as the exercise of powers that are necessary to produce alternative ways of being and living. There may be overlap, but they are not the same. The intensity of their deployment, the rapidity of the events, the concentrated forces, the sudden hybridity of the movement, make them distinct.

Also, in moments like these, the coming together in 'moments of excess' (Free Association 2004) still remembered with emotion ten years later in the accounts of many witnesses (I have spoken to taxi drivers, former students, street sellers, intellectuals, farmers, members of water associations), still allows people not just to see the front line and the powers exercised thereon, but to feel it and feel those powers, together with the sense of belonging to an emergent community. Nevertheless, the powers one feels in these moments of excess risk becoming illusions of omnipotence, because their exercise cannot be sustained in these concentrated forms for long. One cannot draw a direct mapping between the powers exercised on the streets and the powers necessary for livelihoods reproduction in ways that are other than capitalist. The street was joyous, anarchist in spirit, and, in the best sense of the word, communal in values, participative, democratic and terribly seducing. It won a crucial victory.

It opened the way for a political process that ushered into 'power' the first indigenous president in the history of South America, who was a leader of the movement. It brought about a new constitution, one that gave full acknowledgment of plurination-ality and the existence of different circuits of economic power predicated on different value practices, including a communal economy based on the commons. It allowed millions to raise their heads in dignity.

Yet even one of the most vocal critics of the Morales govern-ment and a supporter of communities self-determination had to admit that – in retrospect – there was something else missing to turn the victory of the movement into the opening gate to a completely new society. 'I would have to say we were not ready to build new alternatives,' said Oscar Olivera, one of the spokepeo-ple of the Coordinadora (reported in Forero 2005).

But if one is not ready to build new alternatives, then the 'One lesson of the Water War [that] stands out clearly' is not 'the need to dismantle the existing state' as Olivera also called for (as reported by Solnit 2010). You cannot replace the state or capitalist markets when alternative exercises of political and economic powers are not 'ready'. At the same time, in the devel-opment of these alternatives one has to deal with several aspects of existing states and markets and the circuits they reproduce: we need them to various extents, and fight against them on other occasions. Hence it is necessary to develop a relational stance towards them, a relational stance which is not just to 'say no', but also to engage in constituent practices that try to change them to favour the development of commons, that structurally couple to them but from a position of power and, certainly, while never giving up the autonomy of the commons.

Commons and capital as social systems

When we speak of commons and capital as distinct social systems, the character of this distinction cannot be attributed to the particular structural elements comprising them (see chapters 2 and 7). As already discussed, while in the one case, commons are for commons' sake (and money at most is an instrument for the reproduction of the commons), in the other case capitals are systems in which money is for money's sake (and labour power and ecological systems are only instruments to perpetuate accumulation). This is a crucial difference, a difference that for the commons can be deadly, as in the case of enclosures of commons by capital to facilitate its expansion.

An immediate conclusion about the specific autopoietic requirements of each system is that what we conventionally call 'economic growth' – which incidentally links to growth of greenhouse gases – is only an indispensable requirement for the sustainability of capital systems, not of commons systems. Commons system could survive with alternative means of livelihood and exchange that are not directly measured in terms of economic growth. This idea is captured by what eco-feminist economists and social scientists call the iceberg model (Figure 9.1). The visible part of the iceberg represents the wage labour officially employed in capitalist systems, while beneath the line of visibility are the vast array of other economies, among them the commons (gift exchange, mutual aid, solidarity, household self-provisioning, associations, domestic labour and care, and many cooperatives).

This iceberg metaphor is supported by the sheer size of non-capitalist economy. For example, in 1992, the Canadian government estimated the replacement cost of unpaid work in

Canada to be $284.9 billion, while the opportunity cost – the value of the best alternative to unpaid work – came to $318.8 billion. Volunteers in micro commons around the USA spending long hours 'coaching the local youth soccer team, working at the school book fair, stuffing envelopes for the candidate in the city council race, or going door to door collecting money for

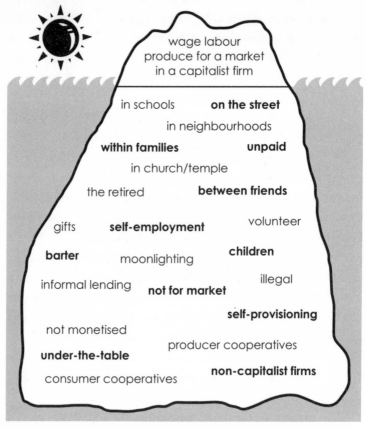

Figure 9.1 Iceberg model of the economy (from Gibson-Graham, Cameron and Healey 2013)

charities all for no pay' accounted for 64.3 million people according to the US Bureau of Statistics between September 2010 and September 2011.

Of course, volunteers also work for many reasons beyond altruism: like hoping to add a line on their CVs in tight labour markets, as in the case of capital/state-promoted mega-events such as the €13 billion Expo held on a 110-hectare site in Milan in the summer of 2015, and sponsored by Nestlé and Coca-Cola among others; social movements denounced the fact that 80 per cent of the workforce was made of up of volunteers (Wainwright 2015)

However, commons cannot be reduced to volunteering. We do not exist as 'volunteers' in our families, or in our neighbourhoods, or in the many associations in social movements or affective networks of friends. Those of us who have been permanently changed by participation in various social movements know that when we do things, we do them as a metabolic exchange with the others in a collective and affective presence. Also, commons, however small they are, produce their own institutions, whether this is a collective meeting, a service to migrants, or a regular convivial meal. Without a regularity underpinning the system's movements, there would be no movement as system.

Commons co-optation

The relationship between commons and capital is necessarily ambiguous, since their co-dependence and co-evolution makes it difficult to point out which of the two systems uses the other. This ambiguity can best be illustrated by looking at the paradigmatic role that the 'village commons' have in relation to capital. In a classic study, the anthropologist Claude Meillassoux argued that the work of reproduction and subsistence going on in the village commons in South Africa during apartheid (mostly carried out by women) allowed male labourers to migrate and be available for employment for cash-crop or other types of waged work. The work in the village commons reduced the cost of reproduction of these male workers since capitalists who hired them did not have to pay for the cost of their upbringing, or contribute to any social security fund in case of illness, unemployment or old age and retirement (Meillassoux, 1981: 110–11). But Meillassoux also recognised the ambiguous character of the contemporary village commons. If the subsistence-producing commons is too 'unproductive', capital loses important aspects of the 'free gift' of labour power, while if it is too 'productive', fewer workers would migrate out of the village commons, pushing wages up (Caffentzis 2004).

At the heart of the relation between commons and capital is the question of struggle for social powers, as each system strives to determine its own (re)production on the ground of its specific value practices. The social contingencies of this ongoing tension or struggle, the forms of its governance that the corresponding force field gave rise to, decides whether a commons can be co-opted or not, or to what extent. The question of co-optation is a strategic field of possibilities, one that requires situated judgements based on context and scale. For example, many would argue that access by commons to markets, for example to meet some of their needs, is by definition contextual evidence of their co-optation, while in fact it could be a contingent strategy of survival and a precondition for their reproduction.

I argued elsewhere (De Angelis 2012) that the current crisis pushes capital to be increasingly dependent on the commons, without however curbing its need to enclose them. The recent EU debt crisis with associated enclosing conditionality's recent waves of land grab on the African continent are two instances of massive enclosures to come. However, the recent enclosures in the EU also are bringing about the formation of new commons, at least, in this phase, to organise subsistence and maintain some degree of social cohesion. Greece has been at the forefront of this movement with the potato markets and self-organised clinics (see boxes 2 and 3). In addition to enclosures, capital also attempts to use commons to fix many social problems created by the crisis and to co-opt the commons as a possible challenge to capital's management. Enclosures (the appropriation and expropriation of commons resources) and commons co-optation (the use of commons to work for capital and not simply for the reproduction of commons themselves) seem to be the two complementary coordinates of a new capitalist strategy (see Box 11).

This can be seen in the World Bank's approach to development in the Global South. For years it has emphasised the importance of some aspects of commons management, such as pooled resources, community participation, and 'trust' as social capital, among others. Whereas communities may create credit associations to pool savings and self-govern their distribution through 'financial money commons' (Podlashuc 2009), development agencies rely on the same principles to tie communities to banks and microcredit institutions and so promote their dependence on global market circuits. In this fashion, bonds of solidarity and cooperation that are nurtured in commons are turned into mutual control and the threat of shame to serve market interests (Karim 2008).

continued on page 327

Box 11 The co-op village, 26 March 2010

It was not easy to get to Salinas, a small town in the Ecuadorian Andes. It is only 90 kilometres northwest of Baños, but the journey took us several hours of detours, some crazy driving on the opposite lane of a road under construction (apparently the only way to get where we wanted to get), and a long wait in a tailback at 3,000 metres altitude caused by a bad accident in front of us. We arrived in Salinas at 10 p.m., but though we felt we had arrived in the middle of nowhere, we were greeted with pizza and beer, some smiling faces and one of the last rooms in the hostel.

Salinas is a small village at 3,500 metres, very close to that amazing volcanic giant that is the Chimborazo (6,267 metres). The Salinas area is much larger, and comprises 32 communities ranging from 600 to 4,500 metres above sea level, thus containing a huge variety of climate and ecosystems (and resources as we will discover later ... an area containing the perfect climate for producing coco beans as well as the perfect climate for processing the beans into fine chocolate).

About 6,000 people live in this area. A middle-aged man working in the youth co-operative that manages the hostel where I stayed with my family told me with some pride that 95 per cent of the population is part of the 'organisation' (the other 5 per cent apparently choose not to be in it, but they have benefited from 'the organisation' nevertheless, since they sell their produce to it). The phrase 'the organisation' actually refers to several associations, foundations, consortia and cooperatives, ranging from cheese producers to textiles, ceramics and chocolate makers, herbal medicine practitioners and trash collectors, a radio station, a hotel, a hostel, and an 'office of community tourism'. To gain a general idea of the scale of this, see www.salinerito.com or the video (in Spanish) at www.youtube.com/watch?v=iUH5HWVH7gQ.

When we woke up early on our first morning there, the small town buzzed with life. From the higher plains, women were descending with donkeys and llamas carrying milk into the town and to the cheese factory. From the lower plains, two coaches brought in teenagers from the technical institute of the town of Guaranda on a study tour. Once arrived, the young people buzzed around the main square, playing volleyball and hanging around in groups, before learning the biochemistry of cheese production at the local cheese factory. One thing you could not fail to notice was that everyone you ran across – whether a woman carrying a baby and pulling a llama, or a man carrying tanks of gasoline, or a teenager passing by wearing a baseball cap, greeted you with a smile and a 'buenos dias'.

There is something intriguing about Salinas, and that is that you do not know where capitalism ends and commonsing begins … and vice versa. You definitely feel the presence of both, which is unsettling and makes someone like me nervous. But I promised myself to keep an open mind: I was travelling to understand commons, the mechanism of their coupling with capital, and the limitations of this coupling, as well as the lines of struggle and power relations that emerge in various contexts of commons. Forty years ago, this had been a very, very poor town. A salt mine, still visible from our hostel room, was the only source of employment. A Columbian family, the Cordovez – who reached the area a few centuries earlier with guns and strange pieces of paper with stamps from the Spanish crown saying the common land around Salinas belonged to them – was the only boss – employing the locals for miserable wages and forcing them into a state of servitute and semi-feudal dependence. Now, all the land we could see belongs to the community by means of 'the organisation': 33,000 acres of it, taken from the Church and from the Cordovez!

But it was taken 'nicely', that is, it was bought. In the early 1970s, in an age of land struggle and land reforms, the Cordovez family could not believe their luck when the newly formed credit co-op – the very first cooperative to be born here – offered to buy the land. The co-op was formed to contrast the money sharks who were preying on the people in times of need (such as funerals, weddings, emergencies), charging the lending rates of usury. Behind the origin of the co-op that initiated the cooperative movement in this remote province, and indeed behind the origin of several other co-ops comprising the 'organisation', is an Italian priest who arrived in Salinas 40 years ago for a three months' mission helping to build a community house – and is still there.

Antonio Polo, an energetic 72-year-old Salesian priest, is a type of 'commons entrepreneur', someone who is in the business of triggering and promoting commoning processes that sustain and consolidate themselves into types of commons institutions. I met Antonio in his house next to the church.

The window of the kitchen faces the square, so it was possible to see all the goings-on down below. The kitchen seemed to be an open house, with people coming in and out, someone waiting for dinner, and another selling eggs at a good price. Antonio explained to me that the original choice to buy the land from the Cordovez, rather than taking back the land the family had effectively stolen, was moral and economically rational. It was moral because it was an anti-violent choice. And it was economically rational because when people buy land they have a vested interest in making it productive for them (at least in the sense that they have borrowed money to buy it and they have to repay the loan with interest). I had my doubts, as the reasons given seemed to me too ideological. After some probing it seemed to me that the Cordovez family was interested in selling – and selling at a relatively good price – because of the broader context of land struggle and talks of land reform, hence of 'violence' against the private property of the big landowner. The 'peaceful' choice was therefore dependent on the 'violent' context, making the moral distinction between the two quite narrow, and leaving the distinction relevant only from a strategic point of view, that is, contingent on the existing condition and opportunity to claim commonwealth (whether human resources or money resources). Antonio explained how through the years the different cooperatives, foundations and consortia were formed to give work to local people after the salt mine was closed. He is definitely an engine of ideas for imagining new productive enterprises.

The cheese factory pools milk from the surrounding areas (and the cheese from the different cheese factories that have been established in local communities). The chocolate factory got its coco beans from the subtropical areas where the climate does not allow processing of the coco into fine chocolate.

The annexed Italian Torrone factory – which regularly exports its products to fair-trade shops in Italy – allows the use of the abundant local honey. The herbal medicine laboratory pools together herbs and plants brought in by local people, and the mushroom-drying facilities use the mushrooms collected under pine trees that were planted in deforested areas – with some environmental concerns, given the fact that pines are not really local species. All the social enterprises' of the Gruppo Salinas – the name that was used to brand the activities of the area for reasons of commercialisation and export – plus its 'strategic allies' employ overall 434 people, but the total number of producers involved is far higher, ranging from 1,600 to a few thousands (opinions differ). But it is clear that the cooperatives have a core of workers employed at the centre, and a range of other members with a different contractual arrangements. The system at times resembles a textbook case of the 'putting out' system, in the sense of a method of production dispersed in the homes of workers, who mostly work part-time for money, alternating this paid work with subsistence agricultural production. The important difference from the capitalist pre-industrial version of 'putting out' is that the organising tasks of the 'boss are in the hands of the employed members of the co-op, and the pay rates, pace of work and general rules for delivery times of the other members are negotiated in co-op assemblies (subject, of course, to the external constraints set by the market).

For example, the textiles co-op comprises a few full-time workers designing sweaters and hats and organising distribution of the wool to be turned into finished products. They represent the meeting point between the needs of the market and the bulk of the knitting workers of the co-op. In the room at the entrance of the shop, I witnessed a moment of exchange between the full-time workers and the part-timers (incidentally, the very fact that this exchange occurs under everyone's eyes – including those of consumers' – and not in some back room is a plus in terms of transparency). Two women pulled out some sweaters and hats from a plastic bag. The women on the other side of the counter weighed them and checked the weight against the numbers in a register to check that the weight of the finished products was pretty much the same as that of the wool originally issued. Then they briefly checked the quality of the products, searching for irregular stitches, for example. There seemed to be some discussion with respect to the value of the product, and an agreement was quickly reached and recorded in the register, and new wool was weighed, recorded and issued.

I was told that there is generally no pressure for a worker to finish a job at a given time, except when there is a big commission and the workers agree to commit to a deadline. All payments in all the co-ops are generally made through the credit co-op. Assemblies of co-op members occur every couple of weeks to discuss matters of work organisation, and the assembly for the cheese factory was advertised – by a big, handwritten poster showing the agenda – both in front of the place where milk is collected and in front of the credit union.I asked to be given some examples of how the principle of solidarity works within the Gruppo Salinas. In the case of the cheese co-op, every farmer who is a member is paid the corresponding amount for the milk she brings in for the production of cheese. However, at the end of the year, the monetary surplus is not distributed among co-op members on the basis of their contribution of milk, but is shared among them for common projects: it is either used to buy new equipment or transferred to community funds. This way, as our guide told us, 'the farmer who has ten cows is helping the farmer that has only one cow', which enables some redistribution. Another example is the use of *mingas*, a form of unwaged community work used throughout the Andes (see Box 5). Infrastructure works such as road maintenance, irrigation, planting, digging, and also garbage collection and street cleaning are all types of work that call for *mingas* of different sizes, and these *mingas* are used in Salinas too. Yet another example is the important use of foundations that channel funds earned in social enterprises for community projects.

Salinas uses, therefore, a mix of organising principles between private and community production, adaptation to the market and its needs for 'competitiveness' and solidarity and communitarian values, a mix that would be interesting to deconstruct and study with more lengthy field work in terms of how power relations are reproduced or diffused, and how the distribution and control conflicts inherent in market-oriented arrangements are dealt with. But the overall basic question in the back of my mind is this: what is co-opting what? Is capital co-opting the commons or is the commons co-opting capital? My impression is that, taken as a whole, Salinas offers a context in which dignity is definitively at the centre of doing things, and capital is not all, and perhaps – perhaps not yet – not even the most important thing. However, the limitation of Salinas' coupling of market and competitive principles with solidarity and community ones becomes more evident, the more we look at this experience from the perspective of scale. A few observations on these follow.

First, one of the largest acquisitions was an old manufacturing plant to turn the abundant wool from the area into yarn, and thus vertically integrat it with the artisan production of sweaters.

Although part of this plant was donated, other parts of it were bought on credit. Furthermore, the amount of energy it costs to operate is quite high, and the community does not have access to a source of cheap renewable energy. All this and taking into consideration all the other costs implies that the break-even point (the point at which the plant does not lose money and does not make any) is 10,000 kg of wool thread a month. However, the international solidarity fair-trade circuit can afford to buy only 500 kg a month of sweaters at the given fair-trade price (which, although higher than the market price, obviously has an upper limit, because the fair trade operators too have a business to run and a commodity to sell). This implies that the rest of the wool production of wool (up to 20,000 kg a month, which is the maximum capacity of the plant) enters the normal market circuits and provides the raw material for underpaid and overexploited textile workers around the world. This is one way in which the damned capitalist 'law of value' enters Salinas.

Second, one of the most recurring themes in conversations, literature and videos relating to Salinas is that its experience can become a model for other poor rural communities. It could, of course, but the more it becomes so, the more the rule of the 'fallacy of composition' would apply: you cannot infer that something is true for the whole from the fact that it is true of some part. No longer able to use a market niche (that is, an area of the market which is relatively free of competition), the salineritos workers would set their products against the products of other cooperatives around the world, thus undermining their livelihoods (and of course, this is already happening to some extent). The same is true of the 'success' of fair-trade coffees in our supermarkets, which obliges the 'ethical' consumer effectively to choose which 'fair trade' community to help building its school or hospital, a choice often influenced by the relative price of the different 'community brands'. I think the world we seek is different, is one in which everybody should have access to health and education irrespective of the price of the commodity they sell. The capitalist ideologues' solution for this conundrum is the same as its solution for the conundrum that emerges from the polarisation of incomes and wealth: the dogma of the necessity of aggregate growth, which implies the search for always new areas of commodification of life and, as its by-product, would destroy communities and the planet. At the systemic level, the Salinas experience is not the solution, although within it there are definitively important aspects of the solution.

Third, in the history of the Salinas social enterprises, there is and there has been from the beginning not only a strong reliance on international solidarity and donations – often but not only channelled through institutions and organisations within the Catholic Church – but also an important reliance on debt. With the use of debt to promote purchases of capital (and hence extend the scale of production), comes the need of selling to repay debt, and the subjection of local people to the meeting of market deadlines. This is inevitable, because to the extent that we rely on market mechanisms for our reproduction, we are subjected to its rules and general laws of operation. Obviously, in the history of Salinas there have been some problems with individuals' and co-ops' delays in making a payment, and perhaps some default. In this context, one of the aspects that most attracted my attention is the use of participation in *mingas* as one of the criteria for classifying co-op members as 'serious', and hence for the extension to them of credit and other co-op services (an instance of subjection to the market through a disciplinary process) (see Polo 2006: 64). I am not sure how and to what extent this has been the case, but what this reveals to me is the co-optation of commoning to promote capitalist market values and not vice versa.

I have mixed feelings about this Salinas experience. There is no doubt that the 69 agro-industrial and 38 service community enterprises are quite a means for the local population to meet reproduction needs in ways that shield them from the most exploitative practices of other areas in the region and make them active participants in commoning processes centred on dignity. But the increasing reliance on, and strong preoccupation with, global export circuits and the markets seems excessive, with the risk that experiments like these really become vehicles for commons co-optation. Also, although there is a clear environmental sensibility in the discourse of this community in the brochures and book I have read (for example, there is an awareness that excessive expansion of cheese production has some environmental impact), there is too much concern about finding new sources of revenues by 'adding value' to local resources processed into export products, and none at all about the environmental problematisation of global production chains and one's own role within it. There is definitely no consideration for 'Pachamama' ('Mother Earth', according to indigenous cultures of the Andes) in the celebration of mushroom or snail meat exports towards European and Asian markets, products that both the Europeans and Asians could and should produce themselves if they so much desire them: a basic element of critical food sovereignty discourse.

This opens up to another critical issue, also recognised by Antonio Polo in our conversation: that the process in Salinas has started from agri-industry rather than agriculture. The discrete amount of common land available could perhaps have been used more for the community, and only now are some experiments being carried out with greenhouses and different types of plants. I wonder whether the Salinas reality would be any different today if in the 1970s priority had been given to the food self-sufficiency. In any case, Salinas deserves more attention and study, because it helps us to pose the big questions we need to pose if we are preoccupied with processes of radical social transformation: How can local commoners be agents of their own social renewal? How and to what extent can they access the social wealth they need for the pursuit of a better life through their commoning rather than their work disciplined by the market? How can they access circuits of wealth generation outside their local circuits? What forms of distribution and exchange can they invent with other commons? To what extent can the existing market circuits be safely used as a means to access wealth? How can these limits be defined?

In Britain, a coalition government of Conservatives and Liberal Democrats oversaw massive cuts in public spending between 2010 and 2016 (continued from 2015 on by a solely Conservative government), and promoted a vision of 'the Big Society' that claimed to support community empowerment to address social upheavals. The agenda of the neoliberal era is continuing apace, as if no crisis has happened, even as the ruling class clearly recognises the social and environmental problems caused by this agenda. Unlike Margaret Thatcher in the 1980s, who said that society 'does not exist', the Conservative prime minister David Cameron wanted to turn it into a 'Big Society' – continuing a strategy of community involvement already pursued by New Labour in the UK, as well as by governments in the USA and Canada (De Filippis, Fisher and Shragge 2010: ch. 4). According to Cameron, governments urgently need to 'open up public services to new providers like charities, social enterprises and private companies so we get more innovation, diversity and responsiveness to public need' and to 'create communities with oomph' (Cameron 2010).

But this approach requires recognition that resources are not simply financial, and that the resources that lie dormant in fragmented and atomised communities need to be activated through some form of commoning. People need to take matters into their own hands by, for example, connecting diabetes patients, the elderly or the marginalised youth into self-help groups. There is of course nothing new about the idea of mobilising communities for whatever social or ecological end. But what seems to be emerging in discourses such as the 'Big Society' is a commitment to a faster speed and scale of change, since, as widely recognised, social innovation can take a long time to be adopted. The Big

Society project capitulated to the same government's enclosures strategy in the form of tripling university fees to £9,000 a year and cleansing London boroughs of their poor through tight cuts in social housing. It still survives in the corrupted form of social enterprise where a social bond is paid by the state to investors if specific targets are reached. Here, however, we are abandoning the world of commons measures and re-entering that of capital (Dowling 2012).

Another discourse pioneered by capital in order to use the commons to serve its interests is the idea of 'sustainable communities'; a term used in urban planning and design circles when proposing new financial centres, shopping malls or mega-venues such as the Olympics. The basic idea of 'sustainable communities' is that they 'can stand on their own feet and adapt to the changing demands of modern life' (ODP 2003). In other words, they do not decline while facing the ongoing transformations that the relentless, ever-changing requirements of the global economy impose. But this idea – with its emphasis on education, training, environment, governance, participation and, of course, sustainability – amounts to an oxymoronic utopia. It is a vision in which communities never seem to tire of playing competitive games with other communities somewhere else in the world in order to overcome the disruptions and inequalities of wealth and income inflicted by competitive markets. In this way 'commoning' is annexed to a divisive, competitive process in order to keep the whole game going. This oxymoronic ontology of our condition seems to be the key to sustainability for capital (De Angelis 2007b).

In all these cases, commoning is turned into something for a purpose outside the commons themselves. The main purpose in all these cases is not the autopoietic reproduction of the commons themselves, their multiplication and expansion, thus providing an alternative to capital, but to make a particular node of capital – a region or a city – more competitive, while somehow addressing the problems of reproduction at the same time and at a fraction of the cost for capital.

However, it is also important to take heart from the fact that, in spite of capital's strategies of using a commons fix for the problems it creates, while never really solving them, commons may well be part of a different historical development I will trace in the next chapter. I should point out one thing, however. In Chapter 8 I discussed Campi Aperti, the Bologna association of farmers and consumers practising participatory guarantees. This association often entered in deals with the city council of Bologna, often after the city conceded central space for markets or in relation to council tax levels. One thing I noticed was that each deal obtained was preceded by a struggle, either actualised or threatened. So, each deal between the council and the farmers–consumers association gave the council at least a degree of social peace, and gave the association more resources and prime space to put forward their food sovereignty values and self-organised and horizontal form of association. I asked my informants what it was that prevented their deals with the state from being co-opted. The answer was easy: whatever the deal, whatever the level of taxes they had to pay, their own organisation was autonomous, they could self-manage themselves and set their own quality and price standards independently of state guarantees and constituted through their own practices. This is precisely the autonomy of the commons that I discussed in Chapter 7.

Structural coupling between capital and commons

The cases discussed in the previous section are a few of the cases that can be made to illustrate the question of common's co-optation. However, whether capital co-opts the commons or the commons are able to use capital will be a key strategic question of the near future. Examples of symbiotic relations between capital and commons are all situations of interdependence and positive feedback loops between the two systems; that increases the dependence of the commons on capital. This is evident, for example, in the spiral between the production of commodities, consumerism patterns and the growth of debt and financial industries. Another example of symbiotic relations between capital and commons is parasitism, getting value for free: an example is the 'cognitive capitalist' value-capture from social networks such as Facebook selling targeted ads to advertisers; another example is clothing designers checking grassroots street clothing culture for packaging and branding purposes (Fisk 1989). This form of parasitism is analogous to the use of the atmosphere or rivers or the seas as sinks of profit-making activity. Capital cost externalisation is parasitism, and if capital

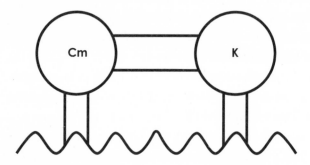

Figure 9.2 Capital-commons structural coupling

had to pay up for all its cost externalisations, the bill would mean the death of this mode of production and social form. From the point of view of capital, all activities of the commons as well as of ecological reproductive systems are targets for its parasitism.

As I argued in Chapter 8, a key phenomenon of relations between systems is 'structural coupling', that is, the intersystem relation among systems that are environments to each other, such as commons and capital. As I argued, one of the key things about structural coupling is that the other system boundary becomes a strategic object since 'the boundaries of one system can be included in the operational domain of the other' (Luhmann 1995: 217).

To include the boundaries of one system into the operational domain of the other is for a system to make its own complexity 'available for constructing another system' (Luhmann 1995: 213). Since social systems here are understood in terms of their autopoiesis, to make this 'complexity' of capital available for the commons is to make the 'sense' of capital available to that of the commons, 'and with it indeterminacy, contingency, and the pressure to select' (ibid.). This is crucial. Take for example the discussion of property rights and boundaries in Chapter 7. To regard property as a bundle of rights allows us to manipulate – in given situations – these rights and include the boundary of a state/legal system based on private property within the domain of a commons. For example, a garden community association can be set in place on land owned by people who give use and access rights to the members of the association. A boundary of capitalist-system-based property rights is included into the operational domain of a commons system. Another example is the creative commons licence also used by this book (https://creativecommons.org/). This takes on the boundaries of the private property within the operational domains of the commons and both allows the creative product to be reproduced as commons and uses the protection of the state against profit-based use of that creative product. Clearly, the opposite can be the case, that is, capital that can use the boundaries of the commons in its own operational domain. The net result, who uses whom, is only given by the relation of power and the force field.

Using the other's complexity: a new commons deal?

What does it mean to see ourselves strategically within structural coupling, that is within an interaction among autopoietic systems? It means to pose questions and find situated answers that allow us to enlarge the spheres of the commons, that allow us to connect and reproduce commons autopoietic systems into a transformative, that is, conditioning, social force. Making capital and state complexity available for commons development is a key point. It is a way to enlarge the sphere of the commons and be aware of the risks of co-optation. In Table 9.1, I propose a few simple intuitive examples of how capital and commons use the complexity of the other for their own purposes. This, of course, is in a derivative sense, that is, in terms of resources produced by the other system. I am very hesitant to even think that the commons could directly use the organisational methods of both state and capital, as for example Lenin (1918) did in celebrating Taylorism. Often commons can use this complexity of capital because there is an echo of the commons inside capital or state systems, and thus it is possible to define meta-commonal relations across capital, state and commons.

Table 9.1 Using the other system's complex products

Commons ...	... using the products of capital complexity
Wikipedia	depends on a distributed infrastructure including mainframes, cables, privately produced electricity etc.
Community-supported agriculture networks	trucks, fuels, electricity, road networks
Cochabamba water associations	trucks, fuels, some equipment, pipes
Massimo's local community garden	tools, irrigation equipment, some borrowed tractors
Reclaimed factory (Rimaflow)	capitalist detritus, fuel, trucks

Capital/state ...	... using the products of commons complexity
Large event (Milan, Expo)	volunteers and their support households
Any skilled occupation	'good will': nurtured in the commons
Public parks	increasingly tended on 'ecological days' by volunteers mobilised in the community
Police	use information from neighbourhood watches, 'civic' behaviour ....
Labour power	Reproduced in households

In Table 9.1 there is a series of examples in which commons use capital and capital uses commons. Table 9.1 shows how commons and capital/state use each other's complexity in the form of existing products requiring complex operations for their production. Commons and capital are autopoietically closed in the sense that while they use and rely on resources from their environment, those resources take up a different social dimension when inserted in their system's operations: within capital social systems they become capital and labour power, and in commons social systems they become commonwealth and commoners. Both capital and the commons rely on resources produced outside themselves and their specific value operations. While the commons require a range of products of capitalist industry, capital depends on the resources created by peer-to-peer networks in cyberspace which have become necessary for capitalist innovation; and the basic work of reproduction in households that is necessary to re-create the conditions for having bodies and minds available to join the labour market. It also relies on basic operations of socialisation that are the offspring of commoning, such as trust, which capital turns into a means of accumulation in the form of social capital. On the other hand, commons also rely on resources produced outside their functional operations. The vast array of useful products that commons do not have any other ways of procuring but through engaging in monetary payments for them, hooks them up in a variety of degrees to global market loops. These products have been produced as commodities, that is, not only as useful products, but also as exchange values that feed into the profit system and serve the autopoietic reproduction of capital. However, the social labour producing them springs out of commons around the world.

Also, both capital and commons rely on materials created by ecological processes for which they are both responsible, but while the capitalist mode of production is responsible for the largest chunk of environmental devastation, by and large commons systems seem to meet their ecological responsibility. Ecological resources around the world are maintained and reproduced by communities, as in water and forest management (Deb 2009) that contributes to the maintenance of the ecological presupposition of life upon which also capital depends.

Another difference between the commons using capital complexity and capital using commons complexity is that capital/state does not pay for this use, while the opposite is true, commons often pay, if not directly, at least indirectly in terms of environmental, social cost and taxes. It is for this reason that, all in all, capital/state symbiosis with the commons is parasitic.

One way to counter the parasitism of capital/state in relation to the commons would be to establish a universal basic income to cover at least the basic subsistence level in a market society. If subjectivities mutated towards commons this universal basic income not only would prevent large numbers of people from experiencing poverty and hunger, but could open the way to pool basic resources and extend the sphere of commons ecologies within society by turning public/private wealth into commons wealth.

The fact that commons are compatible with capital through money allows a strategic space. Outer incompatibility would imply cutting off many communities from the economic system and access to its complexity, and their inability to access any objects of use on the market produced by social labour, an element of the social commons, hence restricting their ability to select forms of development and reproduction. There are, of course, several types of these communities. Amish communities, deep ecologists and no-contacts indigenous communities are examples of commons that choose to cut off in varying degrees from the economy and therefore, directly or indirectly, from capital's circuits. But these extreme cases are obviously not the rule. Other and more problematic cases include those who are excluded from the economy not out of choice, but as a condition of their lives: the world hordes of the poor, the stigmatised migrants, the pauperised middle class, and the hungry. Commons among the poor are part of the struggle for life and death that often turn into massive powerful movements. To guarantee access to the social wealth necessary for the commons (re)production and development, the commons both struggle against capital and then make pacts with it. But in this way the commons at the same time construct its force to fool capitalism. As in Goethe's *Faust*, the key is to lose only half the bet with the Devil, and by commoning strive find 'redemption' from the hell of the social and ecological injustice of capitalism.[5]

Capital/state and commons mutual conditioning

In systems thinking, conditioning emerges from the consideration that social systems are not merely relations among elements. 'The connection among relations must also be regulated. This regulation employs the basic form of conditioning. That is to say, a determinate relation among elements is realised only under the condition that something else is or is not the case' (Luhmann 1995: 23). Conditioning also 'concerns the availability of specific elements' (ibid.).

Thus, for example, both capital/state and commons aim at introducing and making effective constraints to limit each other's operations, and therefore give rise to determinate relations between the two systems. On the side of the commons, one need only think of the systems of labour rights that limit the working day or limit the power of management to demand compulsory overtime, or hiring and firing at will and precarisation. To the extent that they are effective, these are constraints on the operations of capital that allow different commons-based autopoietic systems (such as labour unions or households) greater operational freedom. On the other hand, on the side of capital, the dismantlement or reinscription of these rights into patterns of greater commons dependence on money allows capital greater operational freedom through precarity, such as in hiring and firing, lowering wages, lengthening working hours, all practices that, other things being equal, strengthen capital's functional autopoiesis (accumulation).

A classic form of conditioning of commons by capital is of course enclosures. Here the expropriation of commons resources, whether direct (by force and legal measures) or indirect (by externalities such as pollution etc.), conditions the commoners into determinate patterns of development or destruction. Communities (a structural element of commons) here go through processes of fragmentation and regeneration into new determinate conditions, for example from rural areas into favelas and shanty towns. Commons as a social force is not destroyed here; only specific commons are, while commoning is reconfigured in new conditions, with new communities and new elements selected by its evolution into new forms. Otherwise we would not understand the long history from the early phases of capital-dominated industrial societies to today, a history of struggles, movements and rights obtained, lost and reconfigured through struggles which have always involved some form of commoning.

Another example of capital conditioning the commons are many of the health and safety rules introduced over broad regional areas such as the European Union. In the EU, 'health and safety' rules are set in such a way as to make it financially impossible for a small community to sustain the rules designed for big corporations. Many forms of commoning or resource pooling into commonwealth thus are forced to become illegal. Different households are discouraged from trusting each other when they cannot share at a school party their cakes and biscuits made at home, but instead have to show that they have purchased the produce. Often commoners challenge this. In my experience, rural areas are where this challenge becomes the common sense of an entire town rather than a self-aware political act as in certain cases in cities; this is because the state is further away from the rural areas than from the metropolis and other cities. As I argued in Chapter 5, the interrelated conditioning of commons and capital also occurs via the structural coupling between the two that gives rise to the 'economy'. The selling in order to buy circuits of daily life (C-M-C) and the buying in order to sell circuits of capital accumulation (M-C-M') are structurally coupled. By and large, we could safely understand C-M-C operations as the circuits through which broader commons circuits (remember the commons formula shown in Figure 5.4) engage in market operations and functionalise the medium of money for their own autopoiesis. The latter is closed, limited by the reproduction of needs. Money is a medium for the commons' operation, but not the only medium. Think of the use of money in a household, an association, a social centre, or a Community Supported Agriculture scheme. On the other hand, M-C-M' indicates the circuit of capital, and here money is not only a medium for its autopoiesis, it is the end, the bottom line deciding its preservation. The end of the commons circuit is its own reproduction – in dignity, love, solidarity and conviviality – at least when the commons is not lacerated by its internal struggles, but these latter are used instead by its institutions to drive the commons' evolution.

Thus the commons can condition capital via the economy and, vice versa, capital can change the commons via the economy. Wage rates, strikes, patterns of consumptions, levers of employment induced by capitalist technology and automation, or capital flight are all instances of this. But the relation between capital and the commons is also constituted through other mediations and corresponding codes. For example, it is a legal relation, as in the case of wage or family laws, or contract laws, which filter access to the wage by members of the commons. It is a legal relation too in the case of property laws or even company laws. The relation between commons and capital is also constituted through politics, that functional system that makes laws, or, in the case of countries strangled by debt, is the mediator between a supranational enclosure decision and local and national resistance to it. The relation between commons and capital is also constituted through the justice system that interprets the law and administers punishment, and it is even constituted in the media system that selects types of information and analysis constituting particular cultures favouring capital or the commons. The commons could condition capital through all these systems and its own code, if only it had the social power, if only it commanded networked communal and reciprocal labour to reach the social force to influence these systems to its advantage and for its own development without losing the sense constituting its autopoiesis and autonomy. In short, if only we had a strong worldwide commons movements.

'Commonisation'

A commons movement is not simply a movement against the valuation processes and injustices of capital as well as the hierarchies of the state, but a movement that seek to *commonalise* many functions now both in private and state hands, especially those functions that have to do with social reproduction, and that define the quality and the quantity of services available. It is clearly a movement that, together with social and ecological justice and a good life, also has the expansion of *resilience* as a goal – that system quality that allow commons systems to adapt to or more easily recover from stress, crises and adversity. Since commons also relate to ecologies, the need to increase the resilience of ecological systems is part of the same horizon. If environmental, economic and social crises deepen, together with the collapse of welfare systems of many states, it becomes necessary to begin to pose the question of commonalisation of many private and state institutions providing services that are vital for the reproduction of life.

Aside from the strategy of creating commons from the ground up (as I have assumed so far), another strategy is to commonalise existing private or public systems and transform them into resilient organisations, which in turn imply, much deeper democratisation and cooperation, namely basic commons coordinates.

The objective to turn more and more spheres of societies into sustainable and resilient spheres thus coincides with that of adopting commons as a central kernel of the architecture of a new mode of production integrating many types of modes of production. This can only be brought about by a commons movement embedding the necessary knowledge, experience and exemplary practice.

In this sense, *omnia sunt communia* is only a horizon through which we regard an existing private or public institution as the object of commonalisation strategies and as interlinked with an ecology of the commons. This would be a constituent process driven by commoners' own democratic evaluation that particular currently private or public institutions do not serve the commons but only authority for authority's sake, accumulation, and environmental destruction.

Commonalisation means to shift a public or private organisation into a commons or, more likely, into a web of interconnected and nested commons giving shape to metacommonality, with the overarching goal of resilience. Resilience in turn embeds a series of features that allows a more effectively pursuit of social justice, ecological sustainability, and the good life for all (Table 9.2).

For a public institution or private corporation, commonalisation does not mean that a given final result is optimal, but that a process has begun along which there is a collective effort, through the commoners' democratic management of constraints, costs and rewards, to increase all sorts of commoning across different social actors involved in the corporation or public service. Thus commonalisation means essentially beginning to increase three attributes of resilience in a particular institution (Table 9.1):

Table 9.2 Principles of a commons resilience

Transparency	The participants know of each other what they are doing and can react accordingly and cooperate instantly. There is no room for secret committees and boardroom politics.
Communication	The participants are ready to communicate effectively and inclusively, online (as it were) and as personally as possible.
Cooperation	The participants benefit from the mutual use of their capabilities and talents. The overall benefit of cooperation is greater than the mere addition of individual contributions.
Democracy	The participants create systems of collective benefits on the basis of equal rights. The actual democratic systems are all oligarchic, as the so-called private sector is excluded … Democracy makes identification and a sense of responsibility possible. Dictatorships and other hierarchical systems are notoriously unstable.
Modularity	Resilient systems consist of well-defined interchangeable modules which support each other. Redundancy is enhanced by modularity.
Decoupling capacity	Modules can survive on their own for a certain period of time. Defects can be repaired without endangering the whole system.
Decentralisation	Decoupling presupposes decentralisation. Local self-sufficiency within a defined context makes democracy more manageable.
Relocalisation	Multifunctional local systems correspond to local needs. Modules need proximity to support each other and to create local/temporal synergies. Transportation must be minimised because it consumes energy and therefore fuels.

Ecological design	Sustainable systems can only work with a new ecological design of things used by them. Instead of planned obsolescence, ecological engineering has as its basis robustness, repairability, reusability ('cradle to cradle'), combinability etc. According to Stahel (productlife.org) the material throughput could be reduced by a factor of ten and still achieve the same level of utility. Such products/processes are poison for growth, of course, and have been kept off the market so far. Our future will be based also on low-tech or a return to the Middle Ages (or the Palaeolithic). instead of consumer goods for strictly individual use, we'll develop tools, machines and other goods suited for communal and cooperative use, for the synergic luxury of neighbourhoods.
Adapted size	Size must be adapted to function. 'Big' is not always the most effective, just as 'small' is not always beautiful. On the whole we could speak here of adaptive basic patterns. (This is also linked to the 'dance of measures' conceptualised in Chapter 7, which would also imply the choice of a particular institutional organisation, and hence size.)
Cognitive diversity	A variety of methods, ways of thinking and cultures is needed, Diversity itself is an important feature of stable systems. Our current monomaniacal system (valorisation of capital) must be replaced by a variety of relatively independent systems.
Graduated commitments	Resilient organisations are based on grades of varied intensity of commitment. There is always a core group with a higher degree of commitment, surrounded by circles of varying participation. Not everybody must do everything. Division of labour can be a good thing. (This clearly is true to the extent that turns are taken on communal chores – which guarantees enormous reduction of labour time. See Chapter 6 on the question of communal labour.)
Belonging	The feeling of belonging to a community improves resilience. It also improves health and happiness

Source: P.M. (2014: 12).

1. the parameter of *democracy*: democratisation of a state service or a corporation along a scale that has at its two opposite poles management versus direct democracy; this democratisation of management can be the basis through which to expand cooperation through belonging;
2. maximum *accountability* and transparency and the ability to recall every public servant (starting from the top) and other stakeholder involved in the production of the service;3. *opening the boundaries* between different type of practices and subjects thus allowing maximum cognitive diversity as well as increasing the porosity of the system boundaries to a variety of subjects, knowledges and practices, thus leading to a commoning of the maximum potential creativity and resilience.

Diversity, like variability, increases systems resilience because 'it is essential for their maintenance', especially in managing 'interactions among slow and fast processes, large and small' (Gunderson and Holling 2002). Thus, for example, in health services all schools of medicine should be welcomed and work synergistically together, including conventional medicine – sanitised of its most profit-driven practices, such as its pricing policies and excessive investment in vanity products at the expense of essential medicines for more widespread life-threatening diseases such as malaria – and also alternative medicine. This holistic and inclusive approach to health is already being pursued by many cooperatives, and it should become standard in *commonalised* health services.

Thus three principles, *deep democratic management, accountability* and *loosening boundaries (DAB),* and the principles associated with these, are the basic goals for a strategy of commons vis-à-vis state and corporate property, on the basis of which the other principle of resilience could be adopted in different conditions and contexts. They indicate not the end point, but simply the road to take.

For instance, take *Win Barcellona* (Guanyem Barcellona), the basic programme of Barcelona en Comú whose leader Ada Colau took the mayoral office in May 2016 and came from the grassroots radical anti-evictions movement PAH. The programme embedded all three of the basic DAB elements I outlined above, and although, precisely, it has the uncertainty of a programme, significantly it aligns to our discussions here. So for example, the programme states that the deepening of democracy is relevant in

> recognising and promoting local initiatives and networks of self-managed public goods and services. From cultural and social centres to consumption cooperatives, community gardens, time banks and early childhood facilities for families. Public institutions should give these groups spaces, resources and technical support while respecting their autonomy and not instrumentalizing them. (Guanyem Barcellona 2015)

Here existing commons are considered a subsystem participating in the overall production system of the public commons. Added to this is the proviso that 'Citizens have the right to make decisions about the things that affect them' and the consequent policy of extending the mechanisms of 'citizen participation' and the promise that 'we have to ensure that public institutions respond to the will of the people rather than the interests of major economic powers or a handful of leaders used to working behind closed doors' (Guanyem Barcellona 2015).

The programme stresses accountability as a reinforcing aspect of democracy: 'all municipal bodies and management positions must be audited immediately', etc. Finally, the opening up of the existing state boundaries as organisation is clear in the basic objectives anticipated by the group. In the first place, 'winning to guarantee basic rights and a decent life for all ... decent housing, education, health, food ... and winning to push for a socially and environmentally fair economy', which essentially means a resilient economy in the terms I discussed above (Guanyem Barcellona 2015). Whether *en Comun* has got DAB principles is pretty much clear; only history will tell us, however, how and how much, together with social movements, this political organisation and corresponding movements will be able to radically change Barcelona within fields of opposing forces of constituted power. What is certain is that what happens in Barcelona is entangled with what happens in Spain, Europe and in the world, and, moreover, that the possibilities of radical system change and transformation also depend on how the different scales are nested, and on what are the principles regulating such an interaction among scales, which are nested systems whose destiny is shared but have different movements and momentum (Gunderson and Holling 2002).

Obviously, one cannot demand transparency of a commons, unless its activity creates negative externalities on other commons; this is because a commons is not a public institution, and the boundary around it – in spite of the different degree of porosity and the possibility for an individual to go through it – generally has a rational kernel: it represents the contextual limit of the sphere of its activity. On the other hand, we can legitimately demand transparency of a public institution because such institutions ought to benefit all of us, and not only a part of us, ought to be our commons, however idealistic such an expression may be. Hence, our demand for DAB implies a demand that we should all be part of the public institution's relational field and be able to exercise control over it, whether by sending people's representatives to its board of directors with effective powers, or as social movements contesting the effects of its managerial and top-down administration. This is the same as regarding public institutions as distorted commons, that is, as regarding them in an aspirational way – as what, from the commons perspective that understands commons through the lens of commoning and grassroots democracy, they ought to be, in spite of their present distortions as commons.

The complexity of social transformation

Any commons movement that aims at the transformation of the state and public institutions is preceded by the emergence or intensification of social movements and, more so, commons (community) movements. Most likely, a massive social movement would be necessary to commonalise institutions and functions of public services. Thus, it is when the school become a 'key location in the battle between the community [commons] and the state' that the battle takes on not only 'a territorial character' as highlighted by Zibechi (2012: 18), but also a potential movement in the direction of commonalisation of state school institutions. The school can, then, be either a site of struggle between the community and the state or a site of civil war among children and families, for example competing for grades and hence placement in government-ranked 'good' schools as in the case of London's schools. The school can be either a place in which commonalisation is taught and prac- tised, or one in which competition begins to exclude and divide. The choice cannot begin from the top, but must be practised from below: by families and children, by teachers and headmasters. The choice is increasingly between either autonomous and autopoietic schools, hospitals, clinics, child- care, and so on – extending the climate and the structure for emancipation and social conviviality – or state or privately run services, in competition with one another, creating further alienation, exclusions and divisions instead of eliminating the gigantic ones we have already.

Yet something is missing from this basic characterisation of change as a purely bottom-up process – two things specifically, a question of value and a question of organisation and coor- dination on a very large scale. The question of values is about the types of values pursued by struggles. Are these *always* radical, progressive and transformative of social structures towards resilience as indicated in Table 9.2? Or, rather, are they building up strong boundaries, xenophobia, sexism, racism, homophobia and so on, that divide and constitute wage hier- archies, rather than connecting across commons? Commons values can evolve towards the resilient systemic objective as in Table 9.2 if social movements develop a twofold goal (already enacted in many instances): one, to set in train a resistance to neoliberal capital, and, two, to constitute many alternatives – 'one no many yesses', as anticipated by the Zapatistas move- ment already in the mid 1990s. We know now, though, that the many yesses will have sufficient power to build the good life and to resist capitalist power only if we build their interconnections and systemic structures.

The evolution of struggles in this direction, seeking both to politically limit capital and to construct alternatives, implies a reconceptualisation of the subjectivities enacting this. In Chapter 5 I discussed some aspects of this reconceptualisation, in that I derived the commons as something *including* a relation to capital but not being exhausted by such a relation to capital. This relation to capital is obvious by the fact that commons are often creators of the commodity labour power, and not just in the household dimension, but also in schools, collectives, neighbourhoods, staff canteens, etc. Thus, within the commons is reproduced what traditional Marxism called the *class in itself*: ready-to-go-to-work labour power, then working, then coming back and being reproduced to to go back to work, with a particular social composition. However, if this loop of reproduction of labour power is only one aspect of what goes on in the commons, the other being the exercise of autonomous and autopoietic powers as in commoning, then inside commons there is also something else than class in itself. There is also the *class for itself*. There is thus a relation between the commons discourse and class discourse which is crucial.

In so far as commons are in relation to capital, they are the social producers of *class*. Whether this class is only in itself or for itself is decided by the form, magnitude, and strategic direction of commoning and struggles. In Box 12, I summarise some key directions of this struggle starting from a world in which power is unevenly divided in several domains. Box 12 is borrowed from a publication I also contributed to by Midnight Notes and Friends.

continued on page 353

Box 12 The point of struggles
[Source: Midnight Notes and Friends 2010: 14–15.]

Social movements and commons: towards commons movements

1   The struggles subvert class hierarchy – between those who are working class and those capitalist class, within the working class, and within nations and internationally; racially; between women and men; between immigrants and citizens; and between diverse cultures. Their demands lead to greater equality if won (and perhaps even if not won) because of how the battle is fought. The needs of those 'on the bottom' (the poorest economically, least powerful socially or politically) are to be put first in an explicit way that builds unity and sustainability. Social democratic demands continue generally for access to wealth: wages and income, work time, job security, pensions, health care, housing, food (which may mean land in many cases), and education. (Some of these comprise the indirect wage – which is more apt to be in some ways socialised, a form of commons, even if within capitalism). Do such struggles privilege the already relatively privileged/powerful, would 'victory' lock into place greater inequalities? Similarly, do autonomous actions include or exclude the least powerful socially or economically?

2   The struggles increase class unity, bringing together different class sectors in positive, mutually strengthening relationships, overcoming divisions among the class. They go beyond single issues, connecting them, without diminishing the significance or value of those issues. This unity must become planetary, hence the importance of deepening and expanding global networks through struggles towards constituting long-term autonomous and decentralised livelihoods based on collective relations of production, exchange and consumption that are based on dignified livelihoods of all commons.

3   The struggles build dignified inclusion in community. The walls of exclusion and apartheid come down in revolutionary

struggles – including, in our time, the walls against immigrants, prisoners, gays and lesbians, and historically oppressed races and peoples. They respect the otherness and commonness of the other so as to be more aware of her/his needs, especially the less powerful at present. They aim to ensure that we all treat one another with dignity.

4   The struggles strengthen the commons and expand decommodified relationships and spaces. The commons is a non-commodified space shared by the community. Social democratic versions include such things as health care, education, social security – however imperfectly realised. However, does the struggle also support bringing the bottom up, expanding inclusiveness and participatory control? On the other hand, are autonomous sectors able to avoid commodification (avoid being turned into business products or services for sale)? Even if they cannot do so completely, can they maintain a political stance and active behaviour that pushes towards non-commodity forms? More generally, how can the working class on small or large scales create forms of exchange that are or tend towards being decommodified? Create markets (forms of exchange) that do not rule lives and livelihoods? Reduce the reach of commodification and capitalist markets into people's lives?

5   The struggles enhance local control and participatory control. 'Local' is not a geographical term, it means that decisions are taken as close to those involved as possible; participatory means that all those affected have a real voice in the decisions. This puts on the table the issues of who makes decisions and how. Much of what we know as autonomous action is local and almost definitionally includes 'local control' of some sort. Social democracy historically does not. Indeed, one of its hallmarks is reliance on a large, bureaucratic, intrusive, and hard-to-influence state apparatus. This state was the target of a widespread working-class attack in the 1960s, which, however, was turned against the working class and used by the right wing to promote neoliberalism. Can the working class make social democratic demands/struggles that include the demand and fight for local and/or participatory control? (There were aspects of this in some early 'war on poverty' programmes, but they were eliminated or co-opted once the US state saw danger in its 'miscalculation' on this.) More generally, do 'inside' struggles help support 'outside' struggles? Are there ways to move social democratic struggles towards more autonomous action? Example: battles for government support of urban gardening may also push for control through local, participatory democratic bodies, rather than city or state government. Factory struggles may begin as 'inside' but the participants may come to organise themselves in assemblies, etc., take over and control production cooperatively, and then set up cooperative support across factories and other sectors (as happened in Argentina after its economic collapse in 1998–2002). Indeed, many union struggles (the quintessential 'inside' struggle) reached a turning point that transformed them into outside struggles, as an examination of general strikes will show. However, even in autonomous developments, participatory control is not guaranteed, either at the level of writing the rules or in ongoing practice. So in the various areas of reproduction (health care, food, education, housing) and production, what would participatory democratic control look like, and how can it be fought for in ways that win in the specific area and decrease divisions in the class?

6 The struggles lead towards more time outside capitalist control. In particular, this means a shorter working week for the waged and unwaged. It means recognising 'women's work' as productive, creating income for those doing this work as well as expanding who does it. How can we ensure that a shorter waged-work week does not further empower men relative to women? Or some class sectors over other class sectors? That is, how can victories in the realm of time be egalitarian?

7 The struggles reduce the staggering wastefulness and destructiveness of capital, of lives, time, material wealth, health, and the environment (air, land and water), but these reductions happen in ways that do not penalise other workers ... What will have to be done so these people are not economically destroyed? Of course, from a working-class perspective, things like the military and weapons production are destructive to the point of insanity, so should be eliminated. Reducing waste of some sorts may benefit some while not benefiting others (for example, if it leads to a reduction of waged-work time, it may not help mothers with kids) – so inclusion must be considered when 'capitalist wastefulness' is addressed.

8   The struggles protect and restore ecological health. Struggles facilitate a healthier, more holistic approach to the planet. For example, battles to save jobs in industries that foster ecological disaster need to be addressed; there are now and will be such battles. Land, air, and water are of crucial importance. Agribusiness, global commodification, bioengineering, and war lead to pollution, erosion, dams, flooding, deforestation, global warming, diminishing diversity, and the death of land and oceanic ecosystems. In replacing agribusiness as the mode of food production, closer human relations to food production are to be fostered.

9   The struggles bring justice. Too often, exploiters and oppressors have acted with impunity. Thus the real criminals must be brought to justice for healing to occur. Revolutionary justice is bottom up, and new forms of enacting justice should be consistent with the other revolutionary characteristics, for example 'No' to capital punishment even for capitalists.

The bottom line of Box 12 is a Marxist understanding of what postcapitalist transformation is: in a class society there is no change or transformation without class conflict vis-à-vis capital and the state but also among different sections of a working class very much divided along wage, gender, race and other lines.

These principles indicate the huge complexity of transforming the dominant mode of production, a complexity caused by the difficulties not only of constituting commons ecologies, but also of overcoming the multifaceted real divisions that exist among commoners and commons movements and between both these and capital and the state.

Complexity is a feature even of small communities. Commons, even small ones, are complex phenomena. Many communities show characteristics of complex systems. In the first place, they are heterogeneous, with different values and interests influenced by gender, age, class, ethnic group, etc. Communities at large, beyond those belonging to specific commons but within proximity to each other within a territory, may comprise competing groups, and differences may be great to the point that a particular locality may be thought of as containing different communities, as in the caste communities in many parts of India (Berkes et al. 1998) or in semi-segregated areas of Western metropolises where migrants live, or when a village in Europe is ripped apart by divisions over whether to welcome or not a few refugees. Other communities may share some rules useful when beginning commons systems, or they may simply be an environment to one another, at times even a conflicting environment (Berkes 2006). But where commonalisation of private and public systems is concerned, and the overall problematic of social transformation or social revolution, we are dealing with a massive increase in the level of complexity since we are talking about the articulation and coordination of different scales of commons; invariably, therefore, complexity skyrockets to the point that it appears unmanageable. One seems to need a simple rule, say capitalist market money, or the authority of the state, to manage complex systems, but this is to forget that the subjugation of a multitude of subjectivities to a simple rule is simply not beneficial for most of the people at the bottom or for human freedom, and is also not *viable* in term of addressing the very complex problems facing humanity: environmental disaster, catastrophic poverty, and monumental injustices.

Chapter 10

Towards postcapitalism

Everybody is a manager, the law that governs from an evolutionary perspective in nature is – self-organisation.

HEINZ VON FOERSTER

And when everyone is Super (chuckle) no one is!

SYNDROME, *THE INCREDIBLES*

How can the social form shared by households, community
gardens, neighbourhood associations, reclaimed factories,
social centres, and commons ecologies in general become a force
of social revolution, of radical emancipatory change towards
postcapitalism? What is emancipation?

Emancipation

Emancipation has to do with the *process of liberation,* of being
set free. But to emancipate ourselves from capital and the
current forms of the state we need a form of emancipation
that is obtained through wider spheres of autonomy and autopoiesis of the commons. Only in this way can we emancipate
ourselves from state and capital, and from the problems they
create (war, global warming, control obsession, poverty in the
midst of plenty, expropriations and exploitation). Nevertheless, we cannot emancipate ourselves from the vertical state and

exploitative capital tomorrow or in a year's time; rather, we must see emancipation as a *process of growing commons powers vis-à-vis capital and the state*. These powers, in turn, are the power fields out of which the commons draw their social forces in the process of their development and dealings with capital and the state at any given time and and in any given context – that is, in the process of emancipation.

Are the commons emancipatory? In this book I have not assumed they are, merely distinguishing commons from corrupted commons, the latter being those commons systems that reproduce oppressions and the claustrophobic sense of boundaries. But can a commons be emancipatory? Well, can social movements be emancipatory? Actually no. Emancipation is not a matter of social systems, only of individuals. Zibechi (2012: 26), reflecting on the writing of Jacques Rancière filtered by the pedagogical experience of the social movements in Latin America, argues that 'Emancipation does not allow for prescriptions or model; it is a process that is always unfinished and must be experienced individually.' But if it is true that 'one can only be emancipated by oneself,' it is also true that there is a context, a 'space–time marked by the logic of emancipation and not by the logic of 'first in the class' – that is, a climate conducive to emancipation – that climate does not fall from the sky but is created by the collective activity of the social movements that are, to paraphrase Braudel, the 'home of the common people'. Zibechi is here reflecting on social movements, but, I would argue, commons also are space–times, are the contexts of subjects. Remember Figure 2.1, tracing the subject's path jumping from system to system. From the perspective of the individual subjects experiencing emancipation, social movements and commons are two systems, both contexts in which individual subjects operate. To talk about emancipation from capital/state, or from its effects (poverty, stress, imposed work, global warming and ecological genocide, crap food, advertisements and plastic culture, consumerism, fear, egocentrism) is thus to talk about a collective process that creates a context in which individuals emancipate themselves.

Thus, if commons ecologies become the context in which individuals and communities experience their process of emancipation, our effort will be to problematise emancipatory commons, that is commons that, from the perspective of individuals within them, constitute not simple rules to be obeyed in order to get benefits, but contexts in which the subjects learn and experience for themselves the meaning of empowerment: 'emancipation is not an objective but a way of life' (Zibechi 2012: 49).

Commons are located within an environment which often is not emancipatory. In this sense, commons find themselves constrained by this environment, either because state/capital limits the imagining of the possible, or because the fear of overcoming constraints imposed and normalised by state/capital is so big. The commons themselves then need to forge a different environment, changing their relations to the social systems within it, like capital and the state. This happens in waves, through social movements, unpredictable in timing and in form, but always bringing new energies inside the commons, rearranging resources and subjectivities, creating new common wealth together with new perspectives, affects, horizons and yet, in turn, depending so much on the commons themselves for life and reproduction, and care, and energy. A lot has been written about social movements, about their resources, about identities, about their relation to power, about their defeats and victories.[1] But only a tentative link has been made between commons and social movements in terms of them both being social systems, in terms of their reciprocal influence and dynamics.

Authors such as Zibechi do not explicitly comment on the distinction and articulation between commons and social movements, yet this is highly visible in the practice of social movements that he describes that show few key commons characteristics. In the first place,

> territorialisation of the movements, that is, they have roots in spaces that have been recuperated or otherwise secured through long (open or underground) struggles. This reflects a strategic response of the poor to the crisis of the old territoriality of the factory and farm and to capital's reformulation of the old modes of domination. (Zibechi 2012: 15)

Territorial rootedness is a feature of several movements: the movement of the landless in Brazil, who seize lands and self-manage them including all aspects of care and education; indigenous peoples of Ecuador who expanded their communities to rebuild their ancestors' territories of ethnicity; indigenous people in Chiapas who populated the Lacandon jungle; anti-dam communities in India who seek to reclaim their lands and rivers; Ogoni people in Nigeria who seek different distributive arrangements for the revenue from oil extracted in their territory and a different ecological practice that prevents destruction of lakes and lands; social centres in urban areas that seek to revitalise solidarity community links in their area. In South America in particular:

across the continent, the poor have recuperated or conquered millions of hectares, creating a crisis within territorial order and remodeling the physical spaces of resistance. From their territories, the new actors consolidated long-term projects, most notably the capacity to produce and reproduce life, while establishing alliances with the middle class. The experience of the Argentine piquateros [unemployed workers] is significant, since it is one of the first instances of an urban movement with these characteristics. (Zibechi 2012: 15)

Territorial rootedness is also the future of several of the movements we have been discussing. The case of Genuino Clandestino was discussed in Chapter 8, a networks of farmers and consumers who depend on territorial rootedness to sustain interactions. The successful social centres are also reliant on committed and territorial rooted subjectivities, even if only to relate to and help subjects who, because of their migration status, are not territorially rooted. Their purpose in seeking asylum or a residence permit is to increase their territorial rootedness, to be able to operate within a territory.

The radical character of *rootedness* becomes clear when we appreciate that the neoliberal era has coincided with a great movement of people, labour, and, mostly capital, in terms of both financial and productive capital. Both these forms have allowed the constitution of the greatest-ever disciplinary machines such as the working-class debt machine and global capitalist markets, entangled disciplinary machines that regulate the life activity of people and communities all around the world in a giant disciplinary panopticon (De Angelis 2007a).

There are two main ways in which commons can escape this panopticon.

In the first place they can escape it through migration, a strategy of deterritorialisation in search of better wages and the opportunity to access education. Migration and refugee movements in the global factory may allow individual subjectivities to obtain emancipation from political and religion persecution or economic destitution. But it is also increasingly risky and not always successful, especially since the intensified construction of walls and detention centres by states around the world and especially the states of the Global North. In many cases, the deterritorialisation of people corresponds to a new reterritorialisation, in which first- and, especially, second- and third-generation migrants build networks of solidarity in the new areas. Migration is also often linked to expanded territorialisation in the original communities, which benefit from remittances. International migrants in 2016 are believed to have sent $601 billion to their families in their home countries, about two thirds of which was received by countries of the Global South. This figure is three times the size of development aid (KNOMAD 2016).

The second way of escaping the disciplinary panopticon is through commonalisation, and one crucial aspect of this is linked to territorialisation. This is the side linked to survival, to subsistence, to the material reproduction of bodies in terms of food, housing, education, health and care. This trajectory also emerges because in times of crisis there is simply nothing else around, maybe just charity. 'Developed' countries that experience economic collapse like Greece witnessed from the early years of the crisis a sudden increase in the commons because they become a survival strategy for many. While the Troika (the European Central Bank, the European Commission and the

International Monetary Fund) have been imposing austerity on Greece to repay European banks, in only a few years, between 2009 and 2014, the effect was to force down wages by 38 per cent, to reduce pensions by 45 per cent, and to cut household incomes by 30 per cent (to less than €4,400 per household); and an increase in 400 per cent in overdue mortgages. At the same time, between 2008 and 2012 child mortality increased by 42.8 per cent, and the number of living children with both parents unemployed grew by 331.8 per cent. Meanwhile there have been social insurance cuts in the proportion of people's hospital and extra-hospital care costs that are funded by insurance (30.5 per cent and 34.8 per cent), maternity, family and birth allowances (14.9, 23.5 and 52 per cent respectively), unemployment benefits and disabled allowances (11.7 per cent and 15.8 per cent), and a massive 58.6 per cent in all forms of social housing and subsidies (all 2013 figures). The capitalist crisis has its own rationales, it seeks to devalue anything that can be repurchased from distraught, desperate people (the suicide rate from 2007 to 2011 was up by 43 per cent; the incidence of depression in 2013 amounted to 12.30 per cent of the population, up from 3.30 per cent in 2008).[2] Labour power and capital are devalued so that a new wave of accumulation can begin on the basis of cheap sale prices and higher profitability for international investors. It is in contexts like these that commons develop as a survival strategy (see boxes 2 and 3).

However, territorialisation in the sense of building commons systems of solidarity in the midst of crisis in a particular area is also linked to deterritorialisation of values, especially when the creation of commons is linked to the evolution of perspectives and horizons that see private and public resources as commons and regard the 'other', regardless of gender, ethnicity, age or sexual preference, as a commoner. Emancipation is always linked to a particular struggle. The struggle of individuals to do things in common in spite of the 'habitus', to overcome cultural boundaries and prejudice to perceive hope despite the creation of oppressive conditions and to overcome cynicism: this is an emancipation journey of individuals within the emancipation climate of the commons, which in turn can rest on the emancipation climate of social movements.

Commons and social movements are different, however, in their provision of a context for emancipation. Social movements are an environment to emancipation, which is lived and experienced by subjects but not necessarily delivered by the social movements themselves. Commons are emancipatory only when their practices are emancipatory. Thus, a generalised critique of the political economy of food can be at the basis of a social movement against genetically modified organisms (GMOs) or more trade-liberalising laws (hence campaigning for an emancipation from neoliberal laws). However, this is not sufficient for the commons to be an environment to emancipation, which would include the actual promoting of local food sovereignty systems and networks, agroecological educational projects and new types of participatory market structures. For the commons, the critique of health and the medicalisation of life is only necessary and not sufficient: emancipation will require instead the establishment of practices re-appropriating healthcare through the knowledge of plants in the surrounding region and their transformation into therapeutic or preventive medicines. In this sense, commons can be an environment of individuals' emancipation, because they provide alternatives to the subjects who created them, while social movements simply demand these alternatives. Or, to quote Zibechi once again, reflecting on the Latin American experience:

> A community has an emancipatory approach to health care when it recovers its own healing powers, which are been expropriated by the industry and the state, and liberates itself from the control that capital exercises over health care through multinational pharmaceuticals. Zapatista medical health care practices, as well as those of many indigenous peoples and piqueteros groups, share many commonalities despite their enormous cultural differences. (Zibechi 2012: 31)

I have argued in this section that commons and social movements are often interrelated, and they both define environments in which emancipation takes place. But what is their difference, and how can their difference been articulated in such a way as to push society towards a postcapitalist era?

Commons, social movements and social fabric

Social movements both present themselves as a system/environment relation and have boundaries. But while commons as such are preoccupied with their reproduction qua commons, social movements' reproduction is projected onto society. This projection has a twofold aim: to act as an attractor of subjectivities to reach a critical mass for change vis-à-vis politics, and to be recognised by larger and larger spheres of society as one of its legitimate components (in terms of the values practices guiding them and in terms of sense horizon). In the latter case the operation is of course very much at risk of co-optation, although that may at times be a necessary risk. Recognition always passes through a particular field of representation. However, 'this places the movement in a difficult position. In certain periods, it cannot afford to make concessions to visibility or escape intervening on the political stage' (Zibechi 2012: 19). These concessions are, at a given time and place, deals with its counterpart, whether capital and/or state. The need to reach deals often raises the issue of what is the form of organisation of the social movement, whether centralised or, at the other end of the spectrum, diffused and discontinuous. The first case would allow the presence of a highly visible organisation, at the cost of the virtues of internal democracy and decentralised autonomy. The second case would take stock of the benefits of decentralisation and inclusion, at the risk of lack of effectiveness and direction in the negotiations. I agree with Zibechi that there is no optimum form that can be decided a priori, and that much depends on context: 'The debate or whether to opt for a centralized, highly visible organization or a diffuse discontinuous one presents the two extremes of the question, although there are no simple solutions to the matter and it cannot be settled for once and all' (Zibechi 2012: 19).

Having made such a disclaimer regarding the organisation of social movements, let me return to the relations between commons and social movements. These are two modalities of social systems within what we call society, the social broth that includes all social systems. Within this social broth we find social systems such as commons and capitals that reproduce themselves or die out all the time. The process of birth and development of social systems gives rise to a social fabric, while the dissolution of social systems gives rise to any form of material or biographic detritus. By social fabric I mean *the social space constituted by the multiplicity of social systems in their structurally coupled interactions, or deals.* We can have structurally coupled interaction among individual capitals (through market exchanges, partnerships, collusions, etc.) or among commons (networks of households, associations, etc.), and across capital and commons (for example a deal between a company and a trade union, a community association and a local council). A social movement is a wave in the social broth that results in change, to varying degrees, in the quality of the social fabric, and the different couplings among social systems.

Ultimately, there are four ways to change this social fabric: (1) through systems' perturbation; (2) through changes in the patterns of structural coupling; (3) through decoupling and autonomisation of systems; and (4) through destruction of systems.

None of these ways are more 'politically correct' than others, as they all depend on the particular situation and balance of forces in which social movements find themselves. What we can say is that social movements acquire a class meaning when the change in the social fabric that they give rise to provokes a change in the way capital has to strategise its own reproduction and when the commons can find new room and resources for their (re)production, development and formation of commons ecologies.

Each social movement is a succession of waves and cycles that is a recomposing and decomposing force; it favours certain types of connections and destroys others, and it creates sociality and creates alien differentiations with the 'enemy' while at the same time overcoming alien relations among commoners. But if social movements favour connections and sociality, it does not mean that they create a new social fabric that can reproduce and sustain itself in characteristics that we may recognise as fundamentally alternative to the current one dominated by capital. Actually, capital's own development occurred as a result of the struggles for wages, working conditions, employment and environment. Capital has adapted to many of these struggles in the course of the centuries, although this does not mean that it solved many of the issues posed by the struggles.

Precisely because of their own limited characteristics, social movements can only contribute to the making of alternatives; they themselves are not the alternative. The latter requires different types of temporality and cycles, cycles with different objectives and rhythms. By cycle I mean the temporal sequences in which human activity turns things and relations into something else. In the first place, from the perspective of their preconditions, both social movements and commons presuppose one another, and both cannot be conceived without a commons basis for the reproduction of the lives of the subjects participating in them as well as for the form of their sociality. We would not be able to understand the labour movement without thinking about the practices of commoning, of sharing resources, of solidarity, of affects, of gift, and about the work of reproduction in households, which allows the workers as a social body to express their force in the struggle against capital, or without the reproduction of these bodies within the households, neighbourhoods and associations.

Recent movements such as the Occupy movement in New York City or the Arab Spring in Cairo or Tunisia would not have been possible without a commons basis in which material and immaterial resources were shared in different modalities: social movements need to organise their own practices of commoning necessary for resources and the reproduction of their members – food, security, logistics, tents, fundraising, and so on. Clearly, in social movements subjects also practise alternatives, even if only educational alternatives, since to participate in social movements is an ongoing process of self-education. Yet, these forms of commons are sustained so long as the movement lasts; the subjects are enriched, but at the same time the intensity and potential extension of new emancipatory social relations decline massively with the vanishing of the movement, especially when it is hit by repression.

Many contemporary social movements are also the forms that the commons take when they resist enclosures. Whether it is resisting the redevelopment of a neighbourhood of social hous-ing in anticipation of a large event such as the Olympic Games, or the expropriation of community land to build a dam or a high-speed train line, movements articulate families, networks and associations – commons – in defensive struggles and in so doing weave a social fabric across the commons. Hence, although defensive, social movements create the conditions for offensive struggles, through changes in paradigms, redefinition of sense horizons, clarification of the nature and structure of fields of power relations, and new connections with other move-ment through solidarity. The first act of a social movement of this nature is to begin and then to sustain a process of negotiation of meanings across the participating plurality, of singling out what are the commons that they are defending and why, of mapping out friends and foes, of drawing distinctions and of developing a common sense horizon.

Thus social movements embed commons and can be sparked by the defence of commons. However, the reproduction of commons and corresponding communities is often predicated on particular deals with capital, obtained as a result of struggles that have occurred in the past and given rise to particular institutional forms and cultures. Also, social movements and commons sequences have different starting and end points. Their temporal cycle intertwines, and often coincides, but they are not always identical. The starting point of a social movement expresses itself as a concentration of forces in a point, a clashing event, that then opens up to a series of events moving in waves. I indicate this as Event(m), where m stands for *movement*. The end of the social movement temporal cycle is a sort of deal with other social forces of power whether or not the deal brings advantages, whether it is a sort of capitulation or a gain in resources or rights, or a shift in political and cultural horizons. It goes without saying that the type of deal depends on the web of power relations in different contexts. So, a social movement is a system that has a particular cycle – it starts from an event and turns into a deal:

$$\text{Event (m)} \ldots \rightarrow \ldots \text{DEAL}$$

Seen in this light, the commons cycle is just the opposite of the social movement. The starting point of commons in contemporary capitalism is always a given pact with the devil, a balance of forces, a deal. The common resources that can be pooled at that given time is always subject to the power constraints on the commons in a given environment dominated by capital and the state. The end point of the commons instead is its (re)production, and this passes through an event that allows it to do so: the harvest, the payment of a social wage, the sharing of a meal. I call this Event (cm), where cm indicates the commons:

$$\text{DEAL} \ldots \rightarrow \ldots \text{Event (cm)}$$

The process of social revolution therefore must seek ways to couple social movement and commons, to synchronise their respective sequences, to turn the subjects of movements into commoners and make commoners protestors. The process of social revolution can be schematised thus:

social movement cycle   social movement cycle

...Event (m)...→...DEAL...→...Event (cm)...→...Event (m)...→...DEAL...→...Event (cm)...

            commons cycle   commons cycle

This shows how each iteration of the movement increases the power of the commons to develop and (re)produce, and that new, expanded commons ecologies are the basis for a more powerful movement.

If only we could align these cycles into one virtuous loop of social revolution we would have made a giant step towards post-capitalism. Clearly this does not take account what the reaction of the state and capital would be after a few iterations of this virtuous cycle. The probability is that sooner or later some major, violent wave would be unleashed against social movements and commons to limit their power. Yet, if this is a possibility, it does not exhaust all possibilities. Clearly, predicting the future is not my business, but to frame the question of complex social trans-formation is. So, in the next section I want to put into relation this possible virtuous loop of the social movements–commons with the range of actions that the state and capital could adopt against it. Taken as a whole, this multipolar relation between commons and social movements on one side and state and capi-tal on the other entails a disentangling of the complexity of the contemporary problematics of social transformation towards postcapitalism.

Complexity disentangled

How can the plurality of interlaced commons reach a critical mass beyond which it can regulate social reproduction and thus drastically reduce social, economic and environmental injustices, further increase a culture of collective organisation, doing in common and self-management, take a grip on the environmental catastrophe caused by capital's systemic loops, and promise a dignified future for all? In other words, how can we radically change our life in common in order to deepen drastically the horizons of freedom and emancipation?

The big question is not how to create struggles – which sooner or later will develop. But how can the new complexities that struggles generate lead us to seize the opportunity for emancipatory change instead of allowing capital to adapt to the new situation faster than we can ourselves? But first of all, what is complexity?

Complexity is different from *complicated*, as the latter term refers to large systems with patterned behaviour that are predictable. Something may be complicated – such as a large water pipe network below a city, where the flow of water given certain inputs is predictable. On the other hand, a complex system has a large share of unpredictable subsystems. The operations of an air traffic control system are linked to a bunch of unpredictable systems, such as the weather (Sargut and McGrath 2011); or a social movement may be composed of a series of sub-movements that do not always move in the same direction or with the same resolution and impetus.

The original Latin word *complexus* signifies 'entwined', 'twisted together'. This can signify that in order to have a complex you need two or more components (a multiplicity starts with 2), which are joined in such a way that it is difficult to separate them. Similarly, the Oxford English Dictionary defines something as 'complex' if it is 'made of (usually several) closely connected parts'. Here we find the basic duality between parts which are at the same time distinct and connected. Intuitively, then, a system would be more complex if more parts and more distinction among the parts were added. The examples of commons structural coupling discussed in Chapter 8 were examples of complexity. Other examples are contemporary social movements, the current conflicts in Syria, and global capitalist markets.

Distinction and connection are opposite characteristics defining complexity. Distinction refers to variety, to diversity, to what is heterogeneous, to the fact that different elements of the complex behave differently, or have different desires and aspirations. Connection corresponds to some form of constraint, which in the case of structural coupling is a constraint that is constructed autonomously by the autopoietic units. Connection then means that different parts are not independent, but that the knowledge of one part allows the determination of features of the other parts and vice versa. At the limit, distinction without connection leads to disorder, chaos or entropy, like in a gas, where the position of any gas molecule is completely independent of the position of the other molecules, or a room full of roaming children with no common focus of attention. Connection without distinction leads to order or negentropy – like in a perfect crystal, where the position of a molecule is completely determined by the positions of the neighbouring molecules to which it is bound – too boring and unfree a world for current realities or for emancipatory utopians. Complexity can only exist if both distinction and connection are present: neither perfect 'disorder' nor perfect 'order' have got to do with complexity. Complexity is in the middle, above and below, always 'on the edge of chaos' (Principia Cybernetica 1996).

Complexity can be measured in terms of what cyberneticists call variety.

> Given a set of elements, its variety is the number of elements that can be distinguished. Thus the set {g b c g g c } has a variety of 3 letters. If two observers differ in the distinctions they can make, then they will differ in their estimates of the variety. Thus if the set is {b c a a C a B a } its variety in shapes is 5, but its variety in letters is 3. (Ashby 1958:1)

Variety thus 'is a measure of complexity, because it counts the number of possible states of a system' (Beer 1994: 25). Let us take a automobile traffic control system. There are in principle 4 possible states (i.e. variety 4) from the point of view of control variety, i.e. the variety of the control engine, the traffic light. Red, yellow and green are the three main one, indicating stop, careful, go, while the fourth one is when the traffic light does not work. The variety is of course much larger than that posed on the assumption underlying these 4 states of control variety. In the first place, the states of a system under traffic light control presupposes that drivers understand, accept and are disciplined by the traffic rules. But let us assume we move to Cairo or Addis Ababa or another city in the Global South where either traffic lights are scarce, or not working or the trafficlight norms are not completely internalised by drivers. If we were sitting high up on a balcony facing an intersection we would probably see the emergence of a self-organising complexity chaos.[3] The variety of this system would be much higher than one governed by a traffic light, but its effects in terms of traffic regulation are probably the same.

I am about to use now a cybernetic law to argue my case regarding the relation between social movements, commons and capital/state. For the purpose of this analysis, capital/state is called the 'regulator'. There is a law in cybernetic or system theory that is called the Law of Requisite Variety or Ashby's Law, from the name of the person who proposed it in 1957, Ross W. Ashby. This law states that in order to have a system under the control of the regulator, the variety of the regulator must match the variety of the system. Alternatively, the greater the variety of a system in relation to the regulator, the greater is the need of the regulator to reduce the system's variety or increase its own variety. Stafford Beer takes the variety of the system as a measure of complexity, that is, the number of possible states that the system can take.

Thus, to recap, the law of control par excellence states that 'only variety absorbs variety'. This is Ashby's Law. In order to have a system under control, the variety of the regulator has at least to match the variety of the system to be regulated. Let us see the implications of this simple law for the discourse of emancipation, social movements and commons.

Figure 10.1a, contains one system called 'society' and indicated with an oval, while the system indicated by a square represents the regulator. By regulator I mean here the network of capital and state agents and corresponding systems and discursive practices aiming at regulating society in a given period. Note that society here includes 'the economy': capital, families, associations, commons ecologies and the multitude of individual subjectivities and the multitude of those complex relations as defined above. Obviously, even the regulators are part of society as indicated in Figure 10.1a.

One must keep in mind that this illustration, like many cybernetics illustrations, maintain its unity at different scales. That is, Figure 10.1, like other figures, could very generally illustrate a relation at the level of a city council vis-à-vis the city, a company vis-à-vis workers, customers and communities affected by it; a nation-state vis-à-vis society and networks of nation-states; Global capital/state vis-à-vis world societies. But we can also extend the role of regulators as commoners involved in the governance of the commons. To return to Figure 10.1, let us keep in mind that if 'society' is the emergent whole of interconnections and structural coupling or splits among different social systems, it also has an environment, and that is essentially the

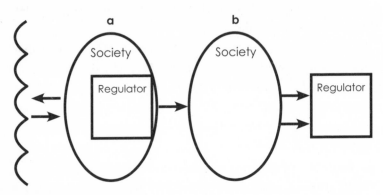

Figure 10.1 A very high bird's eye view of society and regulation

ecological environment of the biosphere as a sum total of the particular environments of situated ecological systems. I have symbolised this with the vertical wave at the left. In other figures, for convenience of illustration, this is not there, even if in reality it is there and it interacts and co-evolves with different systems of society. My point here is, however, different.

For the sake of analytical convenience and following cybernetics practice (Beer 1994), let us separate these two systems as in (b), the right-hand part of Figure 10.1. Let us then make the sensible assumption that society's variety is far greater than the regulator's variety and the more so the more society is complex, that is, numerous and diverse, both in terms of the possible subjectivities, and in terms of the different types of social relations and praxis these subjects entertain. In all types of systems the regulator achieves regulation of variety by two means, either it amplifies its control of variety vis-à-vis a system or it filters system variety. This is a homeostat. All the same, society is a hugely complex system, made of often-struggling subsystems which clash over another high variety of objectives, discourses and reasons. To regulate its effect on capital, the state uses laws restricting other systems from interfering with its own development: laws about strikes, about self-employment, about information, about debt, about money, and now even about seeds. The regulator has a much simplified role now since it can command the huge social force at the disposal of the state and media *to regulate changes in the social temperature:* aspirations, struggles, cultures. So, how would a social homeostatic work?

Let me introduce a second diagram (Figure 10.2), which enables me to begin to discuss the fundamental relations between the regulator and society. Remember that the society oval is in

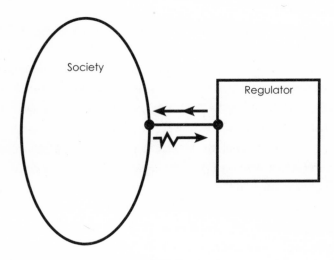

Figure 10.2 Controlled society

turn made of different overlapping system networks each with their force fields interacting with others. Ashby's Law requires that an increase of complexity/variety in society need to be matched by an increase in variety in the regulating system (state/ capital) in order to control the social system (which also, of course, might not happen). Clearly, the past thirty years of capitalist development in the form of modern capitalist globalisation implies an enormous increase in variety of the social system. This means that the global regulator (let us say the USA + G8 + G16 + IMF + EU + central banks + World Bank + corporate Davos, national states and so on) needs to increase its complexity in turn to be able to regulate. Stafford Beer reminds us that the mechanism to manage variety is through a sort of homeostat, that is, the regulator displays two interrelated loops aimed at, first, raising the regulator's variety and, second, decreasing society's variety so as to match the variety of the regulator with that of society. Thus the homeostat is made of one loop filtering the variety of society and selecting what is relevant from it for its own use and adaptation, and another, amplifying loop that amplifies the regulator's variety to society. The filtering loop is marked with the correspondent electric circuit symbol $-\!\!\!\bigwedge\!\!\bigwedge\!\!\bigwedge\!\!-$ while the amplifying loop is marked by the symbol $-\!\!\!\rhd\!\!-$

Among the arsenals of filters in the hands of the regulator there are many practices that are easily recognisable: hegemony on one particular public or economic discourse for example, filters out as 'ideological' any other perspective not sharing the same premises, even more drastically if radical ones. It worked for forty years with neoliberalism, and before that with liberalism with respect to economics, and it worked in different areas including political thinking in fascism, or Nazism, or Stalinism.

In totalitarian systems, indeed, filters are vastly employed not only by discourse, but also by the brutally repressive apparatuses of the state. Bureaucracy, that mostly form-filling stupid time-wasting activity (Graeber 2015), has its rationale for hierarchical societies in that it acts as a big filter that allows a slowing-down of social complexity, and reduces the energy available to fuel it, to increase its level of control. Media manipulation, war, and any activity by the regulator to reduce, select, confine or channel society's movements; police kettling, teargasing, pepper-spraying, shooting of peaceful demonstrators, secret-services targeting of whistleblowers or profiling of black people or Muslims are filtering, as is consequent imprisonment of youth, black people or migrants. The regulator's filter selects out what *it* thinks is proper. Even the exercise of the law and the function of justice have the purpose of filtering out the very general behaviours that the regulators do not desire.

Filtering techniques, those that have been naturalised as just and necessary and those we think are aberrant, are destined to increase with a state/capital-based regulator of an increased social complexity. But all the same, the regulator's amplifier will make its dissonant sound heard. The amplifying loop is also generated by police repression that, being a stick, is always accompanied by a carrot, a method of amplification of action. So the prison is supposed to be accompanied by rehabilitation procedures and officers, the teargas shooting is accompanied by a way out for the demonstrators to run away (often, but not always), taxes are supposedly accompanied by a regime of social welfare with which the state amplifies its operation in society. It is interesting when this is not the case, that is, when police are accused of brutalities, when prison reforms are called for because prisons contribute to the creation of crime, when taxes are defined as robbery. The regulator's filters and amplifiers are supposed to work in tandem, for the sake of the sensibilities of moderate social democrats. And the problem is not really whether there exist filters and amplifiers. The problem is what is constituted through these filters and amplifiers, what social force gains advantage and what instead loses out, what set of values gains prominence and what instead is threatened with criminalisation.

The neoliberal regimes have managed amplification and filtering mechanisms in a very shrewd way. On the one hand, welfare has been brutally filtered out, with corresponding tax cuts, in several countries in the Global North and South. The neoliberal regimes have instead amplified increases in business welfare, in the form of export subsidies and more lenient environmental and tax environments favouring inward flows of foreign direct investment (FDI) – hence amplifying brutal business practices (less strict worker protection laws, social and human rights and environmental laws to mention just a few). These forms of liberalisation, together with privatisations of public assets and enclosures, are basic forms of amplifications and filtering. Many others are associated to it, for example the discourses of Choice and Opportunity (filtered in and amplified in government documents) which correspond to the filtering out of socio-economic and environmental justice and income distribution. This is how different regimes of regulation work.

Now, let us imagine that in Figure 10.2, social movements begin really to move in their upwards cycle. There are clearly many types of social movements in terms of their values and their mode of organisation. However, from the point of view of cybernetics, there are only two, those that manage to increase complexity in society and those that reduce it. In the last camp we have all the xenophobic, racist, sexist and hierarchical movements – from the Ku Klux Klan to the Tea Party in the USA – that, even if funded by millionaires, are expressions of a white grassroots desire to reduce complexity and get to work, *on their own terms,* terms that are happy to put blacks, Muslims and women some steps below their own position on the hierarchical scale. The dark dreams of Daesh belong with this group. This putting down of complexity (for example, the limiting of gay marriage, women's choices, the welfare state, smoking of cannabis, environmental or labour rules limiting business, seed exchanging, freedom of dress, speech and expression and so on) is clearly just the opposite of progressive movements, which fight in the hope of seeing an explosion of complexity, of variability in what is permissible, sharable, walkable in the open. These types of social movements increase the complexity of society in their being, in their doing, and in their purpose, which is a very cybernetic concept since 'the purpose of a system is what it does' (Beer 2004: 861). So, the question is now twofold, one directed to the inside of the movement and the other, looking from the inside perspective, to the regulator. First, can the organisational forms coming from these movements help to regulate this new complexity – even if in new forms of self-regulation – and to shape a corresponding commonsense approach that is able to govern complexity and regulate it in the institutional forms emerging from movements? This is the difficult question that can only be answered contingently, and whose answer depends on the actual relations between commons and social movements discussed in the first part of this chapter. The easy question to frame is the second one: how can the increased complexity brought about by the movements be matched by the increased variety of the state/capital regulator? And how can this be prevented, since if the regulator is able to match the new complexity, emancipatory social change is stopped?

Let us move from this second question. If social movements manage to increase the variety in society, then regulators must either amplify theirs or try to reduce the variety in society. Given Ashby's Law, the capital/state elites will have to decide what to do in order to deal with the increased complexity/variety brought about by social movements. Their control variety must increase. As already noted, in their filtering arsenal there is repression, media engineering and manipulation of the social movement's message. In the amplifying arsenal there is a different type of media manipulation, and co-optation. Co-optation happens when the complexities brought by social movements are in the first place materially divided, and then a good junk of them are absorbed and institutionalised in the complexity of the regulator.

The others are in turn divided, some are turned into subcultural cliché and alternative nodes of resistance, while others are criminalised. The co-optation is not 'progress' per se, but adaptation of regulation within the internal environment of regulation, where the newly acquired variety is moulded within the system of the regulator capital/state.

We can imagine a three-step conscious strategy of growing the commons within a social movements approach. I am following here some of the arguments of Love and Cooper (2007) regarding activists' strategy within complex organisations. Society is, of course, the mother of all complex organisations, since it is itself a social system made up of all the subsystems, including capital and commons circuits.[4] In the first place activists need to 'identify weaknesses in control variety in situations in which activist "owned" sub-systems can expand to fulfil any shortfalls in controlling variety' (Love and Cooper 2007: 9). For example, activists can select those systems having trouble in delivering goods and services at acceptable quality and price but where there is potential for commons to develop and take on the production of those resources (as I have argued above, this often gain momentus under the impulse of crisis). Second, activists can 'undertake acts that will overload existing control variety', for example by increasing struggles over the quality and prices of certain services, the corruption of certain bureaucrats, so that a gap opens between the actual situation and the legitimacy of the demands. Finally, they can 'use "owned" sub-system control variety to stabilise the system. This results in a shift of power towards the activist position' (ibid.); that is to say, forms of commons that replace previous capital/state regulators as 'owners' of that society subsystem.

Clearly thus, from the perspective of radical change, commons and social movements must be aligned here as interrelated sides of the same process, as I have argued in the first part of the chapter. If commons and movements were able to generate themselves endlessly in a virtuous cycle, they would force the overall social system to evolve, and more and more aspects of social reproduction would be *commonised*.

In the case of an increase in variety brought by a social movement, the regulator has two options. One is to amplify its repression, and turn the regulator–social movement–society relation into an increasing hierarchical relation. The other is for it to continuously adapt and co-opt, co-opt and adapt ... but until when? Until when the movement is able to reach a deal, because there are human bodies and reproduction commons that require attention and care. A deal with the regulator is another, often unavoidable, limitation, and if it is a good deal, we call them 'victories'. But the capital/state regulator treats other subjects' 'victories' as barriers to overcome, sooner or later, when the condition allows.

The regulator treats them thus unless, of course, social movements turn into commons movements, that is are able to solve society's complexity with their own solutions – the commons – and thus develop commons social powers: from food and energy to housing, cyberspace and culture (Figure 10.3). Here a subsystem of society is comprising the set of self-regulation of the commons, which in turn also maintains the expansionary and frontline-struggle dynamic of the social movements. This wider commons ecology, defended and enlarged by social movements, reduces the power to regulate complexity of the state/capital regulator, who is left with the increasingly impossible task of

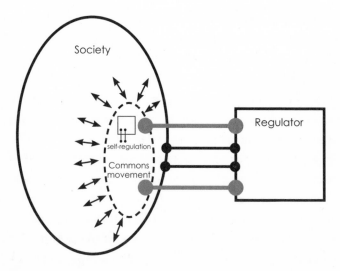

Figure 10.3 Commons movements and social revolution

matching society's variety in order to regulate. This is the case when commons movements outflank the state and capital.

Commons movements

Commons movements are hybrids between social movements and commons, created by repeated and sustained interaction between social movements and the commons, the commons turning into social movements and social movements into commons, in cycles of moving forward and constitution, momentum and consolidation. Commons movements are not just the manifestation of a plurality of subjects expressing their desire for change, but also the explosion of commoning practices shaping commons ecologies that, in the emancipatory environment of social movements, also produces commons institutions able to increase the autonomy and autopoiesis of commons, multiple boundary commoning, and thus the degree of communication, interlaced and networking circuits. Commons movements are able *at the same time to articulate frontline struggles and (re)-production.* There are those in commons movements who are architects of always new commons in always new localities, in order to create, connect, reproduce life in a new way. In commons movements there are commons strategists who see the opportunity to overload state and capital systems with the movement's variety so as to replace the control variety of the capital-state with the self-management control of the commons. There are those in commons movements who are risk analysts not by profession but by inclination, and are the first to alert the commons that they are always at risk of enclosure and that capital encloses as part of its strategy of growth. If commons movements become the expression of a political recomposition that is one with a *mode of production* to expand, to develop and to set against the dominant mode of production, then we have acquired a common sense-horizon, not one that establishes a future model, but a present organisational unit that seeks to evolve and have a place in the contemporary cosmopolitan and globalised world because its power resides in diversity, variety, and complexity.

Commons movements are movements that have the recomposition of the commons as their driving force, and this recomposition is founded on the commons of reproduction: food, care, energy, housing and education. It happens as a result of the evolution of commons and intensification of their interlinkages and presence in society as a particular culture, and as a result of the co-evolutionary relation between the commons and the regulators. It has its great modern examples in the community struggles in Latin America (Zibechi 2012; Sitrin 2012, 2014), where 'societies in movement' are constituted by large grassroots movements made of communities governing large aspects of reproduction and thus developing their distinct social relations. *Commons as systems* is a broader concept that includes social relations and involves also the social practices reproducing those relations, the notion of the production of the boundaries by these practices, and the specific complexity of these systemic forces. I refer, then, to commons movements to point to the complex nature of these social relations that move and constitute the basis of commons as a social force.

Water, land, food and educational commons in regions such as Latin America, or many areas of Asia, Africa and Europe, are developing movements that emerge out of necessity (Greece) and then develop to a higher scale (Argentina, Bolivia, Brazil), or emerge from resistance to enclosure (val di Susa, Italy). They are not movements of fragmented subjectivities sharing a particular passion, but movements of connected subjectivities whose connection is further increased by their social movement. Thus it is not necessarily the case that conflict belong to movements while consensus belongs to commons as Melucci (1996) maintains. When commons develop a consensus to engage in conflict, we have a commons movement. A society is in movement because a large part of it is constituting itself in terms of a growing web of interactive commons, capable of sustaining livelihoods (at least to a degree) and of deploying its social force not only to resist enclosures but to sustain and expand its commons. In short, emancipatory social transformation is predicated not only on increasing complexity, but also on the multiplication of commons governing such a complexity. *Omnia sunt communia.*

Notes

Introduction

1 See the list at minerva.dtic. mil/funded.html

2 'Biodiversity is declining in both temperate and tropical regions, but the decline is greater in the tropics. The tropical Living Planet Index (LPI) shows a 56 per cent reduction in 3,811 populations of 1,638 species from 1970 to 2010. The 6,569 populations of 1,606 species in the temperate LPI declined by 36 per cent over the same period. Latin America shows the most dramatic decline – a fall of 83 per cent. http://wwf. panda.org/about_our_earth/ all_publications/living_planet_ report/living_planet_index2/

1 Commons goods

1 See for example Rete@ sinistra (2010: 18) where it is pointed out that the nexus between 'good' and 'common' is the 'constituting of interpersonal relations among subjects that accept to take charge of a *munus*, a particular gift that obliges who receive it to some ethical constraints in relation to the giver (nature, previous generations, the other from self) and moral in relation to the other effective or potential benefactors. Reciprocity links are therefore created, collective solidarity constraints, norms that create community, cohesion and even identity. It is this nexus that is established between men and women to define the common good. In the collective management of the good, the individuals are united and create *communitas*, they realise a project and give rise to shared experiences and practices.' For an etymological discussion of the term *communitas* and of *munus* from which it is derives, see the work of Esposito (2006).

2 For a systemic analysis along these lines see De Angelis (2007a).

3 The quality of commons as bringing together 'objectivity' and 'subjectivity' has for example been pointed out by Ugo Mattei (2010: 61–2). 'The commons good, differently from the private good (things) and public good (state property), is not a mechanical object and it is not reducible to a commodity. The common good is a qualitative relation. We do not "have" a common good (an ecosystem, water) but in great measure we "are" the common good (we are water, we are part of an urban or rural ecosystem) … the common goods, their perception and defence pass necessarily through a full political implementation of the epistemological revolution produced by phenomenology and its critique of objectivity. The subject is part of the object (and vice versa). It is for this reason that the common goods are inextricably linked to the very fundamental rights of persons, of the ecosystem, of nature and, ultimately, of the living planet.'

4 Elinor and Vincent Ostrom not only introduced common property resources (CPR) as a fourth type of good in this categorisation (rejecting Samuelson's classification and going beyond Buchanan's revision), but also modified the categorisation to pay more attention to how the characteristics of the goods influence individual incentives for behaviour. Specifically, as described by Ostrom (2010: 412), she and her husband: 'proposed additional modifications to the classification of goods to identify fundamental differences that affect the incentives facing individuals (V. Ostrom and E. Ostrom 1977).

- Replacing the term "rivalry of consumption" with "subtractability of use".
- Conceptualizing subtractability of use and excludability to vary from low to high rather than characterizing them as either present or absent.
- Overtly adding a very important fourth type of good – common-pool resources – that shares the attribute of subtractability with private goods and difficulty of exclusion with public goods

(V. Ostrom and E. Ostrom 1977). Forests, water systems, fisheries, and the global atmosphere are all common-pool resources of immense importance for the survival of humans on this earth.

- Changing the name of a "club" good to a "toll" good, since many goods that share these characteristics are provided by small-scale public as well as private associations.'

5 As a simple illustration, take the adjectival table below at www.musicalenglishlessons. org/grammar/rules.htm, and play with the nine categories (the ninth, 'substance', refers in our case to the shared resource).

6 Climate debt is a monetary claim based on a theoretical concept which has been submitted to the United Nations Framework Convention on Climate Change by over fifty countries including Bolivia, Bhutan, Malaysia, Micronesia, Sri Lanka, Paraguay, Venezuela and the Group of Least Developed countries, representing 49 of the world's poorest and most vulnerable countries. It is based on the fact that the poorest countries on earth have left only 20 per cent of global atmospheric space for economic development, while the rich countries, by virtue of the cumulative effect of CO_2 and other emissions, have already 'occupied' 80 per cent of atmospheric space. The climate-debt argument posits that wealthy countries and companies are accountable for the impacts of their historical and continued over-consumption of the Earth's limited resources. Although difficult to calculate, climate debt amounts to three components: the costs of avoiding climate harms and impacts, for example estimated from necessary changes to national planning, projects and programmes; the direct costs of actual (unavoidable) harms, which should be compensated at full costs; and the costs of lost and diminished opportunities in developing countries, caused by having to forgo development pathways followed by the North (Bolivia 2009).

7 Another important case of selection based on strategic grounds is the idea in the Free Software and Free Culture movements that information is a special type of good. The

Free Software Foundation for example rejects private property on intellectual 'goods', while they actually believe that property is a natural right for objects, but not for information. In this way, as convincingly argued by Pedersen (2010), they frame issues pertaining to ideas, information and knowledge – or the intangible realm – in terms of freedom, liberty, human rights, policy, intervention, and regulation. Anything but property, but preferably 'policy'.

8   Dr Julian Lombardi and Dr Marilyn Lombardi of Duke University are the promoters of the development consortium of an open-source peer-to-peer virtual-world application called Croquet, which 'can be used by experienced software developers to create and deploy deeply collaborative multi-user online virtual world applications on and across multiple operating systems and devices' (www.opencroquet. org/index.php/Main_Page). One of the advantage of the P2P technology of Croquet is its cut in potential energy dependence: 'Only 15–25 people can get on a Second Life server at a time. After that you have to use multiple servers to handle it all and it consumes an enormous amount of energy (as much as a real person by some measures). Croquet on the other hand uses a Peer-to-Peer network. The low bandwidth requirement does well on wireless networks and the bigger the better. Those who have spent time in Second Life know that it is prone to sudden failures' (http://edutechie. com/2007/07/7-ways-croquet-is-better-than-second-life/). Yet this development is not around the corner, and the consortium is still at a development stage.

2 Systems

1   'Habitus is the internalised knowledge of a lifetime's worth of external feedbacks, messages and instruction. It is the distilled normalisation of subjects also brought about by the mechanisms of capitalist disciplines' (De Angelis 2007a: 10) Our thoughts and actions are created by habitus, and the habitus guides or constrains our actions (although it does not fully determine them). In Bourdieu the key is the relation between habitus and a field – a notion very similar to 'system' as

I am employing the term here. If habitus and field are aligned, we act and react with ease, knowing what the codes and values of a field are and making them ours. When they are not in some sort of alignment, we have to navigate a field that is unfamiliar and obeys rules we were never taught The other options, of course, are those indicated by Hirschman (1970): either to exit the field or to make our voice heard (but also to make our bodies present, as in direct action) through struggle. In Bourdieu, fields change occurs with the change in the distribution of capitals, an unfortunate name I will only keep for profit-seeking capital. The key change, I will argue, occurs with the transformation of capital into common wealth.

2 See for example the international Expo in Milan in 2015, where up to 18,500 workers were hired as volunteers. http://www.controlacrisi.org/notizia/Lavoro/2015/4/11/44367-expo-forum-diritti-lavoro-presenta-lesposto-contro-il/; Wainwright (2015)

3 Some writers on commons indeed have a truly confused way of approaching the question of capital, labour and reproduction. Take this text from the commons transition document of the P2P Foundation: 'We call the existing economy an extractive economy, because it extracts capital from the commons, but does not directly create livelihoods for the commoners; what is needed is generative capital, that generates capital and livelihoods for the further production of the commons.' First, nobody can extract capital from the commons. At most, capitalist self-valorising value regards the values it appropriates freely from the commons as capital. Second, an economy does not extract anything, since it is the meeting point of demand and supply. Companies extract oil or metal from the earth, and capitalists extract surplus labour from workers. Extraction implies that the object of extraction, whether the earth or labour, is resisting somehow, and capitalist processes deploy a superior force to win the resistance. But they do not extract, say, the knowledge base available on Wikipedia, which is freely available to all, or Facebook-patterned behaviour of a multitude of subscribers that,

packaged as 'big data', the bosses of Facebook sell to advertisers, with almost no resistence from the mass of Facebook users. Third, the term *generative capital* is an oxymoron; capital, as Joseph Schumpeter recognised, is a force of both destruction and creation. It is perhaps better to use the term *commonwealth* to distinguish commons 'stock' in terms of values and goals from capital's specific values and goals. He continues: 'Thus we imagine a connected binary of the commons sphere, in which contributors jointly create commons, AND a cooperative sphere, in which commoners act as cooperators, generating their own livelihood and 'cooperative accumulation' of capital, which funds the continued production of commons, without extracting its value to maximise the profit of shareholders' (Bauwens 2015). I have considered all the commons I know or have participated in, and I did not see any such binary. In most commons, there is no separation between 'contributors' that ' jointly create commons' and commoners that 'generate their livelihood'. They are part of the same process,

as illustrated in the commons circuit in Chapter 4. Also, it is very difficult to conceive how a 'cooperative accumulation of capital' can occur without extraction of surplus value, unless the commoners themselves turn into capitalists, which is beside the point of social transformation. Also, here Bauwens forgets a reference to *work* as social cooperation (Marx 1976: ch. 13). Sometimes, this work is not actually cooperative in the commons, as when my child screams to me from the bathroom that the toilet paper has run out and I have to rush to get some for him. Or when I have just 'collaborated' with the other members of the household in cleaning the kitchen floor to 'accumulate capital' from it.

4 Commons governance

1 What follows is based on my participation in the community parties organised by the people of the small village of Lama di Monchio (Modena), who I thank for sharing their convivial spirit.

2 'In the Japanese mountain commons, for example, appropriation rights and provision duties are assigned

to established family units in a village instead of to individuals. In the Swiss mountains, appropriation rights and provision duties are inherited by individual males who own private property in the village and remain citizens of the village. In eastern Spain, a farmer's right to irrigation water is based on the parcel of land inherited, purchased or leased, not on a relationship to a village. In the Philippines, a complex contract among long-term usufructuary rights-holders determines rights and provision duties. The rules defining when, where, and how an individual's allotted resource unit can be harvested or how many labour days are required also vary considerably across cases' (Ostrom 1990: 89).

3 Caffentzis (2004: 20) calls this 'neo-Hardinian' because 'Just as the neo-Malthusians pointed out, on the basis of demographic trends in Western Europe in the twentieth century, an increase in wages does not necessarily imply an increase in the working class population, so too neo-Hardinians like Ostrom and her co-workers argued that commons situations do not necessarily lead

to "tragedy," they can also lead to "'comedy' – a drama for certain, but one with a happy ending" (Dietz et al. 2002: 4).' In fact, they called one of their books *The Drama of the Commons* – 'because the commons entails history, comedy, and tragedy' (Dietz et al. 2002: 4).

4 (Caffentzis 2004: 23). The omitted text reads '– like scale of the common-pool resource, the costs of measuring its resource units, the renewability or nonrenewability of the resource, the cost of excluding noncommoners, the efficiency, sustainability and equity of the property regime regulating the use of the resource, and the number and uniformity of the participants in the regime –'.

5 The money nexus and the commons formula

1 It is at the level of this commonality that systems thinkers like Nicolas Luhmann (1995) can conceive of the economy as a 'function' system, integrating different social forces.

2 In 1989 Harry Cleaver gave me some typewritten and collaged lecture notes on Marx that he had prepared for his students,

where for the first time I saw the combined circuits of capital and of reproduction. This experience was an absolute revelation, as it smashed any residual Marxist orthodoxy I still held. To bring the two circuits together is to begin to think in terms of the complexity of the two systems from a radical standpoint, and to incorporate both the waged and the unwaged sides of our lives. The first time I used the combined circuits in print was in De Angelis 2007a, to analyse the complexity of capitalist relations of struggle in global capital. I am doing it now to discover the commons hidden within it.

3 The idea of the commons circuit modelled from capital circuits is not new. I was inspired by Nick Dyer-Witheford's (2006) presentation in Cambridge on the topics which I here develop.

4 For discussion of Keynes's views on Marx see Dillard (1984, 1987), Aoki (2001) and Bertocco (2005). Keynes is reported to have written '[Marx] pointed out that the nature of production in the actual world is not ... a case of C–M–C, i.e. of exchanging commodity (or effort) for money in order to obtain another

commodity (or effort). That may be the standpoint of the private consumer. But it is not the attitude of business, which is a case of M–C–M, i.e., of parting with money for commodity (or effort) in order to obtain more money' (quoted in Bertocco 2005: 494 n4).

5 The *centri sociali* (social centres) often emerge with the occupation of old, abandoned buildings by young activists and are transformed into centres for political, cultural, and recreational activities. On this experience see Mudu (2004).

6 Mobilising social labour for commoning

1 www.huffingtonpost. co.uk/2015/05/27/queens-speech-austerity_n_7451008. html?1432738161

2 For a discussion of command labour in the current global political economy see De Angelis and Harvie (2008).

3 Communal labour is a form of collective labour, but it must be distinguished from another form of collective labour, that controlled by the state. The *Mit*a, as they were called in Inca times, the *abati fascisti*, as they were

called in fascist Italy, or some aspects of War Communism, as it was called in the Soviet Union, were all systems more in line with the co-optation of the commons than with their development; they were systems in which the convocation of collective labour was in the hands of the state and outside direct community control. The discussion of this form of collective labour is outside the scope of this book.

7 The production of autonomy, boundaries and sense

1 This broadly follows Luhmann's (1995) idea of social systems as self-referential (operationally closed) systems. Systems consist of operations, while operating is what systems do. Autopoiesis literally means 'auto (self)-creation' (from the Greek: αυτό – *auto* for 'self'; and ποίησις – *poiesis* for 'creation or production'), or auto-reproduction. The term was introduced in 1972 by the Chilean biologists Humberto Maturana and Francisco Varela. It was originally used to explain the emergence and reproduction of biological cells and bodily systems such as the metabolic system.

8 Boundary commoning

1 http://viacampesina.org/en/index.php/organisation-mainmenu-44

2 In English, the word 'genuine' is not usually applied to food. But if I only leave the adjective 'organic', I reduce good food to the food that is certified by the state, which is precisely not the point of the movement I am discussing given the many cases of fraud. After having evaluated other options, I thus must introduce the word *genuine* as an adjective to food, the 'Italian way', which signifies food that – even if does not have an organic certification – is authentic, coming from trustworthy sources unmediated by the state, its natural character preserved without having been adulterated.

9 Commons and capital/state

1 When not otherwise indicated, much of the factual information provided for this account is taken by http://en.wikipedia.org/wiki/2000_Cochabamba_protests#cite_note-CNN_Water-5

2 www.nadir.org/nadir/initiativ/agp/free/imf/bolivia/txt/2000/0417battles_back.txt)

3 www.waterobservatory.org/library.cfm?refID=33711

4 www.nadir.org/nadir/initiativ/agp/free/imf/bolivia/txt/2000/0417battles_back.txt. The law was repealed in a special parliamentary session on 11 April 2000. www.pbs.org/frontlineworld/stories/bolivia/timeline.html

5 In Faust's study, the poodle transforms into the Devil (Mephistopheles). Faust makes an arrangement with the Devil: the Devil will do everything that Faust wants while he is here on Earth, and in exchange Faust will serve the Devil in Hell. Faust's arrangement is that if during the time while Mephistopheles is serving Faust, Faust is so pleased with anything the Devil gives him that he wants to stay in that moment forever, he will die in that instant. Ultimately, Faust goes to heaven, for he loses only half of the bet. Angels, who arrive as messengers of divine mercy, declare at the end of Act V: 'He who strives on and lives to strive / Can earn redemption still' (V, 11, 936–7).]

10 Towards postcapitalism

1 For a broad introduction to social movement theories see Dalla Porta and Diani (2000).

2 Data from various sources, all collated in Solidarity For All (2014).

3 See for example the case in the market square of Addis Ababa in the impressive video at www.youtube.com/watch?v=UEIn8GJIgoE

4 I am here, therefore, distancing myself from Luhmann's formulation that regards modern society as the result of communication functional systems. As shown in Chapter 4, the communication system (economy) emerges from distinct circuits of production (which include a specific mode of communication but cannot be reduced to it) such as the commons and capital.

References

African Centre for Biodiversity (2012). Laying the Groundwork for the Commercialisation of African Agriculture. September. Melville, SA. www.acbio.org.za/images/stories/dmdocuments/AGRA_critique.pdf

Against the Grain (2011). *Food and Climate Change: The Forgotten Link*. www.grain.org/article/entries/4357-food-and-climate-change-the-forgotten-link

Agarwal, B. (2014). Food Sovereignty, Food Security and Democratic Choice: Critical Contradictions, Difficult Conciliations. *Journal of Peasant Studies*, 41(6): 1247–68.

Altieri, M. A. and C. I. Nicholls (2012). Agroecology Scaling Up for Food Sovereignty and Resiliency. *Sustainable Agriculture Reviews*, 11: 1–29.

Anderson, B. (2006). *Imagined Communities*. London: Verso

Aoki, M. (2001). To the Rescue or to the Abyss: Notes on the Marx in Keynes. *Journal of Economic Issues*, 35(4): 931–54.

Arie, S. (2014). Leftwing Looters Raid Shop. *The Guardian*, 8 November. www.theguardian.com/world/2004/nov/08/italy.eu

Aristotle (1948). *The Politics*. Oxford University Press.

Armiero M. and M. De Angelis (2017). Anthropocene: Victims, Narrators, and Revolutionaries. *South Atlantic Quarterly*, 116(2), April.

Ashby, W. R. (1957). *An Introduction to Cybernetics*. London: Chapman & Hall.

Ashby, W. R. (1958). Requisite Variety and Its Implications for the Control of Complex Systems. *Cybernetica*, 1–13.

http://medicinaycomplejidad. org/pdf/soporte/ashbyreqvar. pdf

Azzellini, D. and M. Sitrin (2014). *They Can't Represent Us!: Reinventing Democracy from Greece to Occupy*. London: Verso.

Barbagallo, C. (2016) The Political Economy of Reproduction: Motherhood, Work and the Home in Neoliberal Britain. PhD thesis: University of East London.

Barbagallo, C. and S. Federici (2012). *Care Work and the Commons*. New Delhi: Phomene.

Bardot, P., and C. Laval (2015). *Del Comune, o della Rivoluzione nel XXI secolo*. Rome: Derive Approdi.

Barnes, P. (2006). *Capitalism 3.0: A Guide to Reclaiming the Commons*. San Francisco: Berrett-Koehler.

Bauman, Z. (2000). *Liquid Modernity*. Cambridge: Polity.

Bauwens, M. (2015). *A New Evaluation of the FLOK Experience in Ecuador: What's Next?* http:// commonstransition. org/a-new-evaluation-of- the-flok-experience-in- ecuador-whats-next/#sthash. UJxPfE3V.dpuf. http:// commonstransition. org/a-new-evaluation-of- the-flok-experience-in- ecuador-whats-next/#sthash. WUFYDuJW.dpuf

Beer, S. (1994). *Diagnosing the System for Organizations*. New York: John Wiley.

Beer, S. (2004). What Is Cybernetics? *Kybernetes*, 33(3/4): 853–63.

Bell, P. and H. Cleaver (2002). 'Marx's Crisis Theory as a Theory of Class Struggle', reproduced in *The Commoner*, 5, Autumn. www.commoner. org.uk/cleaver05.pdf; www.commoner.org.uk/ cleaver05_pr.htm. Originally published in *Research in Political Economy*, 5, 1982, pp. 189–261.

Benkler, Y. (2003). The Political Economy of Commons. *European Journal for the Informatics Professional*, IV(3): 6–9. Retrieved from www.boell.org/downloads/ Benkler_The_Political_ Economy_of_the_Commons. pdf

Berkes, F., I. Davidson-Hunt, and K. Davidson-Hunt

(1998). Diversity of Common Property Resource Use and Diversity of Social Interests in the Western Indian Himalaya. *Mountain Research and Development*, 18: 19–33.

Berkes, F. (2006). From Community-Based Resource Management to Complex Systems: The Scale Issue and Marine Commons. *Ecology and Society*, 11(1).

Bertocco, G. (2005). The Role of Credit in a Keynesian Monetary Economy. *Review of Political Economy*, 17(4): 489–511.

Bey, H. (1991). *Temporary Autonomous Zones*. New York: Autonomedia.

Blisset, Luther (2003). *Q*. London: Heinemann.

Bolivia, Republic of (2009). Commitments for Annex I Parties under paragraph 1(b)(i) of the Bali Action Plan: Evaluating developed countries' historical climate debt to developing countries. Submission by the Republic of Bolivia to the AWG-LCA. November. http://climate-debt.org/wp-content/uploads/2009/11/Bolivia-Climate-Debt-Proposal.pdf

Bollier, D. and Silke Helfrich (eds.) (2012) *The Wealth of the Common: A World beyond Market and State*. Amerst, MA: Levellers Press.

Bourdieu, P. (1986) The Forms of Capital. In J. Richardson (ed.), *Handbook of Theory and Research for the Sociology of Education*. New York, Greenwood, 241–58. www.marxists.org/reference/subject/philosophy/works/fr/bourdieu-forms-capital.htm

Buber, M. (1970). *I and Thou*, translated by W. Kaufmann. New York: Scribner.

Buchanan, J. M. (1965). An Economic Theory of Clubs. *Economica*, 32(125): 1–14.

Burzi, B. (2013). Sanità, tra pubblico e privato è concorrenza su costi e tempi. *Il Tirreno*, 13 April, http://iltirreno.gelocal.it/prato/cronaca/2013/04/13/news/sanita-tra-pubblico-e-privato-e-concorrenza-su-costi-e-tempi-1.6874338

Cacciari, P. (2010). Introduzione. In P. Cacciari (ed.), *La societa' dei beni comuni. Una rassegna*, pp. 17–33. Rome: Carta, Ediesse.

CADTM. (2007). Declaration of Nyeleni. http://cadtm.

org/IMG/article_PDF/
article_2464.pdf

Caffentzis, G. (2004). A Tale
of Two Conferences:
Globalization, the Crisis
of Neoliberalism and
Question of the Commons.
San Miguel de Allenende,
Mexico. Retrieved from www.
commoner.org.uk/?p=96

Caffentzis, G. (2012). From
Lobsters to Universities: The
Making of the Knowledge
Commons. *St Antony's
International Review*, 8(1):
25–42. Retrieved from
www.researchgate.net/
publication/263570497_
From_Lobsters_to_
Universities_The_Making_
of_the_Knowledge_
Commons

Caffentzis, G., and S. Federici
(2014). Commons against
and beyond Capitalism.
*Community Development
Journal*, 49. http://cdj.
oxfordjournals.org/cgi/
doi/10.1093/cdj/bsu006.

Cameron, D. (2010). Speech
on the 'Big Society'.
Retrieved from www.
britishpoliticalspeech.
org/speech-archive.
htm?speech=321.

Capra, F. (1982). *Turning Point:
Science, Society, and the Rising
Culture*. New York: Simon &
Schuster.

Capra, F. (1997). *The Web of
Life: A New Synthesis of
Mind and Matter*. London:
Flamingo.

Carlsson, C. (2008). *Nowtopia:
How Pirate Programmers,
Outlaw Bicyclists, and Vacant-
Lot Gardeners Are Inventing
the Future Today!* Oakland:
AK Press.

Carr, N. (2008). *Big Switch:
Rewiring the World, from
Edison to Google*. New York:
W.W. Norton.

Casey, S. P. and G. Z. Foresti
(2014). XM24: Survival and
Inspiration against All Odds.
Roar Magazine, 14 September.
http://roarmag.org/2014/09/
xm24-social-center-bologna/

Castells, M. (1996). *The Rise
of the Network Society*, Vol.
I: *The Information Age:
Economy, Society and Culture*.
Cambridge, MA: Blackwell.

Cleaver, H. (1977). Food,
Famine and the International
Crisis. *Zerowork*, 2: 7–70.
https://la.utexas.edu/
users/hcleaver/Zerowork/
CleaverFoodFamine.html

Cleaver, H. (1979). *Reading Capital Politically*. Austin: University of Texas Press.

Collom, E., J. N. Lasker and C. Kyiriacou (2012). *Equal Value: Community Currencies and Time Banking in the US*. Farnham: Ashgate.

Commons, J. R. (1968). *Legal Foundations of Capitalism*. Madison: University of Wisconsin Press.

Conway, E. (2009) Moody's Warns of 'Social Unrest' as Sovereign Debt Spirals. *The Telegraph*, 15 December. www.telegraph.co.uk/finance/economics/6819470/Moodys-warns-of-social-unrest-as-sovereign-debt-spirals.html

Cox, N., and S. Federici (1976). *Counter-planning from the Kitchen: Wages for Housework: A Perspective on Capital and the Left*. New York: New York Wages for Housework Committee.

Dalla Costa, M. and S. James (1975). *The Power of Women and the Subversion of the Community*. Bristol: Falling Wall Press.

Damasio, A. (2003). *Looking for Spinoza: Joy, Sorrow and the Feeling Brain*. London: William Heinemann.

Daniel, S. and A. Mittal (2009). *The Great Land Grab. Rush for World's Farmland Threatens Food Security for the Poor*. Berkeley, CA: Oakland Institute.

De Angelis, M. (1995). Beyond the Technological and the Social Paradigm: a Political Reading of Abstract Labour as Substance of Value. *Capital and Class*, 57: 107–35, Autumn.

De Angelis, M. (2000). *Keynesianism, Social Conflict and Political Economy*. London: Macmillan.

De Angelis, M. (2004). Separating the Doing and the Deed: Capital and the Continuous Character of Enclosures. *Historical Materialism*, 12(2): 57–87.

De Angelis, M. (2007a). *The Beginning of History: Value Struggles and Global Capital*. London: Pluto.

De Angelis, M. (2007b). Oxymoronic Creatures along the River Thames: Reflections on 'Sustainable Communities', Neoliberal Governance and Capital's Globalisation. *The*

Commoner. www.commoner. org.uk/?p=38

De Angelis, M. (2010). The Production of Commons and the 'Explosion' of the Middle Class. *Antipode*, 42(4): 954–77.

De Angelis, M. (2012). Crises, Capital and Cooptation: Does Capital Need a Commons Fix? In D. Bollier and S. Helfrich (eds.), *The Wealth of the Commons: A World beyond Market and State*. Amerst, MA: Levellers Press.

De Angelis, M. (2014a). Social Revolutions and the Commons. *South Atlantic Quarterly*, 113(2): 299–311.

De Angelis, M. (2014b). Crisis and the Commons Today. In S. Brincat (ed.), *Communism in the 21st Century*, Vol. 3: *The Future of Communism. Social Movements, Economic Crises, and the Re-Imagination of Communism*. Santa Barbara, CA: Praeger, 1–26.

De Angelis, M. and D. Harvie (2008). Globalization? No Question! Foreign Direct Investment and Labor Commanded. *Review of Radical Political Economics*, 40(4): 429–44.

De Angelis, M. and D. Harvie (2014). The Commons. In M. Parker, G. Cheney, V. Fournier and C. Land (eds.), *The Routledge Companion to Alternative Organizations*. Abingdon: Routledge, 280–94.

Deb, D. (2009). *Beyond Developmentality: Constructing Inclusive Freedom and Sustainability*. London: Earthscan.

De Filippis, J., R. Fisher and E. Shragge (2010). *Contesting Communities: The Limits and Potential of Local Organizing*. London: Rutgers University Press.

Delanty, G. (2003). *Community*. London: Routledge.

Deleuze, G. and F. Guattari (1984). *Anti-Oedipus: Capitalism and Schizophrenia*. London: Athlone Press.

Della Porta, D. and M. Diani (2000). *Social Movements: An Introduction*. Oxford: Blackwell.

Democracy Now (2009). 'We Are Not Begging for Aid' – Chief Bolivian Negotiator Says Developed Countries Owe Climate Debt, 9 December. www.democracynow.

org/2009/12/9/we_are_not_
begging_for_aid.

Dillard, D. (1984). Keynes and
Marx: A Centennial Appraisal.
*Journal of Post Keynesian
Economics*, 6(3): 421–32.

Dillard, D. (1987). Money as an
Institution of Capitalism.
Journal of Economic Issues,
21(4): 1,623–47.

Dowling, E. (2012). *The Big
Society, Part 2: Social
Value, Measure and
the Public Service Act.
New Left Project.* www.
newleftproject.org/index.
php/site/article_comments/
the_big_society_part_2_
social_value_measure_and_
the_public_services_act

Dyer-Witheford, N. (2006).
The Circulation of the
Common. Paper presented
at Immaterial Labour,
Multitudes and New Social
Subjects: Class Composition
in Cognitive Capitalism,
29–30 April, King's College,
University of Cambridge.
www.fims.uwo.ca/people/
faculty/dyerwitheford/
commons2006.pdf

Esposito, R. (2006). *Communitas.
Origine e destino della
comunita.* Turin: Einaudi.

FAO (1996). *Rome Declaration
on Food Security and World
Food Summit Plan of Action.*
November.

Federici, S. (2011) Women,
Land Struggles, and the
Reconstruction of the
Commons. *Journal of Labor
and Society*, 14: 41–56.

Federici, S. (2012). *Revolution
at Point Zero: Housework,
Reproduction, and Feminist
Struggle.* New York: PM Press.

Feldman, A. M. (1980). *Welfare
Economics and Social Choice
Theory.* Boston, MA: Martinus
Nijhoff.

Finnegan, W. (2002). Leasing The
Rain. *New Yorker*, 4 August.

Fisk, J. (1989). *Understanding
Popular Culture.* London:
Unwin Hyman

Fiske, A. P. (1990). Relativity within
Moose Culture. Four Models
for Social Relationships. *Ethos*,
18(2): 180–204.

Fiske, A. P. (1991) *Structures
of Social Life: The Four
Elementary Forms of Human
Relations.* New York: Free
Press (Macmillan).

Fiske, A. P. (2004). Relational
Models Theory 2.0. In N.
Haslam (ed.), *Relational
Models Theory: A*

Contemporary Overview. Mahwah, NJ: Erlbaum, 3–25.

Fiske, A. P. and N. Haslam (2005). The Four Basic Social Bonds. Structures for Coordinating Interaction. In M. W. Baldwin (ed.), *Interpersonal Cognition.* New York: Guildford Press, 267–98.

Forero, J. (2005). Who Will Bring Water to the Bolivian Poor? *New York Times,* 15 December. www.nytimes. com/2005/12/15/business/ who-will-bring-water-to-the-bolivian-poor.html

Foucault, M. (1976) *History of Sexuality,* Vol. 1. London: Penguin.

Free Association (2004). *Moments of Excess.* Leeds: Free Association Books.

Friedman, M. (1970). The Social Responsibility of Business Is to Increase Profit. *New York Times,* 13 September. www. colorado.edu/studentgroups/ libertarians/issues/friedman-soc-resp-business.html

Galbraith, J. K. (1952). *American Capitalism: The Concept of Countervailing Power.* Boston, MA: Houghton Mifflin.

Garrett, R. T. Jensen and A. Voela (eds.) (2016). *We Need to Talk about Family: Essays on Neoliberalism, the Family and Popular Culture.* Cambridge: Cambridge Scholars Publishing.

Gartner (2007). Gartner Estimates ICT Industry Accounts for 2 Percent of Global CO_2 Emissions. Press release, www.gartner.com/it/ page.jsp?id=503867

GBN (2011). Court Fines Four Persons over Communal Labour. *Ghana Business News,* 14 November. www. ghanabusinessnews.com/2011/ 11/14/court-fines-four-persons-over-communal-labour/

Giannelli, G. and A. Fumagalli (2013). Il fenomeno Bitcoin: moneta alternativa o moneta speculative? in *Effimera. Critica e Sovversioni del Presente.* http://effimera. org/il-fenomeno-bitcoin-moneta-alternativa-o-moneta-speculativa-gianluca-giannelli-e-andrea-fumagalli/

Gibson-Graham, J. K., J. Cameron and S. Healy (2013). *Take Back the Economy: An Ethical Guide for Transforming our Communities.* Minneapolis: University of Minnesota Press.

Godbout, J. (2000). *Le Don, la Dette et l'Identité: Homo Donator vs Homo Oeconomicus*. Paris: La Découverte / MAUSS.

Gottesdiener, L. (2012). We Win When We Live Here: Occupying Homes in Detroit and Beyond. *Waging Nonviolence*, 28 March. http://wagingnonviolence.org/feature/we-win-when-we-live-here-occupying-homes-in-detroit-and-beyond/

Gottesdiener, L. (2013). The Great Eviction: Black America and the Toll of the Foreclosure Crisis. *Mother Jones*, 1 August. www.motherjones.com/politics/2013/08/black-america-foreclosure-crisis

Graeber, D. (2015). *The Utopia of Rules*. London: Melville House Publishing.

Granovetter, M. (2009). Threshold Models of Collective Behavior. *American Journal of Sociology*, 83(6): 1420–43.

Greenwald, G. and E. MacAskill (2013). NSA Prism Program Taps in to User Data of Apple, Google and Others. *The Guardian*. www.theguardian.com/world/2013/jun/06/us-tech-giants-nsa-data

Guanyem Barcellona (2015). Why Do We Want to Win Back Barcelona? Principles and Commitments to Guide the Way. guanyembarcelona.cat

Gudynas, E. (2011). Buen Vivir: Today's Tomorrow. *Development*, 54(4): 441–7.

Gunderson, L. H., and C. S. Holling (2002). Panarchy: Understanding Transformations in of Human and Natural Systems. Washington, DC: Island.

Hardin, G. (1968). The Tragedy of the Commons. *Science*, 162(3,859).

Hardt, M. and A. Negri (2004). *Multitude: War and Democracy in the Age of Empire*. New York: Penguin.

Hardt, M. and A. Negri (2009). *Commonwealth*. Cambridge, MA: Harvard University Press.

Harvey, D. (1990). *The Condition of Postmodernity: An Enquiry into the Origin of Cultural Change*. Cambridge, MA: Blackwell.

Harvey, D. (2003). *The New Imperialism*, Oxford University Press.

Harvie, D. and K. Milburn (2004). *Moments of Excess.* Leeds: Free Association.

Hess, C. and R. Meinzen-Dick (2006). The Name Change; or, What Happened to the 'P'? *Commons Digest,* 2: 1–4. Retrieved from www.indiana.edu/~iascp/E-CPR/cd02.pdf

Hess, C. and E. Ostrom (2007). *Understanding Knowledge as a Commons: From Theory to Practice.* Cambridge, MA: MIT Press.

Hilldyard, N. (2016). *Licensed Larceny: Infrastructure, Financial Extraction and the Global South.* Manchester University Press.

Hirschman, A. O. (1970). *Exit, Voice, and Loyalty: Responses to Decline in Firms, Organizations, and States.* Cambridge, MA: Harvard University Press.

Holloway, J. (2002). *Change the World Without Taking Power: The Meaning of Revolution Today.* London: Pluto.

Holloway, J. (2010). *Crack Capitalism.* London: Pluto.

Holt-Giménez, E., A. Shattuck, M. Altieri, H. Herren, and S. Gliessman (2012). We Already Grow Enough Food for 10 Billion People … and Still Can't End Hunger. *Journal of Sustainable Agriculture,* 36(6): 595–8.

Ingold, T. (2000). *The Perception of the Environment.* London: Routledge.

Jumbe, C. B. L. (2006). A Short Commentary on 'The Name Change; or What Happened to the P?' authored by Charlotte Hess and Ruth Meinzen-Dick. *Commons Digest,* 2, 5–6. Retrieved from www.indiana.edu/~iascp/E-CPR/cd02.pdf

Jun, N. (2013). Deleuze, Values and Normativity. In N. Jun and D. W. Smith (eds.), *Deleuze and Ethics.* Edinburgh University Press, 89–107.

Karatzogianni, A., and A. Robinson (2010). *Power, Resistance and Conflict in the Contemporary World: Social Movements, Networks and Hierarchies.* London: Routledge.

Karim, L. (2008). Demystifying Micro-Credit: The Grameen Bank, NGOs, and Neoliberalism in Bangladesh. *Cultural Dynamics,* 20(1): 5–29.

KNOMAD (2016). Migration and Remittances Factbook 2016.

http://go.worldbank.org/
QGUCPJTOR0

Koestler, A. (1973). The Tree and the Candle. In William Gray and Nicholas D. Rizzo (eds.), *Unity through Diversity*, New York: Gordon and Breach Science Publishers, Part I, 287–314.

Kollewe, J. (2015). Volkswagen Emissions Scandal – Timeline. *The Guardian*, 10 December. www.theguardian.com/business/2015/dec/10/volkswagen-emissions-scandal-timeline-events

Krippendorff, K. (1995). Undoing Power. *Critical Issues in Mass Communication*, 12(2): 101–32.

Krippendorff, K. (1996). A Second-order Cybernetics of Otherness. *Systems Research*, 13(3): 311–28.

Kropotkin, P. (1902). Mutual Aid: A Factor of Evolution. Retrieved from www.complementarycurrency.org/ccLibrary/Mutual_Aid-A_Factor_of_Evolution-Peter_Kropotkin.pdf

Landauer, R. (1996). The Physical Nature of Information. *Physics Letters A*, 217(4–5): 188–193. doi:10.1016/0375-9601(96)00453-7.

Latouche, S. (2009). *Farewell to Growth*. London: Polity.

Leake, J. and Richard Woods. (2009). Revealed: the Environmental Impact of Google Searches. *Sunday Times*, 11 January. http://technology.timesonline.co.uk/tol/news/tech_and_web/article5489134.ece

Lee, R., A. Leyshon, T. Aldridge, J. Tooke, C. Williams and N. Thrift. (2004). Making Geographies and Histories? Constructing Local Circuits of Values. *Environment and Planning D: Society and Space*, 22: 595–617.

Lefranc, G. (2015) Social Unrest Is Here to Stay: Here's How to Protect Yourself. *Daily Reckoning*, 25 August. http://dailyreckoning.com/social-unrest-is-here-to-stay-heres-how-to-protect-yourself/

Lenin, V. I. (1918). The Immediate Tasks of the Soviet Government. www.marxists.org/archive/lenin/works/1918/mar/x03.htm

Leviten-Reid, C. (2008). The Role of Co-operatives in Health Care: National and International Perspectives. Retrieved from http://

usaskstudies.coop/CSC Research Reports & Other Publications/2009_Role_of_Coops_in_Health_Carel.pdf

Lewin, K. (1997). *Resolving Social Conflicts & Field Theory in Social Science*. Washington, DC: American Psychological Association.

Linebaugh, P. (2008). *The Magna Carta Manifesto: Liberties and Commons for All*. Berkeley, CA: University of California Press.

Lohoar, S., N. Butears and E. Kennedy (2014). *Strengths of Australian Aboriginal Cultural Practices in Family Life and Child Rearing*. CFCA Paper No. 25. www.qldfamilylawnet.org.au/sites/qldfamilylawnet/files/qflpn/cfca25.pdf

Love, T. and T. Cooper (2007). Successful Activism Strategies: Five New Extensions to Ashby. In K. Fielden and J. Sheffield (eds.), *Systemic Development: Local Solutions in a Global Environment* Auckland, NZ: ISCE Publishing.

Luhmann, N. (1995). *Social Systems*. Stanford University Press.

Lukes, S. (2005) *Power: A Radical View*, 2nd edn. London: Palgrave Macmillan.

Lyotard, J.-F. (1984). *The Postmodern Condition: A Report on Knowledge*. Manchester University Press.

Maito, Esteban Ezequiel (2014) The Historical Transience of Capital: The Downward Trend in the Rate of Profit since XIX Century, https://thenextrecession.files.wordpress.com/2014/04/maito-esteban-the-historical-transience-of-capital-the-downward-tren-in-the-rate-of-profit-since-xix-century.pdf

Malinowski, B. (1922). *Argonauts of the Western Pacific: An Account of Native Enterprise and Adventure in the Archipelagoes of Melanesian New Guinea*. London: Routledge and Kegan Paul.

Malinowski, B. (1935). Coral Gardens and Their Magic: A Study of the Methods of Tilling the Soil and of Agricultural Rites in the Trobriand Islands. *Discourse and Society*, 4(2): 249–83.

Malmo, C. (2015). Bitcoin Is Unsustainable. *Motherboard*, 29 June .

Mann, M. (1986). *The Sources of Social Power*. Vol. 1. Cambridge University Press.

Marx, K. (1970). *Critique of the Gotha Programme*. In K. Marx and F. Engels, *Selected Works* Moscow: Progress Publishers, 3: 13–30. www.marxists.org/archive/marx/works/1875/gotha/index.htm

Marx, K. (1973). *Grundrisse: Foundations of the Critique of Political Economy*. Translated by Martin Nicolaus. London: Penguin.

Marx, K. (1976). *Capital: A Critique of Political Economy*. Vol. 1: *A Critical Analysis of Capitalist Production*. New York: Penguin.

Marx, K. (1977). *A Contribution to the Critique of Political Economy*. Moscow: Progress Publishers.

Marx, K. (1981). *Capital: A Critique of Political Economy*. Vol. 3. New York: Penguin.

Marx, K. and F. Engels. (2005). *The Manifesto of the Communist Party*. New York: Cosimo.

Mason, P. (2015). *Postcapitalism: A Guide to Our Future*. London: Penguin.

Mattei, U. (2010). La nozione del commune. In P. Cacciari (ed.) *La societa' dei beni comuni. Una rassegna*, pp. 59-64. Rome: Carta, Ediesse.

Maturana, H. R. and F. J. Varela (1998). *The Tree of Knowledge: The Biological Roots of Human Understanding*. Boston, MA, and London: Shambhala.

McCauley, L. (2014). Detroit Citizens Vow Direct Action to Protect Their Right to Water, *Common Dreams*, 1 July. www.commondreams.org/news/2014/07/01/detroit-citizens-vow-direct-action-protect-their-right-water

Meadows, D. H. (2008). *Thinking in Systems*. London: Earthscan.

Meillassoux, C. (1981). *Maidens, Meal and Money: Capitalism and the Domestic Community*. Cambridge University Press.

Melucci, A. (1996). *Challenging Codes: Collective Action in the Information Age*. Cambridge University Press.

Mezzadra, S. and B. Nealson (2013). *Border as Method, or the Multiplication of Labour*. Durham, NC: Duke University Press.

Midnight Notes Collective (1992) 'New Enclosures', in Midnight Notes, reproduced in *The*

Commoner, 2, September 2001. www.commoner.org. uk/o2midnight.pdf.

Midnight Notes and Friends (2010). *Promissory Notes: From Crisis to Commons.* www.midnightnotes.org/ Promissory%20Notes.pdf

Moeller, H. G. (2006). *Luhmann Explained: From Souls to Systems.* Chicago: Open Court.

Moeller, H. G. (2012). *The Radical Luhmann.* New York: Columbia University Press.

Moore, J. W. (2014). The Capitalocene, Part I: On the Nature and Origins of Our Ecological Crisis. Fernand Braudel Center, Binghamton University.

Mudu, P. (2004). Resisting and Challenging Neoliberalism: Development of Italian Social Centers, *Antipode*, 36: 5.

Müntzer, T. (1988). *Collected Works of Thomas Müntzer*, ed. and trans. P. Matheson. London: Bloomsbury.

Musgrave, R. A. (1959). *The Theory of Public Finance.* New York: McGraw-Hill.

Naidoo, P. (2010). *The Making of 'The Poor' in Post-Apartheid South Africa: A Case Study of the City of Johannesburg and Orange Farm.* University of KwaZulu Natal. Retrieved from http://researchspace. ukzn.ac.za/xmlui/bitstream/ handle/10413/5065/Naidoo_ Prishani_2010.pdf?sequence=1

Nathan, J. (2011). Deleuze, Values and Normativity. In N. Jun and D. W. Smith (eds.), *Deleuze and Ethics.* Edinburgh University Press.

NATO (1996). *Handbook on the Medical Aspects of NBC Defensive Operations*, Section 210: Critical Mass. http://fas.org/nuke/guide/ usa/doctrine/dod/fm8-9/ 1ch2.htm

ODP (Office of the Deputy Prime Minister, UK) (2003). *Sustainable Communities: Building for the Future.* http:// webarchive.nationalarchives. gov.uk/20060502043818

Okia, O. (2012). *Communal Labour in Colonial Kenya: The Legitimisation of Coercion.* New York: Palgrave Macmillan.

Olivera, O. and T. Lewis (2004). *Cochabamba: Water War in Bolivia.* Boston, MA: South End Press.

Ostrom, E. (1990). *Governing the Commons: The Evolution*

of *Institutions for Collective Action*. Cambridge University Press.

Ostrom, E. (2000). Private and Common Property Rights. *Encyclopedia of Law and Economics*, Vol. II: *Civil Law and Economics*, 332–79.

Ostrom, E. (2005). *Understanding Institutional Diversity*. Princeton University Press.

Ostrom, E. (2010). Beyond Markets and States: Polycentric Governance of Complex Economic Systems, in K. Grandin (ed.), *The Nobel Prizes 2009*, Stockholm: Nobel Foundation, 408–44. www.nobelprize.org/nobel_prizes/economic-sciences/laureates/2009/ostrom_lecture.pdf

Ostrom, E., T. Dietz, N. Dolsak, P. C. Stern, S. Stonich and E. U. Weber (eds.) (2002). *The Drama of the Commons*. Washington, DC: National Academic Press.

Ostrom, V. and E. Ostrom (1977). Public Goods and Public Choices. In E. S. Savas (ed.), *Alternatives for Delivering Public Services: Towards Improved Performance*, Boulder, CO: Westview Press, 7–49.

Oxfam (2015). Wealth: Having It All and Wanting More. *Issue Briefing*, January 2015. www.oxfam.org/en/research/wealth-having-it-all-and-wanting-more

Oxfam (2016). An Economy for the 1%. How privilege and power in the economy drive extreme inequality and how this can be stopped. www.oxfam.org/en/research/economy-1

PAH (2013). *Manual Obra Social: Manual e desobediencia civil de la Plataforma de Afectados por la Hipoteca para recuperar las viviendas vacías en manos de los bancos*. https://issuu.com/lapah/docs/manual_obra_social_web__baixa_/7?e=0/3957078

Patel, R. C. (2007). *Stuffed and Starved: Markets, Power and the Hidden Battle for the World Food System*. London: Portobello.

Patel, R. (2009). What Does Food Sovereignty Look Like? *Journal of Peasant Studies*, 36(3): 663–706.

P2P Foundation (2006). Defining P2P as the Relational Dynamic of Distributed Networks.

wiki.p2pfoundation.net/ Defining_P2P_as_the_ relational_dynamic_of_ distributed_networks

P2P Foundation (2010). Section 2, Stefan Meretz. *Commons – Typology.* http://p2pfoundation.net/ Commons_-_Typology.

Parsons, T. (1960). *The Distribution of Power in American Society.* New York: Free Press.

Pedersen, M. J. (2010). Property, Commoning and the Politics of Free Software. *The Commoner,* No. 14 (Winter). www.commoner.org.uk/ N14/jmp-essay-full-the-commoner.pdf

Pedersen, M. J. (2011). Information Sector: A Qualitative Different Mode of Production? Posted on Commoning list, 3 January, https://wiki.p2pfoundation. net/backups/p2p_research-archives/2011-January/011737. html

Pithouse, R. (2010). Peers versus Commoner. Private correspondence, 5 March.

P.M. (2014). *The Power of Neighborhood and the Commons.* New York: Autonomedia

Podlashuc, L. (2009). Saving Women: Saving the Commons. In Ariel Salleh (ed.), *Eco-Sufficiency and Global Justice.* New York and London: Pluto.

Polo, A. (2006). *La porta aperta. 30 anni di avventura missionaria e sociale a Salinas di Bolivar Ecuador.* Quito: FEPP.

Princen, T. (2005). *The Logic of Sufficiency,* Cambridge, MA and London: MIT Press.

PrincipiaCybernetica (1996). *What Is Complexity?* Retrieved December 18, 2015, from http://pespmc1.vub.ac.be/ COMPLEXI.html

Purves, W. K., G. H. Orians, H. C. Heller and D. Sadava (1997). *Life: The Science of Biology.* Sunderland, MA: Sinauer Associates.

Quinn, B. and D. Johnson (2012). Occupy London: Police and Bailiffs move in to evict St Paul's Protesters. *The Guardian,* 28 February. www. theguardian.com/uk/2012/ feb/28/occupy-london-camp-police-clearance.

Rasmussen, M., R. English, and R. Alonso (2013). Who Does Not Become a Terrorist, and Why? Towards an Empirically

Grounded Understanding of Individual Motivation in Violence and Non-Violence. http://minerva.dtic.mil/doc/abstracts/Rasmussen_WhoNotTerrorist_FY13.pdf

Reich, R. (2014). Wealth is Being Redistributed – to the Rich! *Salon*, 7 January. www.salon.com/2014/01/07/the_great_redistribution_is_not_what_you_would_expect_partner/

Rete@sinistra (2010). In P. Cacciari (ed.), *La societa' dei beni comuni. Una rassegna.* Rome: Carta, Ediesse.

Right and Resources Initiative (2011). *Pushback: Local Power, Global Realignment.* www.rightsandresources.org/documents/files/doc_2072.pdf

Roberts, M. (2012). Revisiting a World Rate of Profit. Paper presented at the Association for Heterodox Economics. http://hetecon.net/documents/ConferencePapers/2015/AHERoberts.pdf

Roberts, M. (2014). Profitability, Crises and Inequality: Some Heterodox Views. https://thenextrecession.wordpress.com/2015/07/11/profitability-crises-and-inequality-some-heterodox-views/

Roberts, M. (2016). *The Long Depression*. Chicago: Haymarket Books.

Ross, J. (2005). Celebrating the Caracoles: Step by Step, the Zapatistas Advance on the Horizon. *Humboldt Journal of Social Relations*, 29(1): 39–46.

Ruef, M. (2014). *Between Slavery and Capitalism: The Legacy of Emancipation in the American South*. Princeton University Press.

Ruggieri, A. (2010). *Las Empresas Recuperadas en la Argentina.* Buenos Aires: Programa Facultad Abierta, Facultad de Filosofía y Letras de la Universidad de Buenos Aires. www.autogestion.asso.fr/wp-content/uploads/2012/10/Informe-Relevamiento-2010.pdf

Russon, M. A. (2015). Game Of Thrones season 5 breaks piracy record with 32 million illegal downloads so far. *International Business Times*, 22 April. www.ibtimes.co.uk/game-thrones-season-5-breaks-piracy-record-32-million-illegal-downloads-so-far-1497798

Ruzzene, M. (2015). Beyond Growth: Problematic

Relationship Between the Financial Crisis, Care and Public Economies, and Alternative Currencies. *International Journey of Community Currency Research*, 19.

Samuelson, P. A. (1954). The Pure Theory of Public Expenditure. *Review of Economics and Statistics*, 36(4): 387–89.

Sargut, G. and R. McGrath (2011). Learning to Live with Complexity. *Harward Business Review,* September. https://hbr.org/2011/09/learning-to-live-with-complexity

Sarkal, S. (1999). *Eco-Socialism or Eco-Capitalism?* London: Zed Books.

Schlager, E. and E. Ostrom (1992). Property Rights Regimes and Natural Resources: A Conceptual Analysis. *Land Economics*, 68: 249–62.

Simonsen, S. H., R. Biggs, M. Schlüter, M. Schoon, E. Bohensky, G. Cundill and F. Moberg (2014). Applying Resilience Thinking: Seven Principles for Building Resilience in Social-Ecological Systems, 1–20. www.stockholmresilience.org/download/18.10119fc11455d3c557d6928/1398150799790/SRC+Applying+Resilience+final.pdf

Sitrin, M. (2012). *Everyday Revolutions: Horizontalism and Autonomy in Argentina*. London: Zed Books.

Sitrin, M. (2014). Solidarity Health Clinics in Greece. 19 December. https://zcomm.org/znetarticle/solidarity-health-clinics-in-greece/2014

The Sixth Section (2003). Video directed by Alex Rivera. Produced in association with POV American Documentary. Winner of the American Dream Award. www.youtube.com/watch?v=qss5P2rsFX-0#action=share

Skytter, L. (1996). *General Systems Theory: Problems, Perspectives, Practice*. London: World Scientific Publishing.

Solidarity for All (2013). *Solidarity is Peoples' Power. Towards an International Campaign of Solidarity to the Greek People*. www.solidarity4all.gr/files/aggliko.pdf

Solidarity for All (2014). *Building Hope*. http://issuu.

com/solidarityforall/docs/
report_2014

Solnit, D. (2010). Reflections
from Bolivia: Water
Wars, Climate Wars and
Change from Below.
Upsidedownworld, 7 July,
http://upsidedownworld.
org/main/bolivia-archives-
31/2583-reflections-from-
bolivia-water-wars-climate-
wars-and-change-from-below

Soriano, W. E. (1997). *Los Incas.
Economia, societad y estado
en la era del Tahuantinsuyo.*
Lima: Amaru.

Sraffa, P. (1960). *Production of
Commodities by Means of
Commodities.* Cambridge
University Press.

Steffen, W., W. Broadgate, L.
Deutsch, O. Gaffney and C.
Ludwig (2015). The Trajectory
of the Anthropocene:
The Great Acceleration.
Anthropocene Review, 2(1):
81–98.

The Economist (2013). Protesting
Predictions: Social Unrest
in 2014. 23 December. www.
economist.com/blogs/
theworldin2014/2013/12/
social-unrest-2014

The Commoner, editor's
blog (2009). Granting vs

Confirming Rights; Commons
and Commoning; Invisibility.
www.commoner.org.uk/
blog/?p=207

UNHR (United Nations Human
Rights: Office of the High
Commissioner) (2013).
Unpaid Work, Poverty and
Women's Human Rights.
www.ohchr.org/EN/Issues/
Poverty/Pages/UnpaidWork.
aspx

US Department of Defense
(2015). *National Security
Implications of Climate-
related Risks and a Changing
Climate.* Retrieved from
https://climateandsecurity.
files.wordpress.
com/2014/01/15_07_24-
dod_gcc_congressional-
report-on-national-security-
implications-of-climate-
change.pdf

Van Der Linden, M. (2008).
*Workers of the World: Essays
Towards a Global Labour
History.* Leiden and Boston,
MA: Brill.

Varela, F. J. (1979). *Principles of
Biological Autonomy.* Boston,
MA: Kluwer Academic.

Varela, F. J. (1981). Autonomy
and Autopoiesis. In G. Roth
and H. Schwegler (eds.),

Self-Organizing Systems: An Interdisciplinary Approach. Frankfurt and New York: Campus Verlag, pp. 14–24

Veblen, T. (1973). *The Theory of the Leisure Class.* Boston, MA: Houghton Mifflin.

von Foerster, H. (1974). *Cybernetics of Cybernetics or the Control of Control and the Communication of Communication.* University of Illinois, Urbana.

Wainwright, O. (2015) Expo 2015: What Does Milan Gain by Hosting This Bloated Global Extravaganza? *The Guardian,* 12 May. www.theguardian.com/cities/2015/may/12/expo-2015-what-does-milan-gain-by-hosting-this-bloated-global-extravaganza

Walters, J. (2011). Occupy America: Protests against Wall Street and Inequality Hit 70 Cities, *The Guardian,* 8 October. www.theguardian.com/world/2011/oct/08/occupy-america-protests-financial-crisis

Weber, M. (1968). *Economy and Society.* 3 vols. Berkeley: University of California Press.

Weston, B. H. and D. Bollier. (2013). *Green Governance: Ecological Survival, Human Rights and the Law of the Commons.* Cambridge University Press.

Wissner-Gross, A. (2009). How You Can Help Reduce the Footprint of the Web. *The Times* online, 11 January. www.thetimes.co.uk/tto/environment/article2144224.ece.

Wolcher, L. S. (2009). The Meaning of the Commons. The Law of the Commons conference. Seattle Chapter of the National Lawyers Guild. March. The Editor Blog. *The Commoner,* www.commoner.org.uk/blog/?p=204

Zibechi, R. (2009). Cochabamba: From Water War to Water Management. *American Program,* 27 May. www.cipamericas.org/archives/1723

Zibechi, R. (2010). *Dispersing Power: Social Movements and Anti-State Forces.* Edinburgh: AK Press.

Zibechi, R. (2012). *Territories in Resistance: A Cartography of Latin American Social Movements.* Oakland: AK Press.

Index

About the author

Massimo De Angelis is professor of political economy at the University of East London, and founder and editor of the web journal *The Commoner* (www.thecommoner.org). His previous books include *The Beginning of History* (2007).